North East Vernacular English Online

... to the thoughtful, the meanest *word* has a history. It is instinct with the life of the long generations through whose transmission it has reached our ears to-day; and it may, if we will deal with it in a loving human way, bring strange thoughts to us.
Richard Oliver Heslop, writing as 'Harry Haldane', 1879

North East Vernacular English Online

MICHAEL PEARCE

EDINBURGH
University Press

Edinburgh University Press is one of the leading university presses in the UK. We publish academic books and journals in our selected subject areas across the humanities and social sciences, combining cutting-edge scholarship with high editorial and production values to produce academic works of lasting importance. For more information visit our website: edinburghuniversitypress.com

© Michael Pearce, 2024, 2025

Edinburgh University Press Ltd
13 Infirmary Street
Edinburgh EH1 1LT

First published in hardback by Edinburgh University Press 2024

Typeset in 9/12 pt Noto Serif
by Cheshire Typesetting Ltd, Cuddington, Cheshire

A CIP record for this book is available from the British Library

ISBN 978-1-3995-2017-1 (hardback)
ISBN 978-1-3995-2018-8 (paperback)
ISBN 978-1-3995-2019-5 (webready PDF)
ISBN 978-1-3995-2020-1 (epub)

The right of Michael Pearce to be identified as the author of this work has been asserted in accordance with the Copyright, Designs and Patents Act 1988, and the Copyright and Related Rights Regulations 2003 (SI No. 2498).

Contents

Figures and tables vi
Acknowledgements vii
Abbreviations viii

1 Introduction: *Ready to Go* 1
2 The dialectscapes of North East England 26
3 Morphology 54
4 Syntax 94
5 The dialect lexicon 110
6 Discourse-pragmatic features 130
7 The soundscape 147

References 190
Index 205

Figures and tables

Figures

1.1	Screenshot of part of an RTG thread (desktop version)	4
2.1	North East England showing locations mentioned in this book	28

Tables

1.1	Some morphosyntactic 'vernacular angloversals'	16
1.2	Some localised non-standard features	16
2.1	Counties and districts in North East England	27
2.2	The 'Geordie' repertoire	49
2.3	'Mackem' versus 'Geordie'	50
3.1	Forms of personal pronouns on RTG	69
3.2	Possessive determiners and pronouns on RTG	73
7.1	NEVE variants and respellings of the MOUTH vowel	151
7.2	NEVE variants and respellings of the GOAT vowel	153
7.3	NEVE variants and respellings of the FACE vowel	156
7.4	NEVE variants and respellings of the PRICE vowel	157
7.5	NEVE variants and respellings of the DRESS vowel	158
7.6	NEVE variants and respellings of the LOT/CLOTH vowel	160
7.7	NEVE variants and respellings of the TRAP/BATH vowel	161
7.8	NEVE variants and respellings of the STRUT vowel	163
7.9	NEVE variants and respellings of the FOOT vowel	164
7.10	NEVE variants and respellings of the NURSE vowel	165
7.11	NEVE variants and respellings of the FLEECE vowel	167
7.12	NEVE variants and respellings of the GOOSE vowel	168
7.13	NEVE variants and respellings of the THOUGHT/NORTH/FORCE vowel	169
7.14	NEVE variants and respellings of the PALM/START vowel	171
7.15	NEVE variants and respellings of the CURE vowel	172
7.16	NEVE variants and respellings of the NEAR vowel	173

Acknowledgements

This book owes its existence to *Ready to Go*. I am immensely grateful to the site members who provided the data that I have drawn on so extensively and to the message board's owners and administrators who have kept it up and running as a vital community resource since the turn of the century and who granted me permission to reproduce material from the site. I am indebted to Professor Clive Upton for his generous mentorship and guidance over the years and for his lucid and helpful comments on a draft version of the book. I would also like to thank Professor Joan Beal, whose indispensible work on North East varieties of English underpins so much of my thinking and writing about the subject. Thanks are also due to Laura Quinn, Helena Heald, and Sam Johnson of Edinburgh University Press for getting behind the project and seeing it through to completion so efficiently, and to several anonymous referees for their encouraging responses to the proposal for this volume. I am also grateful to Dr Adam Mearns for assistance with DECTE, Andy Bogle for his insights into the life and times of R. O. Heslop, Professor Angela Smith for enthusiastically sharing her knowledge of local history and dialect with me, Ed of Merritt Cartographic <https://www.merrittcartographic.co.uk/> who made the map in Chapter 2, and my copy-editor Geraldine Lyons. This book would have been impossible to complete without the love and support of my family, so I'd like to thank my wife Clare and my sons Matthew and Adam. Unlike their parents they grew up in the North East and their 'native speaker intuitions' have been invaluable during the writing of this book. Thanks also to my students, who have always been keen to keep me posted on the latest developments in North East Vernacular English.

Abbreviations

BNA	British Newspaper Archive
BNC	British National Corpus
CUD	*Concise Ulster Dictionary*
DECTE	Diachronic Electronic Corpus of Tyneside English
DNED	*Dictionary of North East Dialect*
DSL	Dictionaries of the Scots Language/Dictionars o the Scots Leid
Du.	County Durham
EME	Early Modern English
EDD	*English Dialect Dictionary*
EDG	*English Dialect Grammar*
EDS	English Dialect Society
GVS	Great Vowel Shift
LAE	*Linguistic Atlas of England*
LSS	Linguistic Survey of Scotland
ME	Middle English
Nb.	Northumberland
NECTE	Newcastle Electronic Corpus of Tyneside English
NEVE	North East Vernacular English
NSE	Non-standard English
NW	*Northumberland Words*
ODEE	Oxford Dictionary of English Etymology
OE	Old English
OED	*Oxford English Dictionary*
ONS	Office for National Statistics
OP	Original Post(er)
PDE	Present-day English
RTG	*Ready to Go*
Sc.	Scottish, Scots, Scotland

Abbreviations

SSA	Scots Syntax Atlas
SE	Standard English
SED	Survey of English Dialects
SEDDG	*Survey of English Dialects: The Dictionary and Grammar*
TLS	Tyneside Linguistic Survey

CHAPTER 1

Introduction: *Ready to Go*

Ye canna mak a savaloy out of an alsatian, man haway. ;)¹

The description of twenty-first century North East Vernacular English (NEVE) presented in this book is based on *Ready to Go* (RTG), the website from which this startling injunction comes. RTG is an online forum for *aficionados* of Sunderland A.F.C., a football club located in the heart of North East England. Like many such message boards, it is freely accessible to anyone with an internet connection or smartphone. Registered users can start 'threads' by posting messages, resulting in multi-party asynchronous graphic 'conversations' (Figure 1.1). Interactions are mainly text-based, but it is possible to post pictures, gifs, and videos. The site is enormously popular. On 3 January 2024 there were 14,774 active members, and since 2010 more than 28 million messages have been posted on over half a million threads.² Locales on the 'vernacular web of participatory media' (Howard 2008) such as RTG, exploit the affordances of Web 2.0 technologies, enabling 'communities of users' (Barton and Lee 2013: 9) to engage in relatively unconstrained and informal interactions. This often results in a proliferation of 'spoken-like and vernacular features, traces of spontaneous production, innovative spelling choices, emoticons … and the like', together with the expressive use of regionally marked forms to create localised meanings, to signal participants' origins and affiliations, and to index private, familiar, and intimate domains of social life (Androutsopoulos 2010: 50). An initial glance at RTG would suggest the language on the site matches this description. But to

---

[1] The epigraphs at the start of each chapter are from RTG <www.readytogo.net>. Examples are presented as they appeared online. The original emojis (see Figure 1.1) are reproduced as emoticons in the text. Thread titles are in italics.

[2] *Ready to Go* takes its name from a 1994 song by the alternative rock band Republica, which is played as the Sunderland team runs onto the pitch for home games at the Stadium of Light. The message board has been online since the late 1990s, though only material posted since c.2010 is readily accessible through search engines. RTG has no official association with Sunderland A.F.C.

establish the suitability of such data as the basis for a detailed account of a contemporary regional variety of English, a case needs to be made for its vernacularity – it cannot simply be taken for granted.

Vernacularity is a central concern in sociodialectology because it is assumed that the commonplace speech styles of 'normal' people going about their everyday lives are most likely to contain localised, non-standard forms.[3] Many of the discussions on RTG – though written – are nevertheless *vernacular* in the broad anthropological sense, covering topics of local interest and focusing on everyday concerns. A flavour of the quotidian vernacularity of the site can be gleaned from the titles of some threads started in April 2021: *Rubber roofing kits for a bike shed*; *Making custard from scratch*; *Barry's Bargain Superstore in Consett*; *Best place for timber in Sunderland or South Tyneside area*; *Recommend me emergency boiler cover*. Even when the discussions are about subjects with no directly local significance, they are often contextualised locally, as in this comment about Greta Thunberg: 'if she came from farra nee one would give a fuck' ('farra' refers to Farringdon – a suburb of Sunderland).

The thread from which this remark comes demonstrates something else about the site: the diversity of topics covered. While football is the central preoccupation, discussions range widely, from local cuisine (*Saveloy Dips, a sad demise*) to the UK constitution (*When the queen dies*) via media representations of a Swedish environmental activist.[4] In April 2012 the Higgs boson sparked a lively debate, and the site also hosts a three-page philosophical enquiry into the possibility of unperceived existence. As of January 2024, there are four mentions of Albert Camus (unsurprisingly two of them refer to his goalkeeping prowess), and in a lengthy consideration of existentialism someone paraphrases – in German – a famous adage from Bertolt Brecht's *Die Dreigroschenoper*: 'Erst kommt das Fressen, dann kommt die Moral.' Discussions on RTG often go beyond the local and everyday to explore universal human concerns (*Death*); religion (*Buddhism*); cosmology

---

[3] I use the term *sociodialectology* in preference to the near-identical *social dialectology* for reasons outlined by Kristiansen (2018: 106–107). He argues that in the literature the better-known term is used to mean more or less the same as 'variationist sociolinguistics', so he adopts *sociodialectology* to cover the application of sociolinguistic study to dialectology (understood in its traditional sense of dialect geography). For Kristiansen, the 'particularity' of sociodialectological study is its central concern with the significance of geographical space in 'social, language-ideological, and linguistic processes of variation and change … The focus on *geographical space* should be taken to imply that *dialect* refers to regional varieties, as per traditional terminology' (emphasis in original). Sociodialectology as formulated here is very similar to *sociolinguistic dialectology* as set forth by Upton to describe the 'interface' between sociolinguistics and dialectology (2000: 66–68), which of course includes the impact of the 'Third Wave' and its focus on agency and performance (see 1.2).

[4] A 'saveloy' is a seasoned red smoked pork sausage. *OED* defines 'saveloy dip' as 'a type of sandwich, popular in the north east of England, typically consisting of saveloy, pease pudding, and mustard in a bun, which is dipped in gravy or fat before serving'.

Introduction: Ready to Go 3

(*The Big Bang*); political theory (*The left/right paradigm*), the natural world (*saw a weasel knack a rabbit today*), and so on. However, it should also be noted that the site is imbued with 'Northernness' – what the geographer John Tomaney describes as a form of consciousness rooted in the region's industrial history and the associated values of collectivism, sense of community, hard physical labour, masculinity, and insularity, which distinguishes the North from elsewhere (2010: 83). The historian Dan Jackson is more geographically specific. In *The Northumbrians: North-East England and Its People* (2019) he sets out to explain what makes this part of the north of England and its citizens distinctly different.[5] While Jackson acknowledges that many of the characteristics he cites could also be associated with other places in Britain, the set of traits and dispositions he identifies – forged in a particular history of industrial innovation, expansion, and decline – coalesces to form a unique structure of feeling which values sociability, conviviality, gregariousness, mutuality, solidarity, communalism, toughness, hard work, stoicism, assertiveness, warmth, joviality, independence, candour, and humour (in particular, verbal wit and dexterity).[6] Some of the sentiments expressed on RTG might indeed reflect northern and/or 'Northumbrian' structures of feeling. In threads such as *Who used to work down the pits?* and *The Shipyards and memories of them*, people reminisce about their own or their family's part in the region's industrial history. The valorisation of sociability and gregariousness is reflected in threads such as *Workies or pub*, in which the merits of Working Men's Clubs ('workies') are compared with those of public houses ('I help run a social club like and it's one of the friendliest and best places in town'). North East respect for toughness and hard work is evident in the many discussions about manual jobs, expressed in comments such as 'He said he was the best grafter he'd seen. First in and last home every shift.' Toughness in the sporting domain is also valued, as the discussion in *Sports/pastimes for soft shites* demonstrates. There is also a twenty-page enquiry into *Infamous hardmen of Sunderland*. And running through almost every thread are thick seams of humour. Indeed, if there is one unspoken pragmatic 'rule' of RTG it is 'be funny'.

It seems reasonable then to claim that RTG is a broadly vernacular site in the folkloric sense. Even when the subject matter goes beyond the local

---

[5] What is 'Northumbria'? Jackson uses the term to refer to 'an area of land that now encompasses the post-1974 local authority boundaries of Northumberland and County Durham, Newcastle and Gateshead, North and South Tyneside, Sunderland, Hartlepool, Stockton-on-Tees and Darlington' (2019: vii). The demarcation of territory in the region and its sociodialectological implications are discussed in Chapter 2.

[6] *Structure of feeling* is a somewhat vague but nevertheless useful term associated with the literary historian and cultural critic Raymond Williams. It refers to 'a particular quality of social experience and relationship' which gives a certain epoch or locale its distinctiveness (1977: 131); 'a pattern of impulses, restraints, tones' which imbues the sociocultural artefacts and processes of a particular time and place with a certain flavour (1979: 159).

Figure 1.1 Screenshot of part of an RTG thread (desktop version) entitled *Saveloy Dips, a sad demise* showing turns #61 to #64 in a 'conversation' of 220 turns which took place between August 2018 and February 2022

and everyday, its structures of feeling imbue it with a northern, working-class sensibility. But does that necessarily result in *linguistic* vernacularity? Are the vernacular contents reflected in the forms used to write about them? Should we expect people in such a setting to employ styles of writing that resemble their informal, unmonitored speech? In sections 1.1, 1.2 and 1.3. I explore the nature of the evidence, arguing for the vernacular and naturalistic status of the language, and thus establishing its usefulness as the basis for a description of a regional variety of English. The chapter concludes by outlining the aims, content, and organisation of the volume.

1.1 The *vernacular* status of RTG

It has been a long-held tenet of mainstream sociolinguistics that the naturally occurring, spontaneous, unselfconscious, everyday *speech* of folk in their locally-based communities is the 'holy grail' of the sociolinguistic enterprise, since 'the "secular," everyday linguistic usages that sociolinguists seek have traditionally been concentrated in spoken registers' (Holmes and Wilson 2017: 268; Schilling 2013: 2).[7] Typically, regional dialectologists have been more open in the type of data they have deemed suitable for study, but nevertheless spoken language has also been at the heart of their enquiries. In both approaches there is a tendency to see writing as a secondary, 'composed', self-conscious, and mediated mode of language, which cannot be regarded as anyone's true vernacular. This bias against writing – even to characterise it as 'bad' data – is perhaps not surprising, given the influence the process of standardisation has had on the written mode. Because of the normative pressure writers are typically under to be 'correct' and consistent, it is assumed little of interest from the sociolinguistic perspective will be evident in writing. Does the fact that the language on RTG is written invalidate it as a source of 'real' vernacular English? Not necessarily. In recent years, researchers have begun to pay more attention to various kinds of written material, especially (and of necessity) as their enquiries reach back before the development of sound recording. In doing so, they have had to consider the evidential status of the writing they are looking at. Schneider, for example, lists some 'basic requirements' for [written] texts to be useful for a sociolinguistic analysis (2013: 59–60). The most important of these is that the texts selected should be as close to vernacular speech styles as possible. What in practice does that mean?

In one sense, the idea of 'speech-like' writing appears paradoxical since there is a categorical distinction in the channels through which a linguistic utterance/signal is realised (the phonic/acoustic code for speech; the graphic/visual code for writing). But this traditional dichotomy is being replaced with (or at least supplemented by) a more sociolinguistically and pragmatically realistic view which sees speech and writing as a 'conceptual' continuum, so that, for example, we can imagine a text which might be 'medially' written but is also 'conceptually' spoken/oral, like a private diary or a personal letter/email (Koch and Österreicher 1985). Such conceptions are particularly important for historical sociolinguists, who of course cannot deploy 'standard sociolinguistic methods, such as interview and elicitation' (Nevalainen and Raumolin-Brunberg 2017: 26) and who

---

[7] In her history of variationist sociolinguistics, Tagliamonte remarks that the 'substance of the data is, for the most part, conversational – hours and hours of audio recordings although it can also be comprised of written language of various types as well', though she says very little about writing as sociolinguistic evidence (2016: 107).

are limited to written data. But the same cannot be said for the task of describing a contemporary variety of English. If writing is the primary data, a case has to be made for its suitability. In the rest of this section, I show that much of the language on RTG fulfils the criteria of 'conceptual orality', establishing the grounds for regarding the site as a repository of naturalistic, vernacular North East English.

Readers might intuitively feel that, though (medially) written, the posts on RTG have certain speech-like characteristics. This is perhaps unsurprising given the nature of an online message board. Many of the situational characteristics that give rise to the features we see in typical 'phonic' conversations also hold in relation to RTG. These are interactivity and 'liveness'; shared social and cultural context and stance; the avoidance of elaboration or specification of meaning; and non-standardness (for a functional account of the grammar of conversation, see Biber et al. 1999 and 2002). In the following sub-sections I show the correspondences between 'typical' conversation and asynchronous online message board discourse, arguing for parity of status with speech for sociodialectological study. And in the examples sown throughout the remainder of the chapter I provide a flavour of the character of the material to be found on RTG.

1.1.1 Interactive and 'live'

In a typical phonic conversation, two or more people are involved in an exchange of turns in real time (in other words, they are performing 'live'). These conditions result in the prevalence of linguistic features associated with the structuring and management of interaction, together with performance features and distinctive grammatical structures associated with producing and processing language in real time. To what extent can they also be found on RTG?

While the graphic interactions on an online message board are mainly asynchronous (so not subject to the same production and processing constraints as phonic conversations) nevertheless such interactions can be regarded as 'pseudo-live', at least. Turn exchange does take place, so that in both contexts there are utterances which either form a response or elicit one. This means that on RTG, as in phonic conversations, we see questions (1a,b), imperatives (1c), greetings and farewells (1d,e), response elicitors (1f), and response forms (1g).

(1)   a. Anyone got a bonsai tree?
        b. you're gannin to the match aren't you?
        c. Dinnat say that Marra.
        d. Morning marra, aye we always have a blunder in us don't we?
        e. See yous later lads.
        f. Six beers eh, canny.
        g. Aye, we bought one last year.

Introduction: Ready to Go

In phonic conversation we sometimes need to attract the attention of our intended addressee, often by using special attention-getting forms. We also find these on RTG, sometimes alongside vocatives (2a,b,c), which can perform a similar function. It should also be pointed out that vocatives can also be attitudinal, as with *marra* in (1c,d) and *pal* in (3d).

(2)   a. Hey Hank, just come back from Manchester.
       b. Oi! Watch it sonny!
       c. Me and you should open our own place mate.

Interactivity is also evident in relation to discourse markers which are used in phonic conversation, alongside other inserts (such as interjections, expletives, and hesitators), to manage interaction by signalling relations between the interlocutors and between interlocutors and the ongoing discourse. All these features can be found on RTG.

(3)   a. Reet I'm gannin there tha morra.
       b. I think she hurt him bad like.
       c. Whoops, meant Dickson's.
       d. Oh shit, sorry pal. I had no idea :(
       e. Its Amy and ..er...whatsisname.

The written representations of hesitation in (3e) are perhaps puzzling. While both phonic and graphic conversations share the characteristic of interactivity, only phonic conversations take place 'live' and are therefore subject to 'the demands of real-time language production and processing' (Biber et al. 2002: 436). Interactions on message boards can be rapid, but mostly there is a delay between a post and a response. Nevertheless, some of the 'performance' features we associate with the liveness of phonic conversation are evident on RTG. These can be seen either as 'genuine' responses to the experience of time pressure, or as attempts to represent these constraints in informal writing (perhaps to convey 'rhetorical' liveness).

RTG contains instances of orthographic dysfluencies like pauses and hesitators (3e, 4a), repeats (4b), incomplete utterances (4c), and syntactic blends (4d). Some of the 'typos' on the site might also be regarded as the equivalent of dysfluencies in speech.

(4)   a. his erm.......little error in a certain game in 1985.
       b. But but but I thought anyone from south of the Tyne was a mackem?
       c. Cattermole would probably like it.....:lol:
       d. There's one near me which I must had double figures incidents at.
       e. Nowt wrang with ol Brucey.
       f. Ah's starving anarl.
       g. "Gow on Stowke" or whatever it is the locals sing.

h. Didja hev wine with the bait though?
i. Ross is gonna need big shoes.
j. Whatcha gonna do.
k. Whaddya wanna see like?
l. Gerroff the pitch man Hancock!!

We also see orthographic representations of the natural phonetic changes to conventional word forms which occur in 'allegro speech' (Preston 1985). Alameen and Levis (2015: 161–163) identify four main categories of connected speech processes potentially replicable in orthography: deletion, insertion, modification, and reduction. Deletion involves the loss of sounds. For example, in (4d,f) we see contraction of *is* involving elision of the vowel; in (4e) the spelling <ol> for *old* represents the deletion of a medial consonant in a complex consonant grouping; consonant cluster simplification also occurs in (4f), where the *and* in *and all* is represented as <an>. Insertion involves the addition of sounds, as in (4g) where <w> has been added to *go on* to represent the process whereby glides – typically [w] or [j] – are sometimes used in speech to link vowels across word boundaries. Modification involves the substitution of one sound for another: in (4h) the <dj> in <didja> represents a common pronunciation of *did you* in which the sounds [d] and [j] are replaced with [dʒ]. This spelling also contains an example of vowel reduction, where the use of <a> reflects the fact that in connected speech the vowel in single syllable function words is often reduced to [ə]. A highly salient modification in North East England – illustrated in (4l) – is so-called T-to-R (Wells 1982: 370), in which /r/ replaces intervocalic /t/ in certain contexts, resulting in outputs like *ge*[ɹ] *off*, *ge*[ɹ] *in*, *shu*[ɹ] *up* (7.4.1). Some 'lexical chunks' exhibit multiple connected speech processes (Alameen and Levis 2015: 163). For example, in (4i,j) the spelling <gonna> represents *gonna*, which is derived from *going to* through multiple processes of modification, vowel reduction, and deletion. Multiple processes are also involved in *what are you* → *whatcha* (4j), *what do you* → *whaddya*, and *want to* → *wanna* (4k).

The restricted and repetitive nature of phonic conversation, which also arises as a response to performing 'live', is parallelled on RTG to some extent. So, for example, in phonic conversation speakers often repeat some or all of a previous utterance to relieve real-time planning pressure (Biber et al. 2002: 434). Broadly analogous to this on RTG is the ability for posters to incorporate 'quoted' text into their posts then comment on it, sometimes repeating parts of the quoted text in their own responses (Figure 1.1). Furthermore, in phonic conversations, 'time pressure prevents speakers from exploiting the full innovative power of grammar and lexicon, and so they rely heavily on well-worn, routine word sequences, readily accessible from memory' (Biber et al. 2002: 434). These so-called 'lexical bundles' reflect the habitual repetitiveness of speakers performing live. One of the commonest structural types of lexical bundle contains a pronoun, followed by a verb phrase, followed by part of the verb's complement, as in *I don't know why; I thought that was*. Such bundles are common on RTG.[8]

The pressure of 'liveness' is also responsible for another distinctive feature of phonic conversation: the use of peripheral elements that precede or follow the main body of a speaker's utterance (Biber et al. 2002: 439). Preceding elements have a range of functions associated with 'launching' an utterance. These include 'propelling the conversation in a new direction' and 'providing the speaker with a planning respite, during which the rest of the utterance can be prepared for execution' (Biber et al. 1999: 1073). Devices used to carry out these tasks include the following: fronting, where the typical SV clause structure is disrupted for reasons of topicality as in (5a) – though strictly speaking fronted elements aren't peripheral to the clause; noun phrase prefaces co-referential to a pronoun in the following clause (5b); discourse markers (5c) and other prefatory expressions such as interjections (5d), response forms (5e), and stance and linking adverbs (5f,g). A number of formulaic multi-word expressions also exist in English to launch utterances, and some are present on RTG, with various types of pragmatic force (5h,i,j).

(5)   a. At home I rarely smoked unless drinking.
        b. Newcastle, they go for fat and whiney.
        c. Well there you go, there's me telt. :lol:
        d. Wow wot a cool bloke you are.
        e. Aye ah knaa.
        f. Actually I'm talking shite.
        g. So I'll start off.
        h. No wonder Sunderland is so screwed up.
        i. As a matter of fact, they did.
        j. Like I say, they dont grow cabbages in my back garden for nowt.

As far as peripheral elements at the end of a clause are concerned, in phonic conversation there is a tendency 'to add elements as an afterthought to a grammatical unit' (Biber et al. 1999: 1080). These retrospective qualifications, which are a response to the 'liveness' of conversation are sometimes known as tags and come in a variety of flavours, all of which are evident on RTG. For instance, a comment clause can be added to modify the stance of the preceding clause as in (6a); we can add retrospective vagueness hedges – stance adverbials of imprecision – as in (6b); question tags can be used for retrospective qualification (as well as for eliciting agreement or confirmation) as in (6c). Noun phrase tags are used to repeat a noun phrase with further elaboration (6d) or can be co-referentially linked to a pronoun in the body of the clause, again for clarification, as in (6e). Tags can

---

[8] In the RTG sample corpus (see 1.3) the commonest 5-grams fitting this pattern are *I don't think it*, *I don't think he*, and *I don't think we*.

also repeat aspects of the form or content of the preceding utterance (6f). A speaker might self-supply an answer to their own question – effectively converting a *wh-* question into a *yes-no* question and biasing the response (6g). We can use final vocatives as in (6h) – and (1c), (2b), and (4l) – to retrospectively qualify a message, in particular to signal an attitude towards the addressee.

(6) a. There was a bit of needle there I reckon.
    b. She's right in a way.
    c. They'll be franchises, will they not?
    d. Nah, a buzz man. A geet proper buzz 'cos wa ganna have a fight!
    e. Honestly mate I f***ing detest them. The ones that continually have a negative opinion.
    f. Im never gonna criticise his commentary ever again!
    g. What do you want, a written apology?
    h. It woz class in 1983 marra.

In addition to prefaces and tags, real-time pressures and constraints result in an abundance of other non-clausal units in conversation. These can be divided into inserts and syntactic non-clausal units. Inserts comprise a class of words that are grammatically and lexically peripheral. Indeed, it might be questioned whether some inserts are even words at all (Biber et al. 1999: 1082). Several of the examples given in this chapter contain inserts. The interjections *whoops* and *oh* occur in (3c,d); the greeting *morning* in (1d); the discourse markers *reet* and *like* in (3a,b); the attention signal *hey* in (2a); the response elicitor *eh* in (1f); the response form *aye* in (1g); the hesitators *er* and *erm* in (3e) and (4a); the polite speech-act formulae *sorry* in (3d); the taboo expletive *shit* in (3d).

Syntactic non-clausal units lack finite clause structure (Biber et al. 2002: 440–441). They can be single words, phrases, or unembedded dependent clauses. Condensed questions, especially as noun phrases or as verbless structures (7a), condensed directives (7b), condensed statements, often consisting of a noun phrase or an adjective phrase (7c), and exclamations (7d) are some of the commonest non-clausal units in conversation and can all be found on RTG.

(7) a. What about the bogs in Pan Lane. :eek:.
    b. Heads up lads.
    c. Class choons.
    d. Ha'way the lads!

The real-time constraints of live phonic conversation – such as the need to reduce syntactic complexity and the impulse to speed up communication, avoiding unnecessary repetition – also result in a further feature highly characteristic of spontaneous speech: ellipsis (Biber et al. 2002: 441).

Introduction: Ready to Go

On RTG there are many examples of initial ellipsis, where the subject (8a,b), the operator (8c), and both the subject and operator (8d) are ellipted. We also see medial ellipsis (8e,f) and final ellipsis (8g,h). In some contexts, determiners can be ellipted (8i).

(8)
 a. ^ Saw a puddle on the way home, ^ stopped and ^ plodged.
 b. ^ Never saw nowt.
 c. ^ You serious!?
 d. ^ Got to be up there with the most funniest comedy scene ever.
 e. You ^ better be scared!
 f. Where ^ you gannin?
 g. Aye I did ^.
 h. I'd love to ^ but I do have other commitments tonight.
 i. ^ Real smart move.

Further examples of ellipsis can be found in (1a,f), (2a), (3c), (5h), (7c), (9b,d), (14h), (15a), and (16b).

1.1.2 Shared social and cultural context and the expression of feelings and attitudes

The elliptical nature of phonic conversation is a response to real-time processing and production constraints. A further factor affecting ellipsis is the fact that phonic conversation typically takes place face to face in a shared physical context, between people who know each other well.

Shared context – of the co-text of an ongoing discussion and broader aspects of sociocultural context – gives speakers confidence that their hearers will be able to efficiently recover any ellipted material; similarly, shared context also results in the prevalence of pro-forms in conversation. Furthermore, conversations between people who know each other are often concerned with the expression of feelings, beliefs, attitudes, and so on. This 'affective' dimension of conversation means it is routinely laced with various kinds of humour. Conversations are also shaped by culturally specific politeness constraints. Do these factors influence the interactions on RTG in a similar way?

In phonic conversation we often encounter the substitution of longer expressions with pro-forms (which, like ellipsis, is a structure-reducing device). On RTG too we see pronouns substituting for full noun phrases, pro-verbs substituting for a full verb phrase, and pro-adverbs substituting for an elliptical clause.

(9)
 a. They gave him some stick, then he decided to give them some back.
 b. Never had them ones like.
 c. I'll dee it for £2400.
 d. Hope so mate.

In (9a) the people referred to by the third person pronouns *they, him, he,* and *them* are unrecoverable without knowing what has preceded this utterance in its thread (though we can recover what the second – and pronominal – occurrence of *some* refers to from the sentence alone). In (9b) we don't know what the indefinite pronoun *ones* refers to, and in (9c) the referents of the pro-verb *dee* and pronoun *it* are equally obscure. And what is the content of the clause which the pro-adverb *so* substitutes for in (9d)?[9]

Because participants are constantly referring to themselves and each other, some of the commonest pro-forms found in phonic conversation are first and second person pronouns.

(10) a. Yous telt me all this ages ago, I'm just sometimes a bit slow on the uptake.
b. If Ayr played us you should want yous to f***ing hammer us.
c. That loft of yours must be creaking worse than mine :lol: :lol: :lol:
d. Ah'm booing meself.

The high frequency of first person pronouns in conversation reflects the fact that much everyday interaction is taken up with speakers expressing their personal feelings, attitudes, evaluations, and assessments of likelihood – their *stance* – towards the propositional content of an utterance (Biber et al. 2002: 433). Common ways of marking stance verbally in phonic conversation can also be found on RTG, including evaluative predicative adjectives (11a), stance adverbials (11b), endearments (11c), interjections (11d), and exclamations (11e). In addition to lexical stance marking, on RTG we also see grammatical stance marking in the use of modal verbs (11f) and complement clause constructions (11g,h) – both common conversational markers of stance.

(11) a. Caton Keating, she was really lovely yes.
b. Yeah I'll probably be dead by then.
c. Sorry pet, they're all busy watching the scum match at the moment.
d. Ugh that's terrible.
e. What a bellend!
f. Bloody hell if that's true they must have more money than sense.
g. Very much doubt that they will come back up next season.
h. I'm so glad we never got him as our manager.

Shared context also means that the lexicogrammar of conversation is shaped by politeness – the desire to preserve our face needs and support

---

[9] In (9a) the context is a match between Sunderland and Portsmouth: *they* are some Portsmouth fans; *he* is a Portsmouth player. In (9b) *ones* are gammon and spring onion flavoured crisps. In (9c), *dee it* refers to fitting a staircase, and in (9d) *so* is referring to getting an appointment at an NHS urgent care centre.

Introduction: Ready to Go

the face needs of others. The importance of politeness in conversation is reflected in a high frequency of the speech acts of requesting, greeting, offering, apologising, thanking, and so on (Biber et al. 2002: 433). As in phonic conversations, on RTG we see certain inserts and openings with a stereotypical role in polite speech acts, such as greetings (12a), expressions of gratitude (12b), apologies (12c), and *could you* and *would you* functioning as requests (12d,e).

(12) a. Areet lads & lasses.
      b. Cheers mate, I will.
      c. Aye sorry marra I couldn't resist.
      d. could you hoy up a pic just to check I'm not mistaken.
      e. Would you like a bit of tinfoil?

But conversationalists are not always polite to each other. Indeed, people who know each other well often tolerate high levels of impoliteness. However, much of this is in the form of 'banter', mock impoliteness in which insulting language is used humorously to display social solidarity (Leech 2014: 238–241; Higgins and Smith 2017: 117). On RTG we can only infer that literal insult has not been 'taken' by looking at the extended context – the abuse in the examples in (13) was not experienced as such, indeed some of it was seen by the recipients as a sign of approval, and some posters used orthographic affordances (e.g. <***> and <:lol:>) to temper the insult, showing its bantering nature.

(13) a. Give owa ya styupid gonk.
      b. You're such a boring bellend.
      c. You f***ing idiot man!:lol:
      d. :lol: Yer an Arse.

Alongside banter, other forms of humour are widespread on RTG, just as they are in our everyday phonic conversations, where we routinely encounter 'spontaneous conversational joking ... personal anecdotes, and canned jokes' (Norrick 2006: 335). Humour can be used to convey and build rapport, to express personal and social affiliations, and to act as a vent for strong emotions. Various kinds of word play are associated with humour, including puns and neologism (14a,b,c); formulaic witticisms and sayings (14d,e); and 'typical joking strategies' (Norrick 2006: 335–336) such as hyperbole (14f); allusions (14g) and irony – which in (14h) is only detectable from the context.

(14) a. Stadium Of Shite and Joker Park .... right I'll get me coat!
      b. Whee's this clownshoe?
      c. Arise Sir Pissbiscuit.
      d. Tom couldn't hit a cow's arse with a banjo for months.

  e. Shy bairns get nowt.
  f. Newcastle Brown ale is a million times better.
  g. It was the best of times ... it was the *blurst* of times?!
  h. makes me proud to be British.

In phonic conversations, humour is often accompanied with marked prosody, such as the distinctive intonational patterns associated with sarcastic speech. This is possible because of physical co-presence: speakers can use posture, facial expression, gesture, intonation, and contrasts of volume, tempo, and rhythm to add meaning. We have already seen how graphic conversation can deploy orthography to imply live performance features like pausing and hesitation (e.g. 3e, 4a); orthography can also be used to suggest paralinguistic features associated with politeness, emotion, and stance; features that would have accompanied an utterance if it had been spoken, as in the winking emoji in (15a) and the upper-case spelling used to suggest high volume and an extended syllable in (15b,c).

(15) a. Nee wonder I've got a drink problem ;)
  b. GERRRRRRRIN YOU FISHY f***ing FUCKERS
  c. Cheap signing for TEN MILLION POOND :lol:

There are further instances of these strategies in (4c), (5c), (7a), (10c), (13c), and in the use of italics in (14g).

 Shared knowledge of context also means that participants in a conversation do not have to elaborate on and specify meaning to the same extent as writers of expository prose. Therefore, conversation has a lower lexical density than prose, and speakers tend to avoid noun phrase structures with lengthy sequences of pre- and post-modification. Additionally, conversation often uses 'purposefully vague language' (Carter and McCarthy 2006: 175). In writing, hedges such as *kind of, sort of,* and *like* often provoke criticism for their imprecision. However, in conversation precision is less important, particularly when it might hold things up, so speakers often make 'hints and rough indications, relying on shared knowledge' (Biber et al. 2002: 431). Surprisingly perhaps, in the asynchronous context of RTG we also see vague language.

(16) a. i mean, im not a snob or owt.
  b. Seems a bit crazy that he's came out and sort of doubled down on it all as well.

Here we see a sort of rhetorical vagueness, similar to the strategies in (4) used to convey aspects of the 'liveness' of real speech.

1.1.3 Informal and non-standard range of expression

The examples I have used in this chapter so far powerfully convey the flavour of the RTG data set. Perhaps its most striking overall characteristic is informality and use of non-standard morphosyntax, lexis, and phonology (in the form of respellings designed to capture segmental features of speech associated with a North East accent). Informality and non-standardness are very much characteristics of conversation. As Biber et al. point out, because 'conversation typically takes place privately between people who know one another' it is 'little influenced by the traditions of prestige and correctness often associated with the printed word. Instead, the style of conversation is overwhelmingly informal' (2002: 435).

Formality is an aspect of social behaviour that can be conceived of as a scale, ranging from 'very formal' to 'very informal'. Language is one of the most important social behaviours, and language use can be placed on this continuum. Any 'level' of language may be implicated as a marker of formality (lexis, grammar, phonology, graphology, and so on). External 'triggering' factors of degree of formality in language include the subject matter, the relationship between participants in a situation, their roles and status, the medium of communication, and degree of preparedness. From such a definition it is possible to make some assumptions about where particular kinds of language use tend to occur on the notional formality continuum. From what we have seen of the vernacular context(s) of RTG, we would predict the presence of informal linguistic behaviour and this is what we observe in many of the examples in this chapter. For instance, in almost every case where it is possible to use a contraction, a contraction is used; colloquial words and phrases abound (e.g. *sonny, whatsisname, mate, bogs, stick, cheers mate, soft shites*); taboo language is common (e.g. *shit, fuck, fuckers, f***ing, FFS*). Informal contexts also have a higher tolerance of error than formal ones, hence some posters allow typos to slip through, as in (11a) and the chapter epigraph.

As well as *unintentional* respellings resulting from error, informality can also be signalled through different sorts of *intentional* respelling. These fall into three main categories: 'eye dialect', 'allegro spelling', and 'regiolectal spelling'. Eye dialect, as the term suggests, appeals to the eye of the reader, giving a visual impression of informal vernacularity without conveying any phonological information about a specific accent (Wolfram and Schilling 2016: 345). Examples from this chapter are *what* → <wot>; *was* → <woz>; *tunes* → <choons>; *stupid* → <styupid>; *you're* → <yer>. 'Allegro spellings', which capture connected speech processes (1.1.1), also impart a highly informal flavour to writing, though like eye dialect they do not reveal much about accent, since the modifications implied are heard in most varieties of English. Regiolectal spellings, on the other hand, do attempt to represent localised accent features, and this chapter contains several instances where a poster has respelled a word to give an indication of how it is pronounced

Table 1.1 *Some morphosyntactic 'vernacular angloversals' from the examples appearing in this chapter (see Kortmann 2020)*

Me instead of *I* in coordinate subjects	***Me and you*** should open our own place mate.
Never as preverbal past tense negator	I'm so glad we ***never*** got him as our manager.
Adverbs with the same form as adjectives	I think she hurt him ***bad*** like.
Absence of plural on measure nouns	Cheap signing for TEN MILLION ***POOND*** :lol:
Multiple negation	***Never*** saw ***nowt***.
Degree modifier adverbs lack *-ly*	***Real*** smart move.
Special forms for the 2PP pronoun	See ***yous*** later lads.
Coincidence of perfect and simple past	Seems a bit crazy that he's ***came*** out and sort of doubled down on it all as well.
Double comparatives and superlatives	Got to be up there with the ***most funniest*** comedy scene ever.

Table 1.2 *Some localised non-standard features from the RTG examples appearing in this chapter*

Non-standard morphology	*anarl, mak, nee, nowt, owa, telt, yous*
Non-standard syntax	*ah's, canna, dinnat, ten million poond*
Localised discourse features	*aye, haway, pet,* clause-final *like*
Regiolectal spellings	*dee, knaa, poond, reet, wrang*
Dialect lexis	*bairn, canny, gannin, hoy, lasses, marra, tha morra*

in North East speech (Table 1.2 gives some examples of these respellings, and the subject is given detailed treatment in Chapter 7).

In addition to various forms of respelling, the threads on RTG – like the everyday informal phonic conversations which in some respects they resemble – are rich in morphosyntactic forms and lexical choices deemed to be 'outside the citadel of standard English' (Biber et al. 1999: 1050). This last point is of particular relevance for the main aim of the volume, which is to use RTG as the basis for a description of contemporary North East English. It will have become clear from the examples in this chapter that the site is a topically diverse data set, with a lively vernacular character. But is RTG also a repository of the kinds of features that give a *regional* variety of English its specific flavour? Tables 1.1 and 1.2 provide an initial answer to that question, showing two main types of non-standard features found on RTG, illustrated with examples from the extracts presented in this chapter. Table 1.1 contains a selection of non-standard morphosyntactic features sometimes referred to as 'vernacular angloversals' because they are 'the most wide-spread non-standard morphosyntactic features in the Anglophone world' (Kortmann 2020: 639–640). Table 1.2 exemplifies more *localised* non-standard features of North East English at the levels of morphology and syntax (the subject matter of Chapters 3 and 4), lexis (Chapter 5), discourse features (Chapter 6), phonology and orthography (Chapter 7).

1.1.4 The naturalistic status of RTG data

We have established that posters on RTG often deploy written language in a speech-like way, because the communicative contexts of internet message boards and phonic conversations have much in common, resulting in a similar array of vernacular linguistic features. The cultural and linguistic vernacularity of RTG should go some way to allaying concerns about the appropriateness of the data as a basis for describing a regional variety of English. Its utility also derives from the fact that it is a repository of *naturalistic* language. In linguistics, the term *naturalistic* is applied to language produced in real communicative situations, which has not been elicited for the purposes of linguistic scrutiny. In this sense, the data on RTG is naturalistic – none of the posters knew their words would become the object of academic enquiry.[10] This is not necessarily the case for the human subjects of most sociodialectological research. As we have seen, in mainstream sociolinguistics great emphasis has been placed on the importance of naturally occurring speech – the purported location of the 'best' vernacular data. But the sociolinguistic interview – the primary tool for gathering 'high-quality naturalistic conversational data' (Schilling 2013: 108) – can only be expected to capture *quasi*-naturalistic speech. This is because when someone knows their language is being elicited and recorded to be studied it will inevitably affect what they say and how they say it. While the numerous adaptions and refinements of the sociolinguistic interview have helped mitigate the effects of the so-called participant Observer's Paradox, they have not eliminated them entirely. I will return to this topic in 1.3, but for now the possible 'stifling' or 'suppressing' effect of conventional means of sociolinguistic data collection can be seen when we compare swearing in the quasi-naturalistic speech of sociolinguistic interviews archived in the Diachronic Electronic Corpus of Tyneside English with the genuinely naturalistic speech-like writing of RTG (see 2.2.5 for a description of DECTE). Swearing is a useful indicator, since people are more inclined to swear in informal contexts, in the presence of interlocutors with whom they share interests, sociogeographic background and even certain dispositions and structures of feeling; people are less likely to swear in more formal contexts where they do not feel entirely at ease. In the c.800,000-word DECTE the word *shit* occurs 52 times (approximately 0.065 times per 1,000 words) and *bollocks* twice (0.0025 per 1,000 words). *Fuck* is used 28 times (0.035 per 1,000 words).

---

[10] This might raise some concerns around the notion of consent. Because there are no established ethical guidelines for the treatment of public material on the world wide web, researchers need to come to their own decisions about what is necessary and feasible in terms of gaining consent (Honkanen 2020: 77). I have not sought consent, assuming that 'by performing acts in public, an individual is giving implicit consent to having those actions observed and recorded' (Eckert 2013: 14). Nevertheless, I have tried to avoid using examples that, if traced back to an individual user through a verbatim web search, could unduly embarrass them.

In a 10-million-word sample corpus of RTG (described in 1.3), *shit* occurs 6,113 times (6.1 times per 1,000 words) and *bollocks* 728 times (0.73 times per 1,000 words). *Fuck* is used 5,998 times (6.0 times per 1,000 words). Indeed, the extent of taboo language on the site is greater than these figures suggest, since they do not incorporate the frequencies of spellings like <f**k>, where writers attempt to avoid censure from the site moderators who, according to RTG's terms and rules, are looking out for obscene, defamatory, abusive, hateful, or threatening content. Furthermore, the figures are for word forms, not lemmas (so *fucking, fucks, fucked*, etc., are not included); also excluded are 'expressive' spellings, as in 'Doberman pinschers – fuuuuuck, run.' On RTG swearing is an area of considerable lexical creativity: *fucktards, fucknuts, fuckwittery, fuckface, fucknugget* can all be found in the sample corpus, as can *shitehawks, shitey, shithousery, shitstorm, shitloads, shitsville, shitlips, shitbags*, and so on.

Further evidence for the naturalistic status of RTG data is its generic richness. People's everyday conversation consists of sub-types, like banter, small talk, gossip, verbal play, argument, flirting, storytelling, and so on. The recognition of these sub-types and their associated styles (though they are diffuse and overlapping compared with more institutionalised speech genres such as political speeches, lectures, stand-up comedy routines, etc.) form part of a person's cultural and communicative competence (Coupland 2007). On RTG, just as in everyday phonic conversation, a range of conversational sub-types can be identified. Thread titles indicate, for example, information and advice seeking (*How do you thicken a sauce up?*); offering help (*Anyone need hotel for Blackpool away?*); expressing sympathy and condolences (*Another Sunderland supporter gone to the SOL in the sky*); expressing and soliciting judgments and opinions (*How good is the British Navy? Palace are shite*), recounting incidents and events (*Strange taxi story*); reminiscing (*Can anyone remember the pie shop in Fulwell*); reviewing (*Best Pie*), and so on.

Each conversational genre is associated with a set of different stylistic choices. The style-shifting that occurs as posters move between different genres and topics contributes to the rich naturalistic language environment, as can be seen in the examples in (17), which were produced by the same person.

(17)   a. In other words, religion's purpose is to create illusory fantasies for the poor.
       b. You still not worked out it's your lass knocking on the floorboards to wind you up?
       c. Gonna be an epic shite tomorrow.

These stylistic shifts are a response to the conversational sub-types to which the poster is contributing. Like most literate adults, they understand that a discussion of *Religious beliefs* generally requires a more formal, expository

Introduction: Ready to Go

style than exchanges about mysterious sounds in the night or 'Panackelty' (and its effects on the digestive system).[11]

Such intra-'speaker' stylistic variation is common and widespread on RTG, just as it is in 'real life', where 'speakers design their talk in the awareness – at some level of consciousness and with some level of autonomous control – of alternative possibilities and of likely outcomes' (Coupland 2007: 146). Much of our 'performed discursive practice' (Di Martino 2020: 3) is what Coupland describes as 'mundane performance', which characterises most people's communication, most of the time. The *styling* in (17) exemplifies this quotidian end of the 'performance types' scale, as the poster designs their language according to genre considerations (Coupland 2007: 147). At the other end of the scale is *stylisation* – the 'knowing deployment of socially familiar semiotic material' (Mortensen et al. 2017: 10) often associated with 'high performance', a topic I return to in the next section.

The stylistic diversity of RTG is perhaps most clearly seen when posters use the semiotic resources at their disposal to deliberately represent the spoken (or internal) voice of another person, or persona. These representations can constitute a substantial portion of everyday speech. As Bakhtin claims, 'people talk most of all about what others talk about – they transmit, recall, weigh and pass judgments on other people's words, opinions, assertions, information; people are upset by others' words, or agree with them, contest them, refer to them and so forth' (1981: 338). In phonic conversation we transmit and recollect speech in a variety of ways, 'voicing' people – whether these are actual individuals, invented characters, or notional representatives of wider groups – by quoting them with varying degrees of directness, or simply by suggesting some kind of speech event occurred. Such strategies are also found on RTG.

(18) a. his Mrs kept saying "Joe we have to go now" and he just kept talking and talking.
b. she went off on one, effing and blinding.
c. She told me that he'd died during the night.
d. "If we gan down this season thats me finished ...."

Because representations of the voices of others are an important aspect of everyday conversation, their presence on RTG is further evidence that we are tapping into high-quality, naturalistic vernacular language on the site.

---

[11] Panackelty (or 'panacalty', 'panaculty', 'panack', etc.) is a casserole typically made from corned beef and sliced potatoes, associated with County Durham (Griffiths 2006: 67). RTG posters differ in their understanding of the dish: 'My Mam used to make it with corned beef, sliced potato, carrots, onions and other bits and it was ok.' Some posters object to certain ingredients – 'Nee carrots in a Panack mind' – while others advocate an inclusive approach: 'It's just full of all kinds of stuff found around the kitchen. Corned beef, potatoes, carrots, Bold 2 in 1, mouse poison, sausage. You name it, get it in there.'

This is 'real' English (Milroy and Milroy 1993), encompassing the generic and stylistic range of actual people in their everyday lives. Such language would be difficult to elicit, even in the most extensive and carefully designed sociolinguistic interview.

1.2 Dialect stylisation and dialect writing on RTG

In conversation, speech representations often focus on the propositional content of the reported utterances. It is the *meaning* of another's words that matters to the person conveying them – this seems to be the case in relation to the instances of direct speech in (18a,d). But sometimes the reporting of speech can take on a performative dimension; sometimes, *how* something is said can be as important as *what* is said. This is most evident in the semiotic performances that are incorporated into our everyday conversations, through which we project a persona or play a part (Johnstone 2013: 197). As we have seen, such 'performances' operate on a continuum of awareness and intent. At one extreme, through performance we project quotidian aspects of our identity largely automatically. At the other end we engage in what Coupland (2007) calls 'high performance', in which 'stylised and sometimes extravagant identities are brought into play' (31). And often these performances involve taking on the speech styles of others. When we recount diverting incidents, or tell jokes, or offer evaluations of people we know, or gossip, or construct a character or 'type', we incorporate other voices, often to entertain and amuse our listeners. This is not surprising, given the functional characteristics of conversation outlined in the previous section, where building rapport and affiliation – frequently through humour – is so important. It is therefore not surprising that the vernacular online platform of RTG is a repository of linguistic 'high' performance, as well as 'baseline' linguistic behaviour. For my purposes in this book, the most important kind of performance is what is sometimes referred to as *dialect stylisation* (Coupland 2001).

(19) a. think it was about 3 quid ish for a large kebab like!
     b. i would rather say cheesy chips which is sland slang to GANNAN DOOON THAAA TOOON FAAA AAAA KAAABBAAABBB LEEEEK. FFS GET A LIFE LAD.

In (19a) the language is – given what we already know about RTG – quite typical in its vernacularity. It would be reasonable to assume that this person, when required to convey information about the price of a kebab in phonic conversation, would produce a similar utterance. This is relatively automatic, naturalistic 'behaviour' in which the use of a North East dialect feature – clause-final *like* (6.3.1) – occurs (as far as it is possible to tell) spontaneously. But the sequence in capitals in (19b) is very different.

Introduction: Ready to Go

It is a contribution to a conversation in which the thread starter complained about fans of Newcastle United F.C. mocking the way people from Sunderland say 'cheesy chips'.[12] As the thread develops, some posters add their annoyance to the mix. In the case of (19b), this is expressed through an intentional parody of perceived salient features of Newcastle speech, as spoken by a characterological 'Geordie' type. The respellings of *down* and *town* as <DOOON> and <TOOON> attempt to represent the 'unshifted' [uː] vowel in words in the MOUTH lexical set, a feature often folk-linguistically associated with Newcastle and Tyneside (7.2.1). The spelling of *like* as <LEEEEK> attempts to convey the quality of the vowel in the PRICE lexical set (7.2.4) which in Newcastle and the north of the region is often [ei] or even [εi], while the more 'mainstream' [aɪ] or [ai] has a wider northern distribution, as indeed does the [uː] vowel in MOUTH (Beal et al. 2012: 34–35). A more subtle detail is captured in the spellings <THAAA>, <FAAA>, <AAAA>, <KAAA>, and possibly <-AN>, which reflect the fact that 'the quality of schwa' in Tyneside English has been observed to be 'highly variable' and is 'typically fairly open; [ɐ] is a frequent pronunciation' (Watt and Allen 2003: 269 – see 7.2.18).

The analysis shows that some of the dialect stylisation on RTG is detailed, accurate, and insightful, produced by writers who are attentive to linguistic nuance, and interested in the best way to present these details orthographically. We could claim that such artful representations can be considered as *dialect writing*; that is, they are a conscious attempt 'to represent a nonstandard dialect in written form, at least to some degree and in some portion of a text' (Honeybone and Maguire 2020: 3–15). *Intention* is important. In (19a) the poster does not 'intend' anything with the use of clause-final *like*. This is *not* therefore an example of dialect writing, but an instance of naturalistic written vernacular language which happens to contain a localised feature. But in (19b) the same feature, along with the respellings, 'means' something else. The writer is drawing on their internal representation of a 'Newcastle' dialect to identify salient features, and with the orthographic means at their disposal have written those features down. More examples of intentional dialect writing on RTG are shown in (20).

(20)   a. Shut ya mooth before ah borst it for ya!
       b. Al box yer lugs if yer dinnut givower.
       c. "I was using the front page of the Echo as a bleazer but it took ahad, man!"

While the methods used in these examples are similar to those deployed in (19) it is worth noting that the motivations behind the dialect stylisations

---

[12] A combination of ingredients that, while not unique to Sunderland, is sometimes associated with the city in the North East culinary imagination (especially when washed down with blue pop). For some remarks on the pronunciation of *cheese* see 7.2.11.

on RTG are diverse. For example, in (19b) and (20a) the representations are mocking, and in the case of (19b) abusive. But in (20b,c) they are affiliative and affectionate, appearing in threads called *Things your father used to say* and *Sayings from yesteryear*.

Dialect stylisations can be deployed in performances which tease and demean the social and cultural 'other'; they can also be used in affectionate, and often nostalgic, reconstructions of the speech styles of friends and relatives. Stylisations are also found in another species of dialect writing which occurs frequently on RTG, which we might call 'folk dialectology' (Preston 1993). Research in the overlapping fields of 'language attitudes', 'folk linguistics', and more recently 'citizen sociolinguistics' (Rymes 2020) has revealed the various ways in which people show their knowledge of and attitudes towards sociolinguistic variation. On RTG, this receptivity and interest is implicit in dialect stylisations, but is also made explicit in a variety of ways.

(21) a. There was some old bloke howking (coughing) his guts up outside when I drove past.
b. Kite is your belly.
c. Stotting means like banging. You can stott a ball or have a stotting headache.
d. "Bairn" is nothing whatsoever to do with Danes or Vikings, who had virtually no influence on our dialect. It's from the Anglo Saxon "bearn."

Metalinguistic commentary ranges from simple glosses and dictionary-style definitions (21a,b,c) to well-informed technical explanations (21d). These examples of folk dialectology relating to dialect lexis (see Chapter 5) are illustrative of the wealth of metalinguistic material on RTG.

1.3 RTG as 'corpus'

So far, I have established that RTG is a heterogeneous archive of naturalistic vernacular English. Users converse on a wide range of topics from the quotidian to the arcane, adopting a plethora of styles in a variety of genres, and occasionally displaying their sociolinguistic receptivity by staging dialect performances and/or explicitly commenting on the linguistic variation they observe around them. Most of the examples presented in this chapter and throughout the book have been taken directly from some of the 25 million messages on the site using *WebCorp Live*, a tool which allows concordances of target words and phrases to be made from all searchable pages within a specified website in real time.[13] It performs a similar job to

---

[13] Research and Development Unit for English Studies (2022) <https://www.webcorp.org.uk/lse>.

Introduction: Ready to Go

Google Advanced Search, but with a results page that allows users to choose the number of words or characters to display as the left and right contexts of the search term, resulting in output which is easier to read than Google's. Occasionally I offer an additional perspective by presenting findings from a 10-million-word sample corpus built in June 2021 using *Sketch Engine*, which can automatically harvest and tag material from specified websites and offers an extensive suite of corpus tools.[14] A useful perspective is provided by the keywords function. Keyword analysis can reveal words and phrases whose frequencies are unusually high in a corpus compared with some norm (typically a large reference corpus). *Sketch Engine* reveals that in the RTG sample corpus, amongst the top 100 keywords that help give the site its vernacular flavour (many of which, unsurprisingly, are footballing terms such as *striker, winger, midfield,* and *relegation*) are the following dialect items: *nowt* (see 3.4.5), *canny* (3.7.1.1), *marra* (6.2), *lass, lad* (6.2), *aye* (6.4), *anarl* (3.7.2), *bairn* (5.1, 6.5), *haway* (6.1), *owt* (3.4.5), *knacker* (5.3), *nee* (3.5.2).

In the chapter on dialect variation in the *Cambridge Handbook of English Corpus Linguistics*, Jack Grieve states that 'relatively little research on dialect variation has been based on corpora of naturally occurring language' (2015: 362). Elsewhere, Grieve argues that while dialectologists often 'refer to their collections of transcribed and/or recorded linguistic interviews' as 'corpora', strictly speaking such collections 'do not constitute corpora' because 'the utterances are not naturalistic … Furthermore, such collections … are clearly subject to the Observer's Paradox (Labov 1972), as the informants were aware their language was being recorded for a dialect survey. This is not the case in true corpus-based linguistics' (2009: 79). Grieve's understanding of what 'true' corpus-based linguistics consists of is widely endorsed in the literature. For example, for Mark Davies, corpora are searchable electronic collections of the output of speakers and writers who were – 'ideally' – unaware at the moment of inception that their words 'would later be used in a corpus for linguistic analysis', so helping to preserve the 'naturalness' of the language (2018: 211). RTG's incontrovertibly naturalistic status therefore differentiates it from any other 'corpus' of a regional variety of English within the British Isles, as does its size – even the sample corpus (which represents a small fraction of the RTG site) is ten times larger than the Diachronic Electronic Corpus of Tyneside English (DECTE), the only other archive of North East English remotely comparable to RTG in scale (see 2.2.5).

Size matters. Especially when it comes to the study of dialect lexis (see Chapter 5). In another handbook overview of the field of corpus-based dialect studies, the authors conclude that 'lexis is … a neglected domain … but this neglect is primarily because lexical research requires large corpora, and conventional dialect corpora are simply not large

---

[14] Kilgarriff et al. (2014) <https://www.sketchengine.eu/>.

enough for lexical analysis' (Szmrecsanyi and Anderwald 2018: 310). Take *plodge* for example. This is a widely known traditional dialect word in the North East of England used to describe the action of wading through water or mud (often for pleasure). *Plodge* appears in the 'linguistic landscape', it has been commodified on products, referenced in popular guides to North East dialect and is present in the lexicographical record (Pearce 2017: 74).[15] It even appears in the poetry of the most well-known Northumbrian modernist Basil Bunting ('some steep pool / to plodge or dip / and silent taste / with all my skin').[16] Despite its local prominence, *plodge* only occurs once in DECTE. In contrast, in June 2021 RTG offered up 90 instances of *plodge*, 12 of *plodged*, 56 of *plodging*, and 7 of the agentive noun *plodger(s)*. In 1.1.3 the low level of swearing in DECTE was ascribed to the artificial communicative context of the sociolinguistic interview; in the case of *plodge*, the contrasts between the data sets are likely to result from the difference in corpus size, and the concomitant diversity of topics covered on RTG compared with DECTE. Topic is a fundamental shaper of lexical usage: if a subject does not come up in a conversation, then words associated with relevant semantic domains (including dialect words) won't either. As we have seen, just about anything is up for discussion on RTG. The same cannot be said for DECTE because the data was collected within the constraints of the sociolinguistic interview. It would be difficult to imagine an interview protocol capable of generating the hugely various styles of utterance to be found on RTG. Clearly, *Ready to Go* is a unique resource for understanding contemporary North East English.

1.4 Aims and organisation of this book

The book has three main aims. First, it provides an up-to-date description of the vernacular English to be encountered in North East England as it is represented in an enormous archive of naturally occurring online discourse. I am especially interested in those linguistic forms and functions that serve to distinguish the English associated with the region from English(es) found elsewhere. In this respect, it is a contribution to the grand sweep of dialect study in the British Isles, especially given its focus on 'traditional' dialect features – those forms and functions that have been part of the vernacular English of north easterners since at least the late nineteenth century (though later innovations will also be covered). Second, at various points

---

[15] See Grose (1787) and Brockett (1829: 233). Brockett suggests a link with Dutch *ploegen* ('plough'), though the *OED*'s etymology implies an imitative alteration of *plod*, based on *trudge*.

[16] Bunting – while by no means a 'dialect poet' – did occasionally draw on traditional dialect lexis. Indeed, the epigraph of his greatest work, *Briggflatts* (1966), is 'the spuggies are fledged'. *Spuggy* is a dialect word for 'the house-sparrow, *Passer domesticus*' (*EDD*).

Introduction: Ready to Go

it considers the ways in which linguistic phenomena are represented and evaluated on RTG, and what this reveals about 'folk' (meta)-sociolinguistic awareness; that is, non-linguists' descriptions of, explanations for, and beliefs about the relationship between language use and social context (see 1.2). The interactions on RTG show how sociolinguistic awareness is not simply a 'mental condition that pre-exists discourse' but a discursive phenomenon (Johnstone 2010: 389) that can emerge emically, without the prompting of academic linguists. I show how the creative process of 'naming, signifying and valorising linguistic practices' – what Milani and Johnson (2010: 4) call the 'sociolinguistic imagination' – is dynamically constructed and shared, involving disputation, contestation, and agreement. Such 'talk about talk' and associated dialect stylisations are important in the process of dialect 'enregisterment', whereby a set of linguistic features is 'represented collectively in the public imagination as a stable variety' (Beal and Cooper 2015: 28). Third, the book showcases the potential of naturalistic online vernacular writing as a data source in sociodialectological research, demonstrating how such 'digital traces' – unobtrusive to obtain and on an unprecedented scale – can be 'compiled into comprehensive pictures of both individual and group behaviour' (Lazer et al. 2009: 721). While the value of such an approach has been demonstrated in World English(es) research, where 'dataset[s] of social media interactions' have proved themselves to be a 'rich source for exploring vernacular literacies, orthographic variation and creativity, and the emergence of norms in less regulated linguistic spaces' (Honkanen 2020: 3 and 64; see also Mair and Pfänder 2013), this is the first book-length study to explore an 'inner-circle' regional vernacular variety through its digital traces.

This chapter has laid down the linguistic foundations on which the book is built, describing the data set and justifying its use as primary data in sociodialectological research. The remaining chapters are organised as follows. Chapter 2 embeds the study in its sociocultural and geographical contexts by exploring the 'dialectscapes' of the region and the important role the North East has played in the sociodialectology of England. In Chapters 3 and 4 I offer an account of the morphosyntax of North East English, focusing on localised features but also taking into account vernacular 'angloversals' (1.1.3). Chapter 5 considers the extent and use of traditional dialect lexis on RTG, showing that the rate of 'survival' is perhaps higher than might be imagined, given the conclusions of previous research on lexical attrition in regional varieties of English in the UK. In Chapter 6 I address the rather under-explored topic of regional discourse features, describing ways of organising discourse that are localised to the North East. Chapter 7 engages with the idea that despite consisting of written data, RTG can tell us something about salient features of North East accents, due to the care and interest of the online dialect writers who attempt to capture them orthographically.

CHAPTER 2

The dialectscapes of North East England

I must admit that I prefer Bernicia to Deira.

We saw in the previous chapter that the English on RTG, though written, is highly vernacular: in some respects, it can be regarded as a graphic analogue of everyday phonic conversation. As such, it will inevitably contain regionally marked features. The use of these features by members of a speech community living close to each other (which are absent or infrequent in the speech of people living further away) reflects an empirically verifiable linguistic fact: natural languages display *diatopic* variation; that is, variation in space. Or, more accurately, a person's idiolect (that is, their unique way of speaking) will typically indicate their social background and affiliations, including *where* they spent their formative years. For most posters on RTG, this is of course the English region widely referred to as 'North East England', or 'The North East'.

In human geography, the term *region* is applied to 'a more or less bounded area possessing some sort of unity or organizing principle(s) that distinguish it from other regions' (Gregory 2000: 687). Although the territory contained within the 'bounded area' of North East England can vary depending on who is defining it and for what ends, in this book, when the terms *North East England* and *the North East* are used, they should generally be understood as referring to the official administrative counties and districts given in Table 2.1 and mapped in Figure 2.1. The term *Northumbria* is also sometimes used to refer to this area, which roughly corresponds to the territory covered by the historic counties of Northumberland and County Durham.[1] Compared with other English regions, the population is

---

[1] 'Historic' because when the Local Government Act came into force in 1974 creating a two-tier system of county and district councils, parts of Northumberland and County Durham were subsumed into the new metropolitan county of Tyne and Wear. Some of the changes were even more radical. For example, Cumberland and Westmorland disappeared and were replaced by Cumbria. This rupture in British toponymy was

quite low (approximately 2.6 million in mid-2019, according to the ONS) and spread over a large area (8,500 square kilometres), making it slightly smaller than Corsica and Puerto Rico, but larger than Delaware. Most people live in three urban areas centred on the cities of Newcastle-upon-Tyne (Tyneside), Sunderland (Wearside), and Middlesbrough (Teesside). To the south and north of Tyneside lie the coalfields of County Durham and south east Northumberland, with their ex-mining towns and villages, while the rest of the region consists of wild moor-covered uplands and rich agricultural lowlands (Aalen 2006). This corner of England has played an important – if sometimes overlooked – role in British history. For example, in the seventh and eighth centuries it was at the heart of Norþanhymbra ('Northumbria'), the largest and most powerful of the Anglo-Saxon kingdoms, which stretched from the River Humber to what is now south east Scotland. Northumbria was one of the most important centres of learning in Western Europe, with its intellectual and religious life based at the monasteries and scriptoria of Lindisfarne, Jarrow, and Wearmouth. A thousand years later, as a consequence of the increasing exploitation of indigenous coal reserves in the eighteenth century, North East England became one of the first European regions to industrialise. While coal had probably been dug in the North East since Roman times, the Industrial Revolution led to the employment of thousands of men (and to a lesser extent women and children) in the collieries and ancillary industries of the 'Great Northern Coalfield'. A particularly significant development – the railway – arose from the need to transport the coal rapidly and efficiently from collieries in West Durham and Darlington to the port at Stockton on the River Tees. Later, the North East was at the vanguard of developments in shipbuilding technology, armaments, and electrical turbine generation.

Table 2.1 *Counties and districts in North East England*

County	Districts
Northumberland	Blyth Valley, Wansbeck, Castle Morpeth, Tynedale, Alnwick, Berwick-upon-Tweed
Tyne and Wear	Gateshead, Newcastle-upon-Tyne, North Tyneside, South Tyneside, Sunderland
County Durham	City of Durham, Easington, Sedgefield, Teesdale, Wear Valley, Derwentside, Chester-Le-Street, Hartlepool, Darlington, Stockton-on-Tees (north of the River Tees)
North Yorkshire (part only)	Stockton-on-Tees (south of the River Tees), Redcar and Cleveland, Middlesbrough

Present-day Northumbria has a roughly 'tripartite' structure, reflected in the title of an anthology of poetry from and about the region published by

deplored by the poet C. H. Sisson: 'Swimming the horses at Appleby in Westmorland / – Or Cumbria as they now call it, God damn their eyes' (1998).

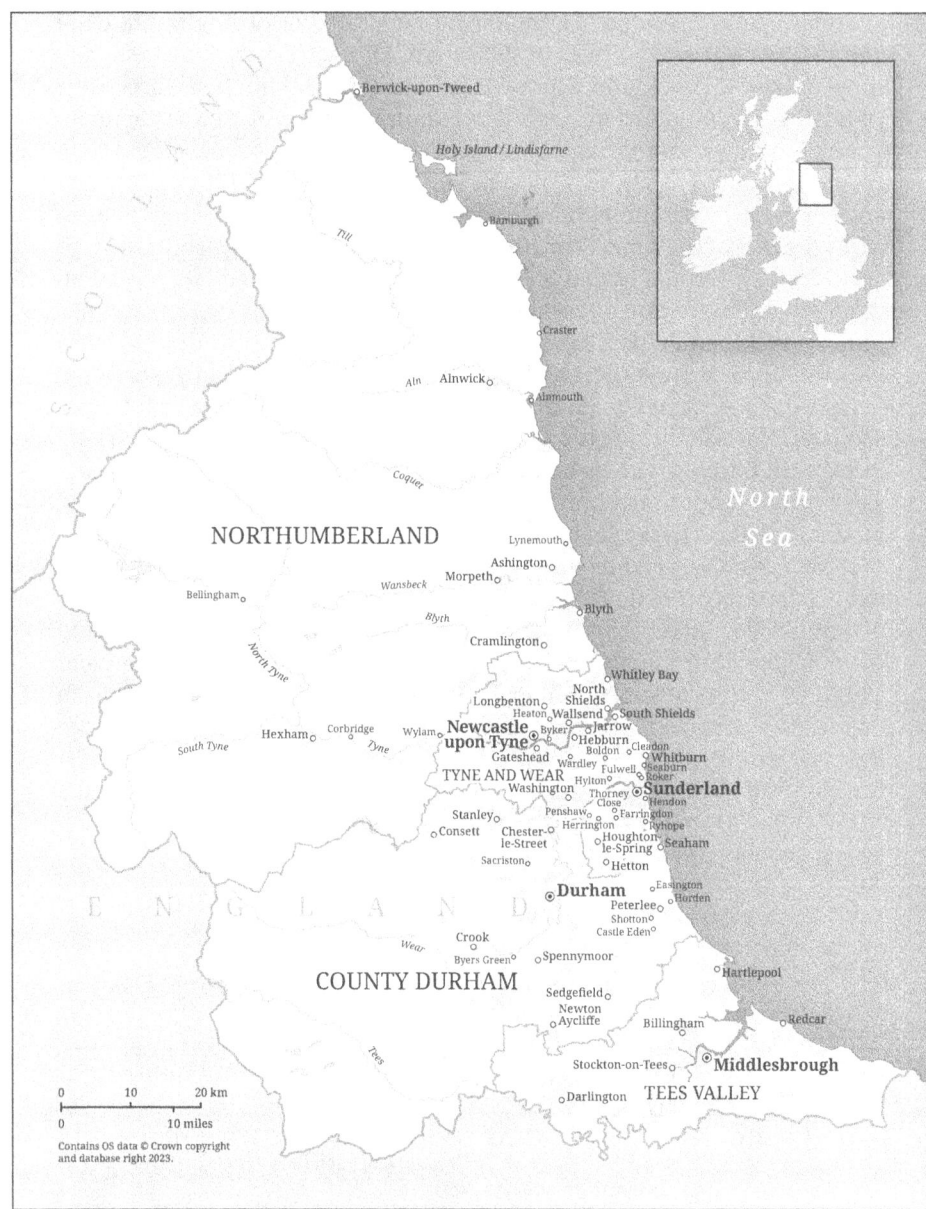

Figure 2.1 North East England showing locations mentioned in this book

North East-based Bloodaxe Books: *Land of Three Rivers* (Astley 2017). The densely populated coastal conurbations associated with these rivers – the Tyne, the Wear, and the Tees – are economic and cultural 'catchments', exerting influence over their respective hinterlands in Northumberland, County

Durham, and parts of North Yorkshire (though Teesside's development and expansion came later than Wearside's and Tyneside's, whose economic rivalry was well-established by the early nineteenth century). According to Milne the North East is

> best visualised as a polycentric space with shifting economic focal points and centres of gravity ... different localities have been prominent at different times ... The towns of Newcastle, South Shields, Sunderland and Middlesbrough have all at some point in the last two centuries dominated one or other element of the economy, only to see that role challenged a generation or two on. (2007: 115)

2.1 The linguistic character of North East vernacular English

The roots of the contemporary vernacular English(es) spoken in the northern half of the North East Atlantic Archipelago are deeply intertwined. Many of the non-standard morphosyntactic and lexical features of NEVE – as represented so dynamically on RTG – can be found in varieties of English and Scots in Scotland and Northern Ireland, as well as in the everyday speech of Cumbria, Yorkshire, and further afield in the north of England. These varieties have shared origins in the Anglian dialects of Germanic peoples from the European mainland who began settling along the east coast of Britain in the fifth century. At its height, the Anglian kingdom of Northumbria – formed when Bernicia (north of the Tees) and Deira (south of the Tees) united in the early seventh century – extended from the Firth of Forth in the north to the Humber-Mersey line in the south, and from the North Sea in the east to the Irish Sea in the west. In other words, it consisted of the whole of what is now northern England and lowland Scotland (before these nations existed as political entities). James Murray – first editor of the *OED* and author of *The Dialect of the Southern Counties of Scotland* (1873) – notes that despite the 'diversifying influences' of a separate culture and history, contrasting legal, ecclesiastical and education systems, and a long record of political and military conflict

> the spoken tongue from York to Aberdeen is still one language, presenting indeed several well-defined sub-dialects on both sides of the Tweed, but agreeing, even in its extreme forms, much more closely than the dialect of Yorkshire does with that of Dorset ... The living tongue of Teviotdale, and the living tongue of Northumberland, would, in accordance with present political geography, be classed, the one as a Scottish, the other as an English dialect: in actual fact, they are the same dialect, spoken, the one on Scottish the other on English territory, but which, before Scottish and English had their political application, was all alike the Anglian territory of Northan-hymbra-land.

Of course, Murray was writing in the mid-nineteenth century. The 'living tongues' he refers to were what have come to be known as – from a twenty-first century perspective – the 'Traditional Dialects' (Trudgill 2000). While some speakers of contemporary NEVE do preserve 'older' features found across a wider vernacular linguistic North which includes lowland Scotland and the historic counties of Ulster, traditional dialects have largely been in recession in Scotland and the north of England and modern dialects on either side of the Anglo-Scottish border have developed differently, with 'different trajectories of language change due to the heteronymic relationship of the vernacular varieties with supraregional forms of English in England on the one hand and with forms of English in Scotland ... on the other'. This has meant that 'the supraregional orientation in both locations has become more dominant' (Hickey 2015: 19; Maguire 2015) and the border has become a more sharply defined linguistic barrier than it once was. Nevertheless, despite the development of supraregional, somewhat 'levelled' forms of English in the north of England, many traditional features are still to be found on RTG, and not simply as fossilised remnants of the linguistic past.

Naturally, Angus McIntosh and his colleagues acknowledged the significance of the vernacular linguistic North when devising the Linguistic Survey of Scotland (LSS) in the 1950s. Like Murray before them, their geographical remit did not stop at the Anglo-Scottish border but extended into Cumberland, Northumberland, and the eastern part of the north of Ireland. It was felt that to understand the linguistic situation within Scotland, the closely related English of these contiguous territories also needed to be surveyed.[2]

While some of the features shared between Northumbrian English and Scots can be traced back to the common Anglian heritage, we also need to take into account the long history of population movement and dialect contact between Northumbria, Scotland, and Ireland which was at its peak in the nineteenth century when the industries of the North East drew in migrants from across the British and Irish Isles. A report on social conditions on Tyneside published in 1928 pointed out that 'the Scotch [sic] element in the population of the two counties [Northumberland and County Durham] is very marked' (Mess 1928, in Watt 1998: 116). In 1841

---

[2] One of the first holders of a Chair in Linguistics at a European university was from Sunderland. Angus McIntosh, who was born in Cleadon and educated at Ryhope Grammar School and Oxford, became Forbes Professor of English Language and General Linguistics at the University of Edinburgh in 1948, aged thirty-four. As well as his work on the LSS, McIntosh is remembered for his scholarship in the history of English which culminated in the publication of *A Linguistic Atlas of Late Mediaeval English* in 1986. He was also a leading figure in Scottish lexicography; indeed, without him 'the *Scottish National Dictionary* could never have reached completion, as it did in 1976, and the *Dictionary of the Older Scottish Tongue* would ... have fallen by the wayside' (Aitken 1981: xxii) – see 2.2.6.

it was estimated that in Newcastle and South Shields the Scots numbered over 5 per cent of the population; and the 1911 census showed that the North East was well represented amongst the administrative counties and large towns with the highest proportions of natives of Scotland (Bueltmann et al. 2013: 156–157). Into the twentieth century comparable maritime industrial sectors on the Clyde, Tyne, and Wear made the North East's shipyards a draw for migrants from the west coast of Scotland, though Highland Scots and east coast Scots were also amongst those employed in North East shipyards. Indeed, the residential area favoured by Scots in Hebburn, South Tyneside became known as 'Little Aberdeen' (Bueltmann et al. 2013: 164). These Northumbrian-Scots connections have continued up to the present day and are sometimes discussed on RTG.

(1)   a. We're more similar culturally than people would like to admit.
       b. I've always thought the NE has the same sort of mentality as the Scots, up against it, sense of humour etc.
       c. We have a lot more in common with the Scots opposed to most home counties wankers.
       d. I generally as a rule prefer Scottish than English.
       e. I identify with the Scots a lot more than I do with Southerners and I admire their national identity.
       f. we have more in common with them than anyone south of durham.
       g. Wouldnt bother me if the border was moved down as far as Yorkshire.

Such remarks reflect 'the continuing close relationship between Scots and Northumbrians' which 'has served to maintain and reinforce the linguistic similarities between their dialects' (Beal 1993: 189–190). The importance of these Northumbrian-Scots affinities is reflected in the abundant references to Scotland, Scots, and Scottish English in this book.

Ireland's contribution to the demographic make-up of North East England is also significant – indeed, after Merseyside, Tyneside has historically been the most important centre for Irish immigration in Britain (Beal and Corrigan 2009). A substantial proportion of immigrants to the North East came from the north of Ireland, where Ulster Scots is widely spoken – a variety which was derived from the dialects of the Scots who settled in the region starting in the seventeenth century as part of British colonial expansion. It can therefore be difficult to determine if a particular feature of NEVE was imported by immigrants from the north of Ireland or was already present in both varieties. The linguistic effect of immigrants from the south of Ireland might in theory be easier to identify since southerners were historically Irish speakers who acquired English as a second language, with the result that southern varieties show Irish substrate influence. Several phonetic, phonological, and morphosyntactic 'parallels' (Hickey 2016: 255) between NEVE and Irish English have been noted (e.g. Beal 1993; Mearns 2015; Hickey 2016). For example, *yous* (3.4.1.3);

ye (3.4.1.3); epistemic *must* in the negative (Beal 1993: 197); 'double' modals (4.2.2); *for to* as an infinitival marker (4.5.2); *needs cleaned*; *wants washed* (4.5.2); /h/ retention (7.3.3); nurse/north merger (7.2.10); T-to-R (7.4.1); epenthetic vowels (7.2.20); alveolar /l/ (7.1). Several of these features are less likely to have been nineteenth-century imports and more likely to reflect the shared origins of the varieties spoken in the north of Ireland, North East England and southern Scotland (reinforced by population movements between the three territories). The same can be said for lexis; indeed, some lexical items widely believed to have Irish origins on investigation turn out not to have. For example, Beal and Corrigan (2009: 248–249) show convincingly that 'contrary to popular perception, *crack* [defined in *EDD* as 'talk, conversation, gossip, chat'] ... cannot be associated with the Irish migration period' and that Irish *craic* was in fact borrowed from Ulster Scots and/or English – a position endorsed by *OED* (see also 5.1.2).

There have been other 'outside' linguistic influences on varieties of English spoken in North East England. Most fundamentally, the Viking incursions and settlements which began in the eighth century affected the southern half of the Kingdom of Northumbria (Deira) more than the northern half (Bernicia), so that Scandinavian influence, though not entirely absent, has been more attenuated in the dialects of Northumberland and the north of County Durham (which remained outwith the limits of the Danelaw) than in those of Yorkshire and the south of Durham (Beal 1993: 187). A further important source of exogenous linguistic influence is the region's long history as a maritime trading economy and the contacts that developed between north easterners and the fishermen, merchants, and sailors from the Low Countries, Scandinavia, and the Baltic (and indeed other coastal locations in the British Isles) who visited the region's ports – some settling permanently. The Romani people have also enriched Northumbrian English and Scots (see 5.1 and 5.2). The earliest reports of Romanis in Britain are from Galloway in the fifteenth century (Matras 2010: 57), and the Scottish Borders and far north of England have been an important cultural centre for Romanichal travellers ever since. It should also be pointed out that the region's mines, shipyards, and their ancillary trades did not only draw in migrants from Scotland and Ireland but also people from the Northumbrian countryside, as well as from further afield in England and Wales. In his account of growing up in the Durham village of Boldon Colliery in the late nineteenth century, the Trade Unionist and Labour MP Jack Lawson was alert to the linguistic dimension of these demographic changes, writing of 'a polyglot population', with Lancashire, Cumberland, Yorkshire, Staffordshire, Cornish, and Welsh 'accents, dialects, and languages' to be heard alongside Scottish, Irish, and local Northumbrian forms of speech (Lawson 1932, in Watt 2002: 51). These conditions of population mixing were of course replicated in other regions; conditions – alongside more diffuse social changes such as the development of the mass media and compulsory state education – which ultimately resulted in a redrawing of the dialect map of Britain. The patchwork of 'traditional' dialects, developed in relatively stable agrarian societies and diverging markedly from SE and each other which we see in the earliest efforts to capture spatial variation in the British Isles (e.g. Ellis 1889 – see 2.2.1) and whose outlines are still very much visible in SED (2.2.3), was superseded (albeit partially) by an array of 'modern' dialects (Trudgill 2000), which are closer to each other and to SE and which I refer to in this book as 'mainstream'.

Present-day NEVE has emerged from a complex set of interacting forces. It owes its linguistic character to 'native' roots in an Anglian dialect of Old English (which it shared with what became lowland Scots), acted upon by a variety of 'external' influences, and shaped by the region's peripherality and its borderland status between Scotland and the rest of England. In many respects it is a conservative variety, with some speakers – even young ones – using features that were once more widespread across the north of England but are now generally recessive. But in other respects it is 'contemporary'. In its supralocalised 'modern' form as an 'urban koiné' (Watt 2002: 44) shorn of some of its most localised features it resonates social attractiveness and 'cool', scoring highly on such values in language attitude research (Di Martino 2020: 70–74). And while the North East is one of the least ethnically diverse regions in England and Wales, and the influence of Empire and Commonwealth immigrants – particularly from the Caribbean – has not been as extensive as it has been in other parts of northern England, there are substantial populations of people of South Asian descent in all the region's main urban centres.[3] However, very little research has been carried out in these communities to discover how the English of South Asians in North East England might contrast with mainstream NEVE (but see Newby 2020).

2.2 Major dialectological and lexicographical sources for the study of NEVE

Since the origins of British scientific dialectology in the mid-nineteenth century, the North East of England has been subject to detailed and sustained scrutiny. In particular, five large-scale projects are important sources of reliable data for the region, spanning a period of collection from

---

[3] In this context it should be noted that one of the oldest Muslim communities in the UK was founded by Yemeni seamen in South Shields in the late nineteenth century (Lawless 1995). The Yemeni role in the history of Tyneside is the probable origin of the ethnonym *Sand Dancer* for the people of South Shields. Although it started out as a racist slur, many townsfolk now embrace it (Pearce 2014). One of the North East's most well-known celebrities, Little Mix singer Jade Thirlwall, is of Yemeni descent on her father's side (see 2.3). We might also note that Gateshead is one of the most important centres of Jewish learning in Europe and that urban parts of the region have substantial populations of Chinese and Eastern European immigrants.

the 1860s to the present day. Their contributions to and significance for the description of contemporary NEVE are outlined below.

2.2.1 Alexander J. Ellis's *The Existing Phonology of English Dialects* (1889)

This monumental work – which took twenty years from inception to publication – was 'the first survey of English dialects based on rich, systematically collected evidence' (Ihalainen 1994: 232). Ellis recruited 811 volunteers to furnish him with examples of local dialect collected in 494 locations across England, the Scottish Lowlands, and some spots in Wales and Ireland (Maguire 2012: 88). Some of his helpers were trained in the use of 'palaeotype' – a transcription system he developed which enabled him to describe sounds in considerable detail. In this work Ellis also published dialect maps of England and Scotland that projected 'groupings of dialect features to geography' (Sanderson and Widdowson 1985, in Szmrecsanyi 2013: 8). The maps show six large 'divisions' further partitioned into forty-two 'districts', 'in each of which a sensible similarity of pronunciation prevails' (Ellis 1889: 3). Most – but not all – of present-day North East England is located in 'the north Northern' district (D32), an area consisting of a 'small portion' of north Cumberland, the north of County Durham and the whole of Northumberland, apart from the northern 'slopes of the Cheviots', which are part of the Lowland division of southern Scotland (Ellis 1889: 637).[4] The south of County Durham is in D31, reflecting later perceptual and socio-dialectological findings about differences in speech between the north and south of the region (see 2.3). D32 is further sub-divided into six 'varieties'. These are not shown on the map but Ellis does sketch out their 'characters'; for example, in relation to the north Durham variety he writes: 'Sunderland can hardly be said to be a dialect on account of the mixed population and

---

[4] Ellis was not the first to produce a dialect map of a British nation. Two others preceded his. In 1873, one of Ellis's chief helpers, Prince Louis-Lucien Bonaparte, had published his 'Classification des dialectes anglais modernes', which had included 'une petite carte des principaux dialects anglais', but the data upon which he based his map was not as extensive or rigorously sourced as Ellis's (Penhallurick 2018: 116–120). Nevertheless, in relation to North East England, there are many similarities between Ellis's and Bonaparte's classification and mapping. 'D32' closely corresponds with a territory claimed by Bonaparte to be home of a dialect which he labels – interestingly, and with, as we have seen, some justification – 'ecossais méridional du nord de l'Angleterre' ('the southern Scots of northern England'). In the same year that Bonaparte presented his map to the Philological Society, James Murray published *The Dialect of the Southern Counties of Scotland* (see 2.1), which included a 'Map of Scotland, shewing the present limits of the Gaelic Tongue, and the chief dialectical divisions of the Lowland Scotch'. Murray's 'southern group' of 'Lowland Scotch' dialects contains 'the border counties in Scotland' but are 'closely connected with the dialects of Northumberland, of Shields, and of North Cumberland in England ... where the affinities between the idioms are to some extent represented in the colouring' on the map (Murray 1873: 237).

influence of Scotch and Irish' (Ellis 1889: 638). Comments like this – in Ellis's work and in 'traditional' approaches to dialect in general – point to the main motivation of such studies, which was philological. Ellis believed that so-called 'mixed' dialects – arising due to the population movements and situations of contact outlined in the previous section – were unhelpful in reconstructing earlier forms of English. Nevertheless, despite misgivings about the 'purity' of speech his fieldworkers were encountering (and their varying levels of ability as phoneticians), accents were often captured in meticulous detail and localised very specifically, and I draw on the material Ellis collected from his survey sites in County Durham and Northumberland in my description of RTG's representation of the North East soundscape in Chapter 7.

2.2.2 The English Dialect Society (1873 to 1896)

The other great English dialectologist of the nineteenth century – Joseph Wright – was also concerned with historical matters, spending much of his academic career as Professor of Comparative Philology at Oxford; but whereas Ellis's preoccupation was phonetics and phonology, Wright will mainly be remembered for his work on dialect words.[5] Wright was the editor of the six-volume *English Dialect Dictionary* (1896–1905), 'the greatest achievement of British dialectological lexicography' (Penhallurick 2009: 291) and the ultimate research 'output' of the English Dialect Society (EDS), which – prompted by Ellis amongst others – had been established in 1873 with the objective of combining 'the labours of collectors of Provincial English words by providing a common centre to which they may be sent, so as to gather material for a general record of all such words' (EDS 1874, in Crowley 2003: 89). The task was to be carried out with some urgency. In philological circles it was a widely held view that traditional dialects were in decline, and the window into the past of the language which they offered would soon be closed forever. In the words of Walter Skeat, Cambridge Professor of Anglo-Saxon and the Society's president: 'The dialects are dying, and the competent helpers who understand them are waxing old. In a few years it will be too late' (in Görlach 1999: 213). The *EDD* and Wright's *English Dialect Grammar* (*EDG*) – which initially appeared as part of the

---

[5] Though united in intellectual capacity and the breadth and depth of their philological interests, the two men emerged from very different social milieux. Ellis 'epitomized the life and career of the liberal-minded Victorian gentleman-scholar' – he was comfortably upper middle class and was supported financially his entire life by a bequest (MacMahon 2006: 114). Wright came from a small village in Yorkshire and as a child worked as a labourer in a quarry and a mill. He did not learn to read until his mid-teens, yet – through extraordinary vigour and assiduity – became one of the great scholars of his age (Kellett 2004). Virginia Woolf admired him and his wife Elizabeth greatly and he is the probable inspiration for the character of Sam Robson in her 1937 novel *The Years* (Periyan 2018: 1305–1308).

dictionary and covers phonology (much of it derived from Ellis) and morphosyntax – remain 'important points of reference for anybody undertaking research into the history of English dialects' (Beal 2004: 206). Inevitably, they are drawn on extensively in this volume. Accessing the riches of *EDD* has been made much easier by Manfred Markus and his team at Innsbruck University, who have produced an 'optimally digitised version' of Wright's work, accessible through a functionally rich interface (Markus 2021: 1).[6]

North East England is well-represented in *EDD*, and for this great credit should go to the antiquarian and philologist Richard Oliver Heslop. His *Northumberland Words* (1892–1893), an 800-page, two-volume work subtitled *A Glossary of Words used in the County of Northumberland and on the Tyneside* provides 'a good idea of the structural characteristics' of North East English in the nineteenth century (Ihalainen 1994: 213) and was one of the most scholarly and extensive local dictionaries of the dozens published under the aegis of the EDS. Many of its findings were incorporated into the *EDD* (the initials R. O. H. occur over 700 times across the six volumes) and it is the source of numerous dialect examples in this book. I have also made use of Francis Palgrave's EDS publication *A List of Words and Phrases in Every-day Use by the Natives of Hetton-Le-Hole in the County of Durham* (1896).

2.2.3 The Survey of English Dialects (c.1946 to c.1978)

The research overseen by Ellis and Wright laid the foundations for the first fully scientific survey of dialects of English in England. The project leaders Harold Orton and Eugen Dieth believed that such a survey was necessary in order to record 'the traditional types of vernacular English' (Orton 1962: 14) typically spoken by older, rural males before they were lost as a result of the social and demographic changes taking place in the period after the end of the Second World War (although it should be pointed out that, like the EDS luminaries before them, who also felt the urgency of their task in the face of rapid change, Orton and Dieth's motivation was to collect reflexes of older forms to help with their historical reconstructions). The main work

---

[6] *EDD* (available online at <https://eddonline4-proj.uibk.ac.at/edd/>) is immense. According to Elizabeth Wright (wife of Joseph) 'there are approximately 1,350 words meaning to give a person a thrashing, and an almost innumerable quantity meaning to die, and to get drunk. There are some 1,300 ways of telling a person he is a fool … There are about 1,050 terms for a slattern … Among animals possessing a large variety of names the smallest pig of a litter holds a very prominent place with over 120 titles … That handsome bird the … green woodpecker … figures under almost every letter of the alphabet; whilst the sparrow and the stickleback also rank high on the list. Among flowers, the ox-eye daisy and the foxglove have the largest number of different names' (E. Wright 1913: 6–7). As well as being her husband's biographer, Elizabeth collaborated with him on a grammar of Old English, and was an accomplished folklorist and dialectologist, playing a key role in the editing of the dictionary (E. Wright 1932: 401–402).

of the Survey of English Dialects (SED) was carried out between 1950 and 1961 at the University of Leeds, during which time eleven professional fieldworkers visited 313 localities, armed with a questionnaire consisting of some 1,300 items, which they completed with almost 1,000 informants (Penhallurick 2018: 144). The wealth of lexical, grammatical, and phonological information generated in these interviews was presented in the thirteen volumes of the *Basic Material* (the survey's main data set). This resource has been a mainstay of research on dialects in England ever since, acting as 'a historical baseline against which future studies could be measured' (Orton et al. 1978: n.p.). In Northumbria (i.e. County Durham and Northumberland) fifteen locations were surveyed between January 1953 and September 1955 and the findings there are drawn on extensively in this book, sometimes directly from the *Basic Material* and sometimes via works derived from it, such as *The Linguistic Atlas of England* (*LAE*) by Orton, Sanderson, and Widdowson (1978) and *The Survey of English Dialects: The Dictionary and Grammar* (*SEDDG*) by Upton, Parry, and Widdowson (1994). Also of great value is the collection of SED recordings with accompanying linguistic descriptions held by the British Library Sound Archive, which includes all those from survey locations in Northumbria. SED material relating to the region can also be accessed through the website of the Leeds Archive of Vernacular Culture.[7] A useful SED-adjacent resource is the 'corpus' collected by Harold Orton in the 1930s from interviewees at some thirty Northumbrian localities (Rydland 1995) which informs some of the descriptions in Chapter 7.[8]

As we saw in relation to *EDD*, the transformation of dialect data from analogue to digital has opened up new ways of interrogating the material, and SED data has been used in a number of mapping projects using advanced statistical methods (see for example the website of the Salzburg dialectometry team at <http://dialektkarten.ch/>), as has data from the *Voices* project (see Penhallurick 2018: 164–165).

2.2.4 *Voices* (2004 to 2005)

Leeds was also the main academic centre for a dialect project in some respects heir to the SED in scope and scale. *Voices* was 'a unique collaboration between the British Broadcasting Corporation, the University of Leeds

---

[7] The British Library material is at <https://sounds.bl.uk/accents-and-dialects/survey-of-english-dialects>. In addition to its SED holdings, the archive also contains the *Voices* recordings (see 2.2.4) and other material valuable for dialect study, including the Millennium Memory Bank recordings and Berliner Lautarchiv British and Commonwealth recordings. The Leeds archive is at <https://dialectandheritage.org.uk/lavc/>.

[8] It is notable that Harold Orton was from Byers Green in County Durham and his Oxford B.Litt. thesis – examined by Joseph Wright – was on the phonology of the dialect of that village (Wales and Upton 1998: 27).

and the British Library to document the linguistic landscape of the United Kingdom at the start of the twenty-first century' (Robinson 2021: vii). Between May 2004 and July 2005 over 80,000 people completed online and paper surveys, while some 1,200 participants took part in group interview sessions carried out by BBC journalists across the country. Data was also gathered from visitors to an exhibition at the British Library. The eclectic range of methods adopted meant that – while the main data set was lexical – information about accent, morphosyntax, and language attitudes was also collected. The richness of the data is shown in the linguistic descriptions of the BBC recordings now held in the British Library and which I refer to in Chapters 5 and 6. *Voices* data has underpinned several important publications in sociolinguistics and dialectology (see for example Upton and Davies 2013). Of particular value in making the data accessible is *A Thesaurus of English Dialect and Slang: England, Wales and the Channel Islands* (Robinson 2021) in which regional distributions of variants of the thirty-eight 'prompt' notions in the lexical component of the *Voices* survey are given.

2.2.5 Diachronic Electronic Corpus of Tyneside English (ongoing)

The large-scale dialect projects outlined so far have been national in scope. In contrast, the Diachronic Electronic Corpus of Tyneside English (DECTE), as the name implies, has a regional focus. The publicly available component of DECTE is a c.800,000-word (and growing) corpus of sociolinguistic interviews with North East speakers, mainly from Tyneside but also from Northumberland, County Durham, and Sunderland, recorded by academics and students at Newcastle University from the early 1970s to the present day (Corrigan et al. 2012). This 'linguistic time capsule' (Allen et al. 2007) combines the Newcastle Electronic Corpus of Tyneside English (NECTE) – which amalgamates recorded material from the Tyneside Linguistic Survey and the Phonological Variation and Change in Contemporary Spoken English project – with NECTE2, a monitor corpus begun in 2007 to allow ongoing changes in their historical contexts to be studied. Particularly valuable features of DECTE are the alignment of sound files to POS-tagged transcripts, and a research-facing and a public-facing website.[9] DECTE is an essential resource for anyone studying the sociodialectology of North East England and has been at the heart of numerous publications (see Mearns 2015 and Mearns et al. 2016).

2.2.6 Additional lexicographical resources for the study of NEVE

While the *English Dialect Dictionary* and its associated glossaries are my main lexicographical resource, I also draw on an important (but often

---

[9] The research interface is at <https://research.ncl.ac.uk/decte/>. 'Talk of the Toon' can be found at <https://research.ncl.ac.uk/decte/toon/>.

overlooked) pre-EDS publication: *A Glossary of North Country Words, in Use* (first edition 1825) by the Newcastle antiquarian John Trotter Brockett (Ruano-García 2014: 537). When it comes to etymologies, the *Oxford English Dictionary* (*OED*) and the *Oxford Dictionary of English Etymology* (*ODEE*) are consulted alongside *EDD*, not because *EDD*'s word histories are inaccurate, but because they can be quite sparse and are perhaps sometimes more confidently expressed than the evidence would support (Chamson 2012). The *OED* online is also, of course, an excellent source of historical examples, as is the *Dictionaries of the Scots Language* (*DSL*) website, which is illustrative of the 'seminal and extensive ... Scottish contribution to lexicography, both within and outside of Scotland' (Scott 2020: 315).[10] It brings together the two major historical dictionaries of Scots: *A Dictionary of the Older Scottish Tongue* (pre-1700) and *The Scottish National Dictionary* (post-1700). An additional source for Scots is *A Concise Ulster Dictionary* (*CUD*). The most scholarly dictionary of North East English since Heslop's is Bill Griffiths' *A Dictionary of North East Dialect* (*DNED*). Mention must also be made of Jonathon Green's online *Dictionary of Slang*, which is an indispensable resource for the study of informal English lexis.[11]

2.3 Geordie(s), Mackem(s), Smoggie(s)

Although its centrality to the dialectological enterprise in the UK makes North East England well-trodden ground for linguists, the region does not typically loom large in the mental maps of outsiders, particularly those from London and the South East, who inhabit what is widely perceived as the cultural, political, and economic 'centre of national gravity' (Wales 2006: 1). Indeed, to many southerners, much of England north of Birmingham, in particular the North East, is *Terra Septentrionalis Incognita*. It is not a major centre for tourism: in 2019 only 4.0 per cent of trips by residents within England were to the North East, compared with 17.0 per cent to destinations in the South West and 28.0 per cent to London and the South East (Great Britain Tourism Survey 2023). Nor is it much of a target for inter-regional migration – according to the ONS in 2019 just 3.47 per cent of the UK's 1.5 million internal migrants moved to North East England (making it the least popular of all the English regions), compared to 32.0 per cent who went to London and the South East. Such facts mean outsiders' perceptions are seldom derived from direct experience but from representations on television, in films, online, and in the national press. These representations can simplify and distort, especially when they focus on Newcastle/Tyneside and its inhabitants (commonly known as 'Geordies') to the exclusion of other places and people in the region. While outsiders

[10] <https://dsl.ac.uk/>.
[11] <https://greensdictofslang.com/>.

tend to perceive the North East as 'a single homogeneous entity dominated by Newcastle and the figure of the "Geordie"' (Beal et al. 2012: 10), insiders tend to see things differently.

(2) a. I gave up a long time ago pointing out to people that I'm not a **geordie**.
b. Outside the northeast, we are all **Geordies** in my experience.
c. I am not a **Geordie**, don't want to be a **Geordie**.
d. I was brought up to believe **Geordies** are from Newcastle.
e. **Geordies** are from Tyneside.

As these RTG comments illustrate, for north easterners, the ethnonym is strongly associated with Tyneside and in particular the city of Newcastle. Insiders are also aware that the North East's ethnonymicon extends beyond *Geordie*, reflecting the region's diversity; and for many inhabitants there is a perceived linguistic dimension to this (3d,e,f).

(3) a. I'm a **Sanddancer**. We have our own local name. We don't need to be saddled by a name for people elsewhere.
b. And what about us **Sandies**? We no more like being labelled Geordies than people from Sunderland do.
c. Born and bred in Fulwell, **Mackem** and hate being called a geordie by any southerner I encounter at work. Always put them right.
d. You're right they're a bit different but his point was **monkey hangers** sound more like **smoggies** than **yackers** which is correct.
e. Moon, spoon, curry why can't **Mackems** say these words?
f. No **smoggies** say dinnar.
g. So, you admit you are a **pitmatic pit-yakker**!

Although all the ethnonyms exemplified here are quite well-known locally, the 'big three' (*Geordie*, *Mackem*, and *Smoggie*) in particular help to shape and reinforce the pluricentric structure of the region.[12]

In an important collection of essays on the history and culture of North East England entitled *Geordies: Roots of Regionalism* (1992, 2nd edition 2005) the editors made the bold claim that the 'book is by Geordies, about Geordies, and we take as our place the whole North East region' (Colls and Lancaster 2005a: xi). *Geordie* is a hypocorism, combining *George* and *-die/-dy* – a Scots variant of the *-y/-ie* suffix added to words or curtailed forms of words ending in *-l* (e.g. *doldie*, *laldie*), *-r* (e.g. *Geordie*, *bardie*), and *-n* (e.g. *bandie*, *Johndie*). According to *DSL* it probably developed through morphological re-analysis of words where the *-d* is organic (as in *Sandy*, *laddie*, etc.).

---

[12] In the RTG sample corpus, *Mackem(s)* occurs 58.01 times per million words and *Geordie(s)* 55.81 times. *Smoggie(s)* is far less common at 3.8 times per million. For comparison, *Mackem(s)* and *fuckers* have a similar frequency, as do *Geordie(s)* and *bollock(s)*, while *cocks* (and *misunderstood*) occur as often as *Smoggie(s)*.

Evidence from birth records suggests that in the late eighteenth and early nineteenth centuries *George* was a very common name in County Durham and Northumberland, and given the frequent, sustained, and multiplex nature of contacts across the Anglo-Scottish border (Llamas 2010) and the historic closeness of Scots and Northumbrian English (see 2.1) it is unsurprising that many a young George would have affectionately been known as 'Geordie'. Indeed, Brockett has *Geordie* as a headword, describing it as 'a very common name among the pitmen' (1829: 131). The assertion that *Geordie* can be used for people from 'the whole North East region' is not *entirely* unjustified: as we have seen, some people outside North East England use *Geordie* like this, mainly because they perceive similarities in dialect and/or social and cultural background amongst the inhabitants; and there is some (albeit limited) historical warrant for such an assertion. For example, a review of the evidence (see Pearce 2015a) suggests that by the mid-nineteenth century *Geordie* was being used collectively for the 'industrial icons' of the North East, the miners who dug the coal and the seamen who transported it (Wales 2006: 135), irrespective of where in the region they were from. But towards the end of the century there are indications of both a broadening of meaning (so that the population at large and not just miners and mariners can be referred to as Geordies) and a narrowing geographical range. In an 1887 essay on 'Geordie' published in *The Star* (Guernsey) the author states that 'strictly speaking, Geordie is a pitman hailing from the north bank of the Tyne'. When *Geordie* is used in its wider ethnonymic sense it also tends to be associated with a specific part of the North East, as in an 1894 article in the *Pall Mall Gazette*: 'The Northumbrian "Geordies" are ... well known, *although the nickname is more especially for Tynesiders* than for the county at large' (my emphasis). Such evidence means we need to reassess claims that *Geordie* 'only became associated with Tyneside in the twentieth century' (Colls and Lancaster 2005b: ix). On RTG, the more generalised meaning championed by Colls and Lancaster often leads to the kind of *ressentiment* expressed in (2) and (3).[13]

Where does this antipathy come from? The fact that the 'incorrect' use of the label *Geordie* rankles with these posters might derive from Newcastle's perceived dominance in the region. The underlying cause is probably the unequal social and economic outcomes of de-industrialisation for different parts of the North East. This process – which began in the 1960s as the effects of the post-war boom faded and has continued to the present day – resulted in massive closures of coal mines and the decline of shipbuilding (the maritime sector is still an important part of the North East's economy, but ships are no longer built in bulk there). In times of prosperity, the predominance of Newcastle as the region's financial, commercial, and cultural capital might not have been a cause for resentment, but as

---

[13] Interestingly, *Geordie* has a different history in Scotland. Now rare, it was occasionally used to refer to miners, but was most commonly 'a soubriquet for a yokel, a rustic' (*DSL*).

governments attempted to ameliorate the effects of industrial decline, some felt – particularly on Wearside and Teesside (Beal et al. 2012: 13–17) – that Newcastle and Tyneside had benefited disproportionately from these interventions: transport infrastructure was improved on Tyneside with the construction of a metro system which took many years to reach Wearside; millions of pounds were spent on the redevelopment of the Gateshead and Newcastle quaysides. At the same time, a perception grew that Newcastle was engaged in self-assertive cultural, as well as economic expansionism, co-opting some of the North East's institutions and symbols for itself: the region's airport was named 'Newcastle Airport' (despite being part-owned by seven North East local authorities); 'BBC Newcastle' was the name chosen for its public radio station. One important symbol – the ethnonym *Geordie* – arguably underwent cultural appropriation by Newcastle. On RTG of course, footballing allegiances play an important role in the shaping of attitudes. Of some concern is what is seen as the 'appropriation' of the term *Geordie* by fans of Newcastle United F.C. (sometimes known as 'Mags' – a clipping of *magpie*, from the resemblance between the plumage of *pica pica* and the club's famous colours). This is of significance for some of the many Sunderland supporters who hail from South Tyneside – an area regarded, as we have seen, as culturally 'Geordie'.

(4) a. the term geordie is not their's [Newcastle United's] to own and never has been.
b. I know plenty Geordie Sunderland fans so I cringe when I hear the likes of "Geordie Nation".
c. the best way to cheese off the mags is to show them Geordies support SAFC.
d. I'm saying that if someone from Washington wants to support them, that doesn't make them Geordies. There are Geordie Sunderland (like me) …

Also of significance in turning some north easterners against *Geordie* might be a certain squeamishness towards the word's associations – epitomised in the popular reality TV programme *Geordie Shore* – with the carnivalesque display of hyper-sexualised, alcohol-fuelled consumerism that has come to characterise Newcastle's night-time economy.[14] This spectacle, best observed in the famous Bigg Market, is rooted in the nineteenth century and the conspicuous consumption of the hard-drinking, flashily-dressed

---

[14] *Geordie Shore* is an MTV programme first broadcast in 2011. The 23rd (!) series aired in 2022. It is a 'structured reality' show in which, according to the TV critic Charlie Brooker 'a gaggle of unbelievable idiots are stuck in a fancy house and intermittently hosed down with alcohol' (*The Guardian*, July 2012). Beal points out that, while some in the region feared the negative publicity the programme would bring, the antics of the cast – while reinforcing stereotypes of drunken, debauched, and disorderly working-class northerners – seem to have boosted the fame and appeal of Newcastle as a 'party city' (2018: 172).

Geordie pitmen (Lancaster 2005: 59–64). The energetic appropriation of *Geordie* by a city whose dominance some north easterners might resent, perhaps underlies the growing currency of other ethnonyms in the region. It is not too far-fetched to claim that some were keen to adopt terms that could be deployed as psychological barriers against the perceived cultural imperialism of Newcastle and Tyneside, even if – as we shall see – these labels were originally imposed on them by outsiders.

An insight into their regional significance can be found in the autobiography of *Geordie Shore*'s Vicky Pattison. Commenting on her female co-stars in the show, she refers to the wider ethnonymic field, while notably placing herself at its centre (2014: 102).

> The definition of a Geordie is someone who lives three miles from the bank of the River Tyne, and that's me. Charlotte Crosby is from Sunderland so she's a Mackem; Holly Hagan is a Smoggie, someone from Middlesbrough; and Sophie Kasaei is a Sanddancer, someone from South Shields. They're not Geordies in the slightest ...

The title of another spin-off book from the series, *Not Quite a Geordie – The Autobiography of* Geordie Shore's *Holly Hagan* is indicative of the complexity of the ethnonymic field. In her account of her arrival in the Geordie Shore house, Hagan describes the response to her revelation that she is from Middlesbrough.

> The group looked at me in shock. I could feel their stares boring into me and my face instantly reddened; it was like I'd just said I hailed from the depths of hell.
> 'You're a Smoggy?' James asked in disbelief.
> 'Yeah, but I act like a Geordie in every way,' I replied and took a large gulp of my drink, embarrassed to look them all in the eye. (Hagan 2014: 109)

These passages are interesting for several reasons. The association Pattison makes between *Geordie* and the Tyne is often found in folk descriptions, as is the willingness to offer precise psychogeographical boundaries for the range of an ethnonym. While Pattison's definitions are couched in relatively neutral terms, her insistence that her housemates from Sunderland, Middlesbrough, and South Shields 'are not Geordies in the slightest' hints at the potency of these terms as markers of socio-spatial territories. For Pattison, the boundaries are self-evident, sharply defined, and closed to discussion; whereas for Hagan, ethnonyms and the identities they index are more nuanced. Although Hagan accepts the label 'Smoggy', she implicitly claims for herself a 'Geordie' identity by associating certain modes of behaviour with being 'Geordie-like'. She does this at the same time as showing an awareness that for many people, 'a "Geordie" is someone born in Newcastle, not Middlesbrough, Sunderland, or anywhere else in the northeast' and that 'thoroughbred Geordies get a bee in their bonnets if you claim to be one of them when you're not' (Hagan 2014: 109). The fact that Pattison and Hagan feel the need to discuss the meaning of these terms in their celebrity autobiographies reflects their popular significance as powerful and complex symbols of identity (though outsiders – and indeed some insiders – might regard such distinctions as exemplifying Freud's 'Narzißmus der kleinen Differenzen').[15]

After *Geordie*, the two most well-known North East ethnonyms are *Mackem* and *Smoggie*.[16] On RTG, many posters self-identify as *Mackem*.

(5) a. I'm a mackem.
    b. I'M MACKEM AND I'M PROUD.

When (and how) was the word coined? Its origins are surprisingly recent – the earliest *OED* evidence is from 1980–1981: 'Steve Cole, John Evans, [etc.] took the field against the "Mackems" in a darts and doms double header.' Interest in the origins and use of the term is sometimes expressed on RTG.

(6) a. I first heard the word '**Mackem**' when I was 11 years old (1981 or thereabouts) while waiting for a woodwork lesson.
    b. Never heard '**Mackem**' until around 80–81, didn't even know what it meant when I was first asked if I was one.
    c. I first heard the term around 1980 from some lad in a bar in Newcastle.

Of course, the word must have been in circulation for some time before becoming more widely known.

(7) a. The word **Mackem** was around in spring 1977, and I suspect it had just cropped up then. I remember it well. I was called it by a Mag from Wallsend in The Sombrero Nightclub, in Chester-le-Street.
    b. In 1971 I worked as 'van boy' for Sykes pop. I was delivering in Jarrow and this young lass says to her ma 'Doesn't he talk funny mam'? Her mam replies 'that's because he's a **Mackem** and Tackem'.

---

[15] In *Das Unbehagen in der Kultur* (1930), Freud used this phrase – usually translated as 'the narcissism of small differences' – to describe beliefs and attitudes that lead members of closely related and contiguous communities to indulge in mutual mockery and feuding as a relatively innocuous way of satisfying aggressive impulses and building in-group solidarity. One of the examples he gives is animosity between 'Engländer und Schotten'.

[16] As we saw in (3) and in the passage from Pattison's book, *Geordie*, *Mackem* and *Smoggie* is not a complete list of North East ethnonyms. In folk linguistic research carried out in the early 2010s, I collected fifty-four different items. Alongside the 'big three', the most frequently attested were *Sand Dancer* (South Shields), *Monkey Hanger* (Hartlepool), and *Pit Yacker* (mining communities in County Durham where 'Pitmatic' – the occupational register of colliery workers – was used). See Pearce (2014) for their etymologies and histories.

References to the phrase 'Mackem and Tackem' are important. It is often said that people from Sunderland are called *Mackems* because of a saying associated with the shipbuilding industry on Wearside: 'we mack 'em and ye tack 'em'; that is, we make the ships and you take the ships. This is part of local folklore, acknowledged in academic texts: a 'widely held popular story holds that the label comes from Wearside shipyards where Sunderland workers would *mak* the ships and then others would *tak 'em* away – hence "Mackems"' (Beal et al. 2012: 17–18). There is some evidence to suggest that this phrase was the origin of the ethnonym, but the connection with shipbuilding is not certain. For example, in 1953 the *Sunderland Daily Echo and Shipping Gazette* published a piece entitled 'Mak'em and tak'em'.

> On Tyneside, Sunderland is often called the place where they 'mak 'em and tak 'em'. Just how this phrase originated I do not know but one explanation is that ships are both built and repaired on the Wear.

The author acknowledges Sunderland's association with the phrase but admits to uncertainty about whether it has anything to do with shipbuilding. What we can infer from this evidence is that 'Mak 'ems and Tack 'ems' was being used to label a group of people during the 1950s by north easterners outwith Wearside ('on Tyneside'), and if we accept the online recollections of the 'van boy' as accurate, it was still in circulation in the early 1970s. We can speculate that in casual speech the phrase would often have been clipped to ['makəm]. During the 1970s, the shortened form seems to have taken off, as revealed in the RTG recollections in (6) and (7). There is also some support for an origin in this decade in an interview recorded in David Hall's *Working Lives,* in which a man from South Shields reflecting on his time in a Sunderland shipyard in the 1970s says: 'The Sunderland lads were called Mackems' (2012: 198).

But why 'Mack 'em' (['makəm]) and not 'Make 'em'? The feature in question here is [mak], the traditional Sunderland/Durham pronunciation of *make,* which according to Kerswill (1987) is the result of lexical variation, with [eː] (the mainstream northern English vowel for words in the FACE lexical set) used in formal situations, and [a] in more informal contexts (a pattern shared with *take*). Eventually, this difference becomes lexicalised in the coinage *Mackem,* which can be categorised as an 'imitative' ethnonym in which the form of the word encapsulates a linguistic feature associated with speakers from a particular area. The *Sunderland Echo* article and the van boy's memories show that between the 1950s and the early 1970s, the 'atypical' pronunciations of 'make' and 'take' ('atypical' for people from outside the area where this pronunciation was used) become associated with people from Sunderland; a semiotic link had been made between linguistic forms ([mak] and [tak]) and social meaning ('coming from Sunderland').

Unlike *Geordie*, the origins of *Mackem* are exoteric. Evidence for this lies in the fact that outsiders are more likely to notice and comment upon what they regard as idiosyncratic speech than insiders (note the way that people's first encounters with the word were often in the mouths of people from outside Sunderland). However, the term has now been widely taken up as an ethnonym: a well-established marker of identity, worn with pride by many (though not all) citizens of the city (and sometimes by people from the wider Wearside area and further afield in East Durham). This is an example of the way a word that starts off being used disparagingly or even abusively is adopted as an in-group marker of resistance and solidarity. The earliest *OED* citation is in the context of football, and while football was not the origin of the term, intra-regional football rivalries have provided fertile soil for its growth. The 1970s saw a dramatic rise in football-related violence which led to increasing animosities between rival supporters. If *Mackem* emerges as an exoteric term of abuse, then an important context for its circulation is within the rituals of football rivalry. It is noteworthy that some of the *OED*'s earliest written evidence for *Mackem* is from the newsletter of the London branch of the Newcastle United supporters' club (1980–1981). The earliest written evidence *OED* has for its use amongst Sunderland A.F.C. supporters is from 1989, suggesting that by then the term had been fully 'reclaimed'. Today, *Mackem* is well known within the region, and recognition is growing beyond the North East. The word appears in newspaper headlines, and not just in the context of football: for example, 'Why aye, wor Nic's a Mackem' (a *Scottish Sunday Express* story about Nicola Sturgeon's family connections with Ryhope, published in May 2015).[17]

Like *Mackem*, *Smoggie* is a 'reclaimed' term. Of the major North East ethnonyms, it is the newest. Evidence for the relatively recent arrival of *Smoggie/Smoggy* in the region's ethnonymicon can be found in the work of sports writer Harry Pearson, who is himself from Teesside. In 1994, it is clear he perceived a potential lexical gap: 'People from Teesside, you see, are rather unimaginatively known as Teessiders; people from Tyneside are Geordies ... while those from County Durham are Mackems' (Pearson 1994: 6). But sixteen years later things have changed:

> A couple of tattooed lads leapt to their feet punching the air when the news comes in that Fulham have taken the lead at Newcastle. 'You're

[17] Newspapers are a useful source of evidence for dialect usage and folk dialectology and their digitisation on platforms such as Lexis®Library News and the British Newspaper Archive (BNA) are opening up new lines of enquiry (see for example Pearce 2013). One largely untapped newspaper resource is the dialect columns which from the mid-nineteenth to mid-twentieth centuries were a popular feature of regional publications (for instance, in North East England, Dorothy Samuelson-Sandvid ('Dorfy') was a fixture of the *Shields Gazette* from the 1930s to the 1960s). Peter Trudgill has revived the tradition, writing regularly for the *Eastern Daily Press* about East Anglian English in his 'Dialect Matters' column (see Trudgill 2016).

going down with the Smoggies/Down with the Smoggies' they chanted at the screen. (Pearson 2010: 41)

Although the Sunderland fans depicted here are using 'Smoggie' to describe their rivals Middlesbrough F.C. and its supporters, the term is now used as an ethnonym for the citizens of Middlesbrough and Teesside in general. In contrast to Geordie and Mackem, there is of now no entry for *Smoggie* in the *OED*; nevertheless, a speculative etymology and history can be proposed. It probably originates in the phrase 'smog monster', a term of abuse for Middlesbrough F.C. supporters coined by visiting fans of other North East football teams struck by the air pollution from Teesside's petrochemical works (Beal 2006: 8). The earliest print reference I have found is from 1994 in *The Sunday Times*: 'The "smog monsters" have metamorphosed into "Robbo's Army"'. Here the football team is associated with the phrase, but by 2000 *The Guardian* is reporting that 'the locals in Boro are disparagingly called Smog Monsters'. It seems the extension of the meaning to the broader population was rapid. Semantic extension was also accompanied by a change of form. At some point – possibly during the 1990s – 'Smog Monster' was clipped to 'Smog' with the addition of a diminutive ending, resulting in ['smɒgiː], which was realised orthographically as <Smoggy>, but more frequently <Smoggie> (probably by analogy with <Geordie>). The earliest occurrence in print of *Smoggie/Smoggy* is in 1999 in the *Newcastle Journal*: 'anyone can win a knock-out trophy – anyone apart from the Smoggies that is'; the earliest attested occurrence in its broader sense is in 2002 in the third series of the popular television show *Auf Wiedersehen, Pet*. This sequence takes place on the Transporter Bridge – an iconic landmark in Middlesbrough. 'Moxey' is from Merseyside:

> MOXEY: Strange part of the world, isn't it? They're not Geordies here, right?
> DENNIS: Certainly not.
> MOXEY: So what are they then?
> NEVILLE: Just people from Middlesbrough.
> DENNIS: Smoggies.

Dennis's remark implies that when this drama was broadcast the word was novel, especially for those outside the region. It is also worth pointing out that in the most extensive study of language variation in Teesside yet carried out, *Smoggie* does not occur as a marker of identity (Llamas 2001). The publication date here is significant; by the mid-2000s *Smoggie* is established enough to secure a mention in Wales's history of northern English (2006: 209). Though it clearly started out as a derogatory label, *Smoggie*, even more rapidly than *Mackem*, has acquired status as a positive marker of Middlesbrough and a wider Teesside identity. Why did this happen? Perhaps the area needed it. Llamas describes the 'transitional nature of the geographical location of Middlesbrough', which, due to various redrawings of local administrative boundaries, means that 'its inhabitants are sometimes uncertain and confused about its precise identity' (2001: 4; see also Beal et al. 2012: 16–17). For some citizens of the region, *Smoggie* is a means of bolstering a specific Teesside identity, which conveniently evokes a proud – albeit polluting – industrial heritage. The term was certainly well established as such by 2011, when Tom Blenkinsop, MP for Middlesbrough South and East Cleveland, made this entirely unhistorical point in the House of Commons: 'in places such as Middlesbrough, Redcar and Billingham, we have *always* referred to ourselves as proud smoggies, in the knowledge that our manufacturing endeavours have far more worth than the machinations of the City' (Hansard, 5 July 2011, my emphasis). Blenkinsop's evocation of a timeless 'smoggiedom' founded on industrial prowess is indicative of the rapid acceptance of *Smoggie* in the twenty-first century.

Geordie, *Mackem*, and *Smoggie* are well-established terms, often deployed in the construction and contestation of regional local identities, though *Geordie*, due to its longer history and association with the North East's largest urban area has, as we have seen, wider national (and international) recognition. They can also be used – as is common with ethnonyms – as a modifier of nouns in the semantic domain of speech and language.[18]

(8)   a. listening to the **geordie dialect** inspired him to write the shipbuilding play.
      b. How do you spell the **geordie word** 'howay'.
      c. It's a **Geordie saying** for little bairns.
      d. His OTT **geordie pronunciation** gets right on my tits.
      e. **Mackem dialect** has obviously changed a lot since I lived there.
      f. A broad **mackem accent** is akin to someone scratching a blackboard.
      g. Is it a **mackem phrase**?
      h. Its that horrible **smoggie accent** of his.
      i. **Smoggy accent** is awful mind.
      j. Beck is a **smoggy word** being part of viking Danelaw.

Geordie can also be used nominally to name the dialect (the *OED*'s earliest record of this is from the 1920s), but such usages are less common for *Mackem* and do not seem to occur at all on RTG for *Smoggie*.[19]

---

[18] The *OED*'s earliest citation for adjectival *Geordie* is from 1903. Using the BNA, I have antedated this by twenty-five years: 'This young lady laid it on very thickly … and spoke to her auditors in what she conceived to be "Geordie" dialect' (*Eastern Argus and Borough of Hackney Times*, 1878). The inverted commas indicate that at the time this was a novel usage.

[19] Though it can be found elsewhere, as in this 2019 tweet: 'Thanks and apologies, but iPhone autocorrect doesn't speak Smoggie.'

The dialectscapes of North East England

(9) a. they have to spoil everything and add **geordie** to it.
b. P.S, glad you're not speaking **Geordie** anymore. :)
c. Weardale is like **mackem** with a Teesdale/Cleveland burr.
d. I learned **Mackem** best reading @Teed on the old Boozer. Did my heed in.

The posts in (8) and (9) exemplify *enregisterment*: the indexical linking – through a variety of discursive and meta-discursive activities (Beal 2010: 94) – of a particular group of people (in this case, those to whom the ethnonym is adjudged to apply) with a repertoire of linguistic norms, features, and practices (a 'register') which serves to distinguish members of that group from others in the wider speech community (Agha 2003: 231). Enregisterment seems to be a scalar phenomenon: some registers are very well-established in the public imaginary, others are 'nascent' (Durkin 2015: 324). *Geordie, Mackem,* and *Smoggie* occupy different points on the scale.

Table 2.2 *The 'Geordie' repertoire with RTG examples (see Beal 2009 and 2017)*

'Geordie' features	RTG examples of 'Geordie' dialect performances
Retention of ME /uː/ in words in the MOUTH set (7.2.1)	*'Fancy a neet **oot doon** tha **toon** bonny lad'.*
Retention of ME /iː/ in words such as *night* and *right* (7.2.4)	*Probably take them more seriously if they didnt have an exaggerated "**reet** aroond tha roondaboot" geordie accent.*
NORTH-NURSE merger (7.2.10)	*"Shoes off, if ya bus **bornt** doon".*
Centring diphthong /ɪə/ in words in the FACE lexical set (7.2.3)	*he said tyek 'ees **nee-am**.*
Retention of ME /aː/ in words such as *know, cold, snow* (7.2.2)	*"ivrybody **nars**, geordies divvent gan any where lookin like casper, not propa geordies any hoo".*
/ɔ/ vowel in unstressed syllable in words such as *letter* and *better* (7.2.18)	***Nivvor** hord of him.*
Retention of OE short /a/ in words such as *wrong* and *long* (7.2.6)	*1pm – get **wrang** off wor lass and gan to the pub.*
divn't/divvent for *don't* (3.2.2, 4.3.1 and 7.4.2)	*We're Geordies and yuh **divvent** understand.*
gan for *go* (3.2.1.1)	*I'm **gannin** doon the toon to pick me giro up pet.*

Beal claims (2009, 2017) that 'Geordie' has been enregistered as a more or less stable variety for at least 150 years. Evidence for this can be found in the rich body of dialect writing – mainly in the form of ballads and songs – that was produced on Tyneside during the nineteenth century (see Beal 2000 and Hermeston 2009). The discursive activity of representing dialect in a popular genre intended for performance helped to establish and circulate a set of linguistic norms that were indexically linked to a particular geographical and cultural milieu. This 'stable core repertoire' (Beal 2017: 22), which can still be found in twenty-first-century sources, is shown in Table 2.2, and exemplified with RTG posts in which the authors are overtly attempting to represent 'Geordie' dialect. Other performative contexts have helped to fix 'Geordie' in public consciousness. TV dramas such as *The Likely Lads* (1964–1974), *Auf Wiedersehen, Pet* (1983–2002) and *Vera* (2011–) have disseminated representations of North East characters, places, and language, while celebrities and popular entertainers such as Sting, Cheryl Cole, Ant and Dec, Sarah Millican, Chris and Rosie Ramsey, Alan Shearer, Jade Thirlwall, Vicky Pattinson, and Sam Fender have incorporated different degrees of 'Geordiness' into their commodified public identities.[20] A further factor in the enregisterment of 'Geordie' can be found in the production of dialect dictionaries – the most well-known nineteenth-century example being Heslop's *Northumberland Words* (see 2.2.2). Its twenty-first century equivalent in terms of scholarly seriousness is Griffiths' *A Dictionary of North East Dialect*. Furthermore, 'Geordie' has – since the 1960s – featured prominently in the genre of 'Contemporary Humorous Localised Dialect Literature', or CHLDL (Honeybone and Watson 2013), the most famous of which is Scott Dobson's *Larn Yersel' Geordie* (1969), a title which has inspired a library of imitators, within and beyond the region.[21] Like the mugs, T-shirts, tea towels, and greetings cards emblazoned with the word *Geordie* and using 'Geordie' dialect that can be found in shops and on market stalls across the North East (and in their associated online outlets), these books are a component in the 'commodification' of 'Geordie' dialect, a process which both reflects and accelerates its enregisterment (see Beal 2009, 2018).

Table 2.3 *'Mackem' versus 'Geordie' (see Beal 2000 and Pearce 2012)*

'Mackem'/'Geordie' contrasts (Beal 2000)	RTG examples of metalinguistic commentary
The NORTH-NURSE merger for 'Geordie' but not for 'Mackem' (7.2.10)	As in "Ma, can wa hev **torkey borgaz** for wa teeee after wav put up tha **porple cortain** purl?"
H-retention for 'Geordie', but *h*-dropping for 'Mackem' (7.3.3)	*If I had a Mackem accent, I'd say, I stopped in an 'otel.*
A 'Mackem' diphthong [ɛi]/[ei] in some words in the FLEECE set in contrast to [iː] (7.2.11)	*They reckon we say* **cheysey** *chips and blew pop. :lol:*

---

[20] In a study of accents and public identity, Di Martino (2020) identifies certain North East celebrities as widely admired 'Geordie ambassadors' in the mass media, who embody well-established values of friendliness and sociability (see 2.1), but also infuse 'new positive values into the Geordie variety', like trendiness and 'cool' (140). Her main example is the singer and TV presenter Cheryl Cole, who has always embraced her 'Geordiness'. She also cites Sting, whom she claims has moved from disaffiliation to affiliation with 'Geordie' and mentions in passing Mark Knopfler, Bryan Ferry, and Brian Johnson (of AC/DC).

[21] The role of the Newcastle-based adult comic *Viz* (1979–) in disseminating representations of 'Geordie' should also be mentioned. Some of its most memorable creations (e.g. Biffa Bacon, Sid the Sexist) hail from Tyneside.

Table 2.3 (continued)

'Mackem'/'Geordie' contrasts (Beal 2000)	RTG examples of metalinguistic commentary
A 'Mackem' diphthong [ɛʊ] in some words in the MOUTH set in contrast to the traditional 'Geordie' [u:] (7.2.1)	*Lerrus tek yer **dewn**, cus I'm gannin ter ... shop in South Shields.*
'Mackem' *dayn't* for 'Geordie' *divvent* (3.2.2 and 4.3.1)	*Three words that seperate Sunderland, South Shields and newcastle. **Dinnit Daint divvent**.*

'Sunderland'/'Newcastle' contrasts (Pearce 2012)	RTG examples of metalinguistic commentary
The vowel in words ending in orthographic <ook> is [ʊ] in Newcastle but [u:] in Sunderland (7.2.9)	*I am 33 years old and pronounce it **"Bewk"** (typical Sunderland pronunciation).*
A contrast in the quality of the vowel in some words in the GOOSE set (especially *school*), with a diphthongal realisation associated with Sunderland and a monophthong [u:] associated with Newcastle (7.2.12)	*I can almost always tell a fellow exile from the way they pronounce 'school'.*
The 'Sunderland' vowel in *make* and *take* is [a], rather than the mainstream [e:] of Newcastle (7.2.3)	*The woman is a great Mackem. **Mak** an **tak** as it should be.*
The possessive determiner *wor* is associated with Newcastle rather than Sunderland (3.4.2.1)	*I actually agree, even Whitburn sounds Geordie to me, and you can walk from Seaburn to Whitburn in about 5 minutes and they say **WOR**.*
The object pronoun *we* (particularly in the prepositional phrase *with we*) is associated with Newcastle rather than Sunderland (3.4.1.2)	*Geordie who sits scross from me say "Yih cummin **wi wuh**?" to mean "Are you coming with us". It can mean Us or Our from what I've heard.*
The pronunciation of the *wh-* words *who* and *whose* as [wi:] and [wi:z] is associated with Sunderland rather than Newcastle (3.4.6)	*Mackems say **wheez** instead of who's.*
Howay in Newcastle and *haway* in Sunderland (6.1)	*Mag alert!! Its **Haway** not **Howay**!!*

Because of their relatively recent emergence as ethnonyms, 'Mackem' and 'Smoggie' are less reified as stable registers than 'Geordie', though 'Mackem' is further along the road. As early as 2000, Beal was able to identify a set of 'shibboleths' popularly believed to 'separate Geordies (Newcastle) from 'Makkems' (Sunderland)' and which she illustrated with dialect representations from a comic strip in a local newspaper and a pub menu (2000: 351).[22] In my research on the perceptual dialectology of Tyne

---

[22] <Makkems> is unusual and indicates that in 2000 'Mackem' was still in an early stage of enregisterment, when <Mackem> had not yet become the accepted spelling (although on RTG we do find a few orthographic variants such as <Maccam, Mackam, Makkam, Makkem>).

and Wear the contrasts identified by Beal were also seen in the responses of participants who were asked open-ended questions about dialect variation between people from Newcastle and Sunderland (Pearce 2012). A perceptual consensus also emerged in relation to several more contrasts which Beal did not mention (see Table 2.3). Further evidence for the nascent enregisterment of 'Mackem' lies in its commodification. Though the process is less advanced for 'Mackem' than it is for 'Geordie', it is nevertheless possible to purchase a variety of items printed with 'Mackem' words, phrases, and respellings, and *The Mackem Dictionary* is now in its third edition (see Swinney 2019).[23] Evidence for the enregisterment of 'Smoggie' is less prominent in the public domain, though online you can buy 'I ♥ parmos' socks and posters featuring 'Teesside slang' such as 'owa mam' and 'heavin' in there like'; and Smoggie canines can be left at 'Smoggie Doggie Day Care' in Middlesbrough.[24] However, as of July 2023 there do not seem to be any CHLDL publications associated with Teesside.

The mental dialect maps of many residents of North East England have a broadly tripartite structure which these three ethnonyms both reflect and help to reinforce. This was revealed in research I carried out in the mid-2000s in which c.1,600 participants from the region were invited to think about the speech of people in fifty-one North East locations, from Ashington in the north to Darlington in the south, assessing the extent of its similarity to or difference from the speech of people in their own hometowns. The aggregated responses revealed a perceptual dialectscape consisting of three 'sectors': a northern sector made up of linked locations across Tyneside and south east Northumberland corresponding to popular conceptions of 'where 'Geordies' consider their homeland to be' (Beal 2004: 34); a central sector roughly coterminous with County Durham and the Wear portion of Tyne and Wear (with dense clustering in the metropolitan borough of Sunderland – home of the 'Mackems' – and neighbouring locations on the Durham limestone plateau); and a southern sector consisting of Teesside – 'Smoggie' territory – and the Tees lowlands (see Pearce 2009 and Beal et al. 2012: 24–26).

2.4 Conclusion

In this chapter I have explored the dialectscapes of North East England, providing context for the description of NEVE which follows. *Dialectscape*

---

[23] Since the dictionary is for general sale and aimed at a non-specialist audience it can be regarded as a commodified dialect artefact, but it should be stressed that royalties are donated to local charities.

[24] *Parmo* is defined by *OED* as 'a dish consisting of a fillet of breaded chicken, pork, or other meat that is fried, topped with béchamel sauce and cheese, and then grilled, typically sold as takeaway food'.

is a deliberate echo of 'landscape', a term used in geography to refer to the distinguishing features and characteristics of a tract of land. Landscapes are palimpsests (Meinig 1979). The textual metaphor is appropriate because like ancient manuscripts made up of partially erased and over-layered writing, landscapes bear the traces of the physical and human processes to which they have been subjected over time. And like texts, they are open to multiple interpretations. 'Landscape' is therefore a word which 'connects the objectivity of the physical/geographical territory with the subjectivity and history of the human observer, who assigns meaning to its features' (Mair 2020: 375). A 'dialectscape' is similarly layered – the living vernacular speech of people inhabiting a particular place at a particular time can preserve traces of earlier influences and forms not found elsewhere. And just like the words of a literary text or the imprint of human activity on a landscape, linguistic evidence can be assigned meaning and interpreted in a multitude of ways. This chapter has provided a sociodialectological reading of the territory, showing some of the linguistic, social, demographic, and historical processes which have led to the formation of NEVE. And by considering practices of (and meta-discourses about) naming, enregisterment, demarcation, difference, commodification, contestation, and affiliation I have also revealed some of the ways the 'folk' – albeit working with different knowledge and background assumptions from the 'experts' and using differently calibrated observational instruments – have read the region's dialectscapes. For a full picture of dialects in situ to emerge (or at least a less partial one), both perspectives need to be taken into account, and at various points in the chapters which follow I draw on the collective sociolinguistic imagination of RTG posters to help understand the linguistic ecology of North East England.

CHAPTER 3

Morphology

I brock me ankle.

In this and the next chapter I identify morphosyntactic features on RTG that contrast with those typically found in Standard English (SE). Of course, a grammatical feature that occurs in both SE and NEVE must also be considered part of North East dialect. But for reasons of economy and focus, these chapters deal only with non-standard elements. It should also be stated at the outset that such features are subject to socio-stylistic variation (see 1.1.4). For every form or structure identified, there will be some north easterners who deploy it frequently in their baseline everyday linguistic performances, while others will rarely if ever use it, though it might be part of their passive morphosyntactic knowledge. For others, the use of a feature might be highly context dependent. For example, if whoever posted the statement in the chapter epigraph wished to communicate the same propositional content more formally (during a medical consultation or in a written insurance claim, say) they would perhaps favour 'I broke my ankle'. We must also acknowledge of course that a person's age, gender, social and educational background, and their geographical location within the region, all interact with context to shape linguistic usage, but the nature of the RTG data means that such information – except in the broadest terms – is largely inaccessible. The features presented here therefore should certainly not be regarded as invariable (see Beal 1993: 191–192).

My description of NEVE morphology as it is represented on RTG begins with verbal features, showing where verb paradigms in NEVE can differ from those in SE, then I look at four lexical verbs whose forms have a particular saliency in the region: *go/gan*, *know*, *make*, and *take*; I also consider variant forms of the primary verbs *have* and *do*. I then turn to nominal features, considering the marking of plurality on nouns, and illustrating further contrasts between NEVE and SE in relation to pronouns, determiners, adjectives, adverbs, and prepositional forms.

Morphology

3.1 Verb paradigms

The three principal parts of the verb in English are the base form, the past tense, and the past participle. In present-day English, most English verbs are regular, with the past tense and past participle formed by adding a dental suffix to the base. The regular past tense allomorph is *-ed*, as in *turn – turned – turned*, but in some verbs the allomorph can undergo final de-voicing, which is sometimes reflected in the spelling (as in *burn – burnt – burnt*) but sometimes isn't (*trip – tripped – tripped*). However, some of the most frequently occurring verbs in English are irregular. Quirk et al. (1985: 102–103) identify six paradigms for irregular verbs: all three forms are the same (e.g. *bet – bet – bet*); only past tense and past participle are identical (e.g. *meet – met – met*); base form and past tense are identical (e.g. *beat – beat – beaten*); base form and past participle are identical (e.g. *come – came – come*); all three forms are different (e.g. *ring – rang – rung*; *give – gave – given*); one or more forms are unmatched, as in paradigms with suppletive forms (e.g. *go – went – gone*). In vernacular English, verb paradigms sometimes differ from those found in SE (see Anderwald 2009: 61–65). For example, some verbs that were historically irregular and remain irregular in the standard have – for some speakers in some vernacular contexts – changed their conjugation class and are regular, as shown in these RTG examples.

(1)   a. Productivity crumbled, competitors **creeped** in.
        b. Derby County have **creeped** right up there unnoticed.
        c. Aye he really **shined**.
        d. The only players to have **shined** were already here.

        e. I know you like that word so I **weaved** it in especially.
        f. Bruce hasn't **weaved** his magic yet.

        g. She **telt** me the other week.
        h. I've **telt** this tale before.

In addition, some irregular verbs with a three-part paradigm in SE can have a two-part paradigm in NSE, a process of levelling listed amongst the most pervasive and widespread of Kortmann's vernacular angloversals (2020: 639–640). In the verbs in (2) the form used as the past participle in SE is used as the past tense.

(2)   a. Been to Alnwick and Alnmouth a few times on camping trips and I was surprised how many SAFC shirts I **seen** up there.
        b. I **done** it last year and loved every minute.
        c. I **drunk** a lot of water!
        d. They **shrunk** and I can barely read them.

Conversely, the form used as the past tense in SE is sometimes used as the past participle, in both active and passive voice.

(3)   a. Mcgeady has **broke** his nose.
     b. When the cricket club got **broke** into the dart board got nicked.
     c. I've just **spoke** to Wes.
     d. Unbelievable constant stress and get **spoke** to like shit on a regular basis.
     e. Gillingham have **beat** a couple of our promotion rivals in recent games.
     f. Horden first team were **beat** by Castle Eden today.
     g. Wish I'd **took** my kids when they were littler.
     h. It was hideous so never got **took** out of the box.

Finally, some irregular verbs with a three- or two-part paradigm in SE can have a one-part paradigm in non-standard English, with all three principal parts of the verb sharing the same form.

(4)   a. Maybe they **come** up from the deepest, darkest parts of the ocean for a bez about in the air?
     b. Kilgallon didn't do anything wrong when he **come** on.
     c. Every time he's **come** off the bench he's been terrible.

     d. They **give** me heartburn so bad but they are so lush.
     e. i was thankful for some of the good times he **give** us.
     f. he's **give** away 2 awful fouls.[1]

The patterns illustrated in (1), (2), (3), and (4) occur frequently in vernacular Englishes. 'Regularised' verb forms of the type exemplified in (1) are widespread in dialects of the British Isles (Upton et al. 1994: 490–491). While Anderwald's work suggests regularisation is commoner in the vernacular English of the south and west of England than the north, the form *telt* (or <tellt>) as the past tense and past participle of *tell* (1g,h) is very much a northern feature. *Tell* forms a small class with *sell* of regularised verbs in which the dental suffix on the past tense and participle forms is de-voiced. Historically, *telt/telled* may show continuation of the Old English (chiefly Anglian) past tense *telede* (*OED*), though it is *telt* (first recorded by the *OED* for the 1500s and labelled 'English regional' from the 1700s) rather than *telled* which has become a shibboleth of English

---

[1] Of course, the same verb can belong to more than one non-standard paradigm. For example, *come* can be *come – came – came* (as in 'he's **came** on against the best team in the league') as well as *come – come – come*. And *give* can be *give – gave – gave*.

Morphology

in the north of England (Anderwald 2009: 74).² In contrast, the paradigm illustrated in (2) – where a form which functions as the participle in SE is used as a past tense by some vernacular speakers – is 'found in the vast majority of all non-standard mother-tongue varieties of English around the world' (Kortmann and Langstrof 2017: 135). The paradigm illustrated in (3) is nearly as common, but in Britain it is particularly associated with northern varieties of vernacular English, especially in North East England and Scotland (see the section on 'Participles' in the Scots Syntax Atlas).³ In the North East these participle forms sometimes appear in the speech and writing of people from a wider social class range than is typically the case in the rest of England, as shown in these examples from a doctoral thesis archived at Durham University and an email from a Cambridge educated academic from North Tyneside.

(5)   a. I would have **went** out and managed it and made decisions.
       b. this is the first time we've **ran** those modules.

For some readers, it will be jarring to encounter 'have went' and 'have ran' in an academic context. However, they simply represent a preservation of variability which was once much more widespread. Such forms have become frowned upon due to the 'pruning away of variation and [the] establishment of norms' associated with standardisation, which began in earnest in the eighteenth century (Lass 2006: 99). When Edward Gibbon was writing his *History of the Decline and Fall of the Roman Empire* (1776–1789) he used some participle forms interchangeably.

(6)   a. ... a strong ray of philosophical light has **broke** from Scotland in our own times.
       b. When he had **broken** the fabric of their ancient government ...
       c. He repeats the words of Lampadius as they were **spoke** in Latin.
       d. But a purer idiom was **spoken** in the court and taught in the college.
       e. The bishops, as well as the rabbis, of former times, have **beat** the drum ecclesiastic ...
       f. ... commanded the priests to be **beaten** with rods.

But when a new edition of this work was published in 1890, 'broke', 'spoke', and 'beat' had all been replaced with forms in *-en*. The internal variability

---

[2] Although examples (1g,h) indicate a relatively 'natural' use of *telt*, in NEVE the form often occurs in contexts where criticism or scolding is implied, especially where a 'lesson' is to be (or has been) learned: 'LEE GET THE BUGGERS TELT'; 'I've telt yeah man. Aycliffe Village.'

[3] The Scots Syntax Atlas (SSA) <https://scotssyntaxatlas.ac.uk/> maps over 100,000 acceptability judgements from over 500 speakers on c.250 Scots morphosyntactic phenomena (Smith et al. 2019).

had been ironed out, with certain variants replaced with those deemed 'proper' for an elite publication.

Because the forms in (2), (3), and (4) also occur in SE, it is only their use which marks them out as vernacular. But some forms found in NEVE do not occur in SE and they are the topic of the next section.

3.2 Verb forms

In *EDG* (1905) the treatment of verbs extends over fifteen pages, listing 'such forms as deviate in some way from the corresponding lit. Eng. forms' (281–296). It reports on an extraordinary abundance. For instance, if we consider only forms of verbs beginning with *b-* attested for Northumberland or County Durham we find amongst them *brang* and *brong* as past tense forms of *bring* (with *brang, brong, brung, brangen,* and *brongen* as past participle forms); and *brack, band,* and *blowed* as the past tenses of *break, bind,* and *blow*. Much of this variety has since been winnowed out of vernacular English (and some of the forms were acknowledged as archaic when Wright listed them), so what is reported here are merely the relicts of a vast system. Nevertheless, there are several 'unusual' forms which have survived into contemporary NEVE represented on RTG.

3.2.1 'Unusual' forms: lexical verbs

Sometimes a verb has forms in NEVE that are not present or are marginal in SE, as for example in the cases of *bring, swing, treat, get, forget, break, froze,* and *shit*. These past tense and past participle forms from RTG were all attested in *EDD*.

(7) a. We **brang** him to England.
 b. Southend probably **brung** more fans last season.
 c. The last couple of weeks has **brung** out some crazy fuckers on here.
 d. he took offence jumped up and **swang** a knife at me.
 e. Think he was having a go at di canio who **tret** him like shit.
 f. He's been **tret** like shit tbf.
 g. where the fuck've they **getten** that from.
 h. My hope is they've **gotten** the picture after yesterday's shit show.
 i. I honestly think SAFC fans had **forgotten** what a good left-back was supposed to be like.
 j. I **brock** me ankle.
 k. You've just **brock** yer leg man.
 l. "Fucking hell, Bally's just **brocken** that lad's foot".
 m. chilled one even further last night n **freezed** a half glass.
 n. Snar down here this morning might be **frozzen** off.

Morphology

    o. I **shat** bricks.
    p. He thought he'd **shat** himself.
    q. We're getting **shat** on here mind.

Gotten and *getten* can be found in the Göttingen MS of *Cursor Mundi* (an encyclopaedic verse history of the world written in c.1300) which is believed to represent a 'Northeast' dialect (Hogg 2006: 365): 'Hu he wald lere vs her vr lai, / þat ebber þat in sine was **gotin**!'; 'Bot crist has nu vs **getten** þar, / vs **getun** in hali gast has he'. The forms *tret* and *brock(en)* are both recorded in *NW*, the former illustrated with a line from a dialect poem published in 1849: "They'll myek the cheps 'mends for the way they been **tret**" (Heslop 1893: 744). In *EDD, frozzen* and *brocken* are recorded for northern England (*brocken* is also found in Scots). We might also note *hing* for *hang*, which represents the maintenance of the midlands and northern *hyng/hing*. Brockett has 'HING, to hang' (1829: 154) and *EDD* records a wide distribution across Scotland, Ireland, and the northern and midland counties of England.

(8)   a. Might not be a bad idea to **hing** on a bit and see what develops.
      b. Tripped over the chord **hinging** from his jim jams.
      c. **Hing** it across our goal, might be handy marra.
      d. Now go and fester back under your rock you monkey **hinger**.

We also find *chow* existing alongside *chew*. *EDD* describes it – like *chaw* – as a widespread dialectal variant of *chew*.

(9)   a. Got a box of assorted sweeties to **chow** through now.
      b. Can't wait to see Madeley **chowing** down on a bulls knacker.

Most of the non-standard forms in (7), (8), and (9) have a wide distribution and are therefore not strongly associated with NEVE, within or outside the region. However, there are four irregular lexical verbs – *go, know, take* and *make* – whose variants are salient as markers of North East dialect.

3.2.1.1 Gan/go

As Beal points out, in North East England the verb *go* 'may be substituted by the lexically distinct verb *gan*, which is obsolete in standard English' (1993: 192). *Gan* is recorded for Northumbrian locations in SED, but not as a separate verb from *go*, whereas *EDD* has *gan* and *gang* as headwords, both attested for Northumbria as synonyms of *go*. We should also note that the earliest forms of OE *go* are in *-a*, as illustrated in this gloss of the Latin *ire trans fretum* ('go across the strait/channel') from the Lindisfarne Gospels: **gaa** *ofer luh* ('go over the lough'). *Gaa* is echoed on RTG, which contains orthographic renderings of the [ga(ː)] or [gaː(ː)] to be found in NEVE speech. SED records *ga* in Northumbrian locations as a third person plural form expressing habitual action, but RTG also has examples of *ga* (spelled <gar>) as a base (10a–c), and a present participle, spelled <garn> or sometimes <gaan> (10d,e).[4]

(10) a. Do the usual places in Roker still have the match on or do I have to **gar** ower the town?
  b. Cannit **gar** wrang.
  c. here lasso will ya **gar** out with is.
  d. Take no notice of me am **garn** senile :D
  e. are yer **gaan** to the match?

In SED, *gan/ga* is categorical for 'go' in Northumbrian locations. For example, when prompted with 'what do good people do on Sunday?' thirteen of the fifteen informants use *gan*, while the remaining two use *ga* in responses like 'they gan to church' and 'they ga to church' (Orton and Halliday 1963: 924). *Gans*, *gannen*, and [ga:z] are also recorded (Orton and Halliday 1963: 937). On RTG *go* and *gan* are broadly interchangeable.

(11) a. Fitness levels would **go** through the roof.
  b. The price of bacon would **gan** through the roof.
  c. If I **go** out with the other half the cost trebles.
  d. if I **gan** out with them somewhere I'll forget something.
  e. so I **goes** into the doctors.
  f. So I **gans** into reception to complain.
  g. the wife **goes** in on Wednesday to get it done.
  h. My wife **gans** there.
  i. we all **went** up Barley Mow with bats and golf clubs.
  j. All **ganned** up Hylton Road bout 1:30 today stinking of wee.
  k. You've **gone** down in my estimation Chubs.
  l. You've **gan** down in my estimations.
  m. I won't be **going** back.
  n. not **gannen** back there again.
  o. We're **going** to get a few more chances here.
  p. Am **gannen** to get some tonight.
  q. I'm **gonna** go and gloat.
  r. If we get beat its **ganna** gan up!

In (11o,p) we see *be ganning to* plus infinitive in parallel with SE *be going to* as a future time expression, with the reduced forms *gonna* and *ganna* in (11q,r). *Ganna* seems to have preceded *gonna* in the history of English: the *OED*'s earliest citation for the former is 1806 (from a collection of Scots verse) and 1904 for the latter.

---

[4] Heslop has *gaan* as a headword and describes it as a present participle of *gan* (1893: 312).

Morphology 61

Etymologically, the relation between *go* and *gan(g)* is uncertain (*ODEE*). The *OED* entry for *go* lists several historical forms which resemble those found on RTG, including the Old English base forms *gaa* (found, as we have seen, in the Northumbrian Lindisfarne Gospels) and *gan* (in Beowulf). By the ME period such forms were becoming more associated with northern varieties. This can be seen when northern versions of *Cursor Mundi* (e.g. Göttingen MS) are compared with midland versions (e.g. Trinity MS).

(12) a. He bad eft **ga** (Göttingen)
b. He bad him efte **go** (Trinity)
c. Four skor and sex 3er ouer **gan** (Göttingen)
d. Foure skore & six 3ere ouer **gon** (Trinity)

By the nineteenth century the northern associations of *gan/ga* are well established. Heslop provides an extensive entry for *gan* (1893: 315) and instances of most of the forms attested on RTG can be found amongst the dictionary's citations (in the following paired examples, the first is from *NW* and the second from RTG).

(13) a. It's time to **gan** hyem.
b. Hope it gans off like, might be able to **gan** home.
c. Aa'll **gan** an *fish* for mesel.
d. Think I'll **gan** and punch one just for fun.
e. Aa gans up tiv him.
f. ah **gans** up to the bully and ah gives 'im a twelve hit combo.
g. He gans skittling aboot.
h. He **gans** on like a twat.
i. He waaks backwards like an aad twiney **gan** doon the grund.
j. im not **gan** to the riverside.
k. **Gannen** down here.
l. We're gutless and shite mate and we're **gannen** down. :cry:
m. Wor aad wife's **ganna** *mask* the tye.
n. I'm **ganna** make a broth on Monday....proper bait.

Gan has particular longevity and saliency in NEVE. Ruano-García et al. (2015) in a study of the lexis of English and Scottish 'Northern texts' list *gang/gan* amongst the 'top ten northern words' in both their Early (1500–1700) and Late Modern English (1800–1900) sub-corpora.[5] Ruano-García et al.

[5] The complete Late Modern list (1800–1900) is: *lad, lass, sel/sen* ('self'), *gan/gang, nowt, mun* ('must'), *bairn, summat, owt, bonny*. Except for *mun*, all can be found on RTG. It is worth noting that *lad, lass, nowt, bairn,* and *owt* occur amongst the top-ten keyest dialect words in the RTG sample corpus (see 1.3).

describe such items as 'lexical pan-northernisms' and stress that because the corpus texts are 'representative of literary dialects' they 'were not necessarily written for a regional audience', concluding that 'writers balanced the number of dialectalisms used so as not to interfere with the readers' understanding of their literary message, and very likely selected terms that readers might have been familiar with' (2015: 145). It would seem then that as early as the sixteenth century *gan* was undergoing enregisterment and has therefore long enjoyed special status in the region.

We should also note the occurrence of nominal *gan* and *ganner* on RTG, which are also recorded in *EDD*.

(14) a. Worth a **gan** like.
 b. Gonna give it a **gan** like :lol:
 c. probably a good **ganner** like.

3.2.1.2 Know

On RTG, *know* is sometimes spelled <kna, knaa, knar, nar, naa> to reflect a vowel in the region of [aː], which is occasionally heard in speech in some words in the GOAT lexical set (see 7.2.2).

(15) a. Nice to **kna** some are concerned about me on here.
 b. As far as I **kna** yes.
 c. aye, a **knar**.
 d. I **nar** who you are anarl.
 e. you **naa** who i mean.
 f. This lad **knas**.
 g. I hope Juan **knars** his PIN number.
 h. You may mock, but he **knarred** about the computer lad weeks ago.
 i. **Knaing** my luck I'll get the sack.

Knar(s) often occurs in NEVE variants of the discourse marker 'you know': [ðəˈnaːz] ('thou knows') and [jəˈnaː(z)] (with an -s morpheme sometimes included on 'you know' by analogy with 'thou knows'). See 3.4.1.3 and 6.3.3.

(16) a. It took me all last night to think that one up **yanaar**!
 b. Booo hooo, it was off side ya **knaas**.
 c. The world will keep turning **the knars**.
 d. ah's not daft **tha knas**.

In SED, when prompted to produce 'I don't know', most of the Northumbrian informants favoured [naː ~ na] rather than [nøː ~ nø ~ nɔː ~ nɔ] for 'know' (Orton and Halliday 1963: 806–807). PDE *know* derives from OE *(ʒe)cnáwan*. *DSL* describes forms in -*a*- as 'northern' and forms in -*o*- as midlands and the south. SE adopts the southern form while the archaic form is preserved

Morphology

in Sc. and NEVE. By Heslop's time it had become a well-known feature of the dialect:

> KNAA, KNAW, to know. "Thoo *knaas* aa like te he' thee near." *Ken* means to be acquainted with a person or thing from observation or from outside view. *Knaa* refers to mental perception. (1893: 428)

For many people of course, the cognate *ken* in the sense alluded to by Heslop has a distinctly Scottish feel. But it was recorded for Northumbrian locations in SED (Orton and Halliday 1963: 807) and it does occasionally appear on RTG.

(17) a. I think I **ken** who he is.
     b. De ye **ken** the "Tute" in Lynemouth, canny drink in there, my marra lives in Albion Terrace.

3.2.1.3 *Make* and *take*

Traditional North East pronunciations of *make* and *take* are [mak] and [tak]. According to Kerswill (1987) this is the result of lexical variation, with [e:] (the mainstream northern English vowel for words in the FACE lexical set) used in formal situations, and [a] in more informal contexts. SED records [mak] and (more rarely) [tak] at Northumbrian locations (Orton and Halliday 1963: 1009, 1011).[6] This variation has become lexicalised, and captured in spellings such as <mack, mak> and <tack, tak>.

These [a] variants are generally base, present tense, and *-ing* participle forms.

(18) a. **Mack** ya mind up.
     b. **Macks** sense really.
     c. i think they just **mak** it up as they gan along.
     d. our lass **maks** it toppa.
     e. just been **mackin'** a cup of tea and a glass of juice at the same time.
     f. People from Sunderland say **mak** and **tak**.
     g. Don't **tack** too long to make up your mind mate.
     h. Roy Wood **tacks** some beating like.
     i. I says come in, **tak** a seat.
     j. **Taks** after his Fatha!
     k. Can someone calmly and without **tacking** the piss explain this one to me?

Forms in *-a-* preserve a pre-GVS pronunciation, echoing the OE verbs *macan* and *tacan*. The historical associations with the north are strong:

---

[6] Interestingly, both are regarded as 'older' by a gamekeeper from County Durham who was seventy at the time he was surveyed in 1953.

as McColl Millar points out 'in all of the dialects' of northern and insular Scots, *make* and *take* are [mak] and [tak] (2007: 34). *EDD* records forms in -*a*- widely across the north, providing a parental admonishment from Durham as evidence for [mak] and a line from a Northumberland song for [tak].

(19) a. A'll **mak** tha' behave thysell.
 b. Sae don your plaid an' **tak** your gad.

Culturally, [mak] is of particular importance because it is the origin of the ethnonym *Mackem* (see 2.3 and 7.2.3).

3.2.2 'Unusual' forms: primary verbs

The primary verbs (*be, have, do*) can function as main verbs and auxiliaries. In both roles, we see some contrasts in *have* and *do* between NEVE and SE (the differences in relation to *be* are largely syntactical, and are therefore dealt with in the section on number agreement in Chapter 4).

Formally, NEVE and SE mainly coincide in relation to *have*. However, SED does record *ha* as a first person singular present tense form in Northumberland, and *ha* (which is widespread in Scotland) is also present on RTG (with both positive and negative polarity).

(20) a. i **ha** absolutely no faith he will learn from his mistakes.
 b. since then i **hant** looked back.

Ha reflects a ME development where in weak-stress conditions the [v] was lost (*ODEE*).

The situation for *do* in NEVE is more complex. Orthographic representations of *do* on RTG reflecting non-standard forms are exemplified in (21–29).

(21) Infinitive
 a. Things to **dee** in Madrid.
 b. needs to **dae** more squat thrusts and star jumps on the touchline.

(22) Imperative
 a. **dee** it yersel.
 b. just **dae** it.

(23) First person singular
 a. Aye, I **dee**.
 b. Only **dae** aboot 10k a year.
 c. He divs. I **div**. We all div. Whoever says we divvent understand is clearly a div.

Morphology

(24) First person plural
   a. I've followed safc long enough to kna we **dee** things the hard way.
   b. oh should we **dae** this Kirsty.
   c. He divs. I div. We all **div**. Whoever says we divvent understand is clearly a div.

(25) Second person singular
   a. Breathe in before you **dee** yasel a mischief.
   b. Av tried the educashun route, but wot can ye **dae**.

(26) Second person plural
   a. Yaz **dee** undastand.
   b. I once asked one "Why do youse actually say it?" and his reply was "Cos vats what yaz all **dey**, eat cheeeezy chips".

(27) Third person singular
   a. She **diz** nowt for me like.
   b. be class if he **diz** mate.
   c. Mind, it'll be chuffing 'ellish if it **diz**, like.
   d. He **divs**. I div. We all div. Whoever says we divvent understand is clearly a div.

(28) Third person plural
   a. There's only one reason they **dee** it.
   b. "AYE BUT A BET WA STILL GET HIGHYA CROODZ THEN THA MACKAMZ **DEY**".

(29) *-ing* participle
   a. Fucking hell man what was he **deeing**?
   b. Clatts is **daeing** the business noo.

The orthographic forms <dee, di> reflect pronunciations – like [di:] and [dɪ] – which developed through the raising and unrounding of the vowel in the GOOSE lexical set (which includes *do*) in Scotland and the northern counties of England, so-called 'Northern fronting' (Johnston 1997: 69). These /i/-forms have been a feature of the English of Scotland and North East England since the Early Modern English period and are well-attested in *EDG* (Wright 1905: 406–407) and SED (Orton and Halliday 1963: 1035–1041). The orthographic forms <dae, dey> reflect a vowel in the region of [ɛi~ei], a development of the FLEECE vowel in some North East locations (see 7.2.11).

The spelling <div> represents [dɪv], where the consonant [v] likely reflects a fortition of the hiatus breaker [w] (Rowe 2007). It should be noted that the examples of *div(s)* in (23c), (24c), and (27d) have a jokey quality, possibly because *div* is commoner in negative clauses in contemporary NEVE than it is in clauses with positive polarity (see also 4.3.1 and 7.4.2).

3.3 Noun morphology

In SE nouns are usually marked as plural with the -s morpheme. A few noun lexemes preserve older forms with mutated vowels (e.g. *mouse – mice*) and the weak plural in -n (e.g. *ox – oxen*); some have the same form for singular and plural (e.g. *sheep – sheep*); a small set reflect a phonetic variation in Old English, where /f/ was voiced to [v] intervocalically, so that for example the plural of *wif* [wiːf] was *wifas* [wiːvəs] (compare *wife – wives*). In vernacular English, there is evidence of a more widespread retention of these older forms. For example, in SED (*SEDDG*: 481–483) the following are attested for Northumberland and/or County Durham: mutation of stem vowel (*cow – kye* [kai]); suffixation of -n (*eyen, shoon, starn*); singular and plural with the same form (*pound – pound*).

While the Middle English -n plurals are no longer seen in NEVE, and few – if any – north easterners still refer to cows as *kye*, there is some evidence on RTG for the analogical levelling of the OE stem alternation -f- → -v- which Wright (1905: 261) particularly associates with southern Scotland and which Miller refers to as 'Scottish plurals' (1993: 107).

(30) a. I hate people who have to use **knifes** instead of fists to settle a problem.
   b. A pleasant Sunday stroll on the hunt for conkers and **leafs**.
   c. I can see why there's an issue with killing bull **calfs**.
   d. There might be dog **thiefs** out there.
   e. And they use to sell "mis-shaped" **loafs** of bread off cheap as well.
   f. The WBA fans even had Wolves **scarfs** on.

A question raised by the examples in (30) is whether they represent pronunciations such as [lɪːfs] or are simply orthographic. SED does record [-fs] in the plurals of *calf, hoof,* and *sheaf* for Northumbrian locations, as well as some use of [-s] rather than the more typical [-z] in *cows, fleas, peas, shoes,* and *slugs* (*SEDDG*: 481–482).

A further form of levelling is to be seen in the regularisation of irregular nouns, a phenomenon often associated with child language acquisition or L2 varieties of English, but which is also present in L1 vernacular varieties (though some of the examples in (31) represent jocular stylistic choices rather than habitual vernacular usage).

(31) a. Drill it in there man, they're lumbering **oxes**.
   b. One in the eye for them Sunderland folk and their little **aircrafts**.
   c. Being just the same but killing **mooses** and seals and stuff.
   d. Play up you handsome young **swines**.

Some 'double plurals' (Wright 1905: 263) – in which the -s morpheme is added to an already plural form – might have a similar stylistic function on

Morphology

RTG, though *folks* is a common and widespread vernacular word, particularly as a vocative, as in (32d). Also of note is the *-s* morpheme sometimes found in *shows* and *cinemas*, where the referent is singular. *Shows* (to refer to a travelling fair) is recorded in *DNEE*; *cinemas* was perhaps coined by analogy with *shows*.

(32) a. The body in question was under **feets** of snow.
b. Ill be on tonight from like 10 if **peoples** are on.
c. Time to move on like **peeps**.
d. What's on the menu today **folks**?
e. "All together like the **folks** of shields" Me ganny used to say when everyone turned up for dinner at the same time.
f. and if you couldn't afford the **shows** you'd gan to the park.
g. me munching a pack of fruit pastilles at the **cinemas** in the metro centre.

Finally, (33) exemplifies a widespread pattern in vernacular English in which nouns – in certain contexts – have the same form for both singular and plural. Mustanoja suggests that many of these – such as *year* and *month* – are survivals of OE unchanged plurals, 'or of OE plurals ending in *-u*, *-e*, and *-an*, like *hundred*, *lode*, and *tonne*, or of OE genitive plurals, like *mile*' (1960: 57). Other nouns with identical forms for singular and plural include *foot*, *fathom*, *pound*, and *stone*. What they all have in common is that they denote number, size, length of time, amount of money, and so on, and are preceded by an expression of number or quantity.

(33) a. Lived in Stanley a few **year** now.
b. I went part time when the bairn was about nine **month** old.
c. About two **ton** of cheese melted under the grill on them.
d. basically I walk ten **mile** every day with the dog.
e. About a foot wide and eight **foot** long.
f. Got one with two fat ladies, won 15 **pound** in the club.
g. "Then when I said I couldn't afford the 32 **poond** ya laffed arriz!"

Such plurals reflect a 'linguistic phenomenon of universal occurrence' in which 'no plural ending or other sign is needed to indicate the number of the governing noun' if 'the idea of plurality is obvious from the attributive numeral or adjective' (Mustanoja 1960: 58). Murray comments that 'the same distinction has prevailed from the earliest appearance of northern literature in the 13th century' (1873: 162). While uninflected quantitative nouns in these contexts are non-standard, they are permissible in some standardised Germanic dialects. For example, the German translation of the title of the Spanish language film *Tres metros sobre el cielo* ('three **metres** above heaven') is *Drei **Meter** über dem Himmel*.

Another aspect of measure phrases shared between NEVE and other Germanic dialects (including Sc.E, but not SE) is shown in these RTG examples.

(34) a. Love a **bit cheese savoury**.
b. Two grown men hitting a **bit rubber** over a fence with a **bit string**.
c. cut a **bit cake** up and stick icing sugar over it.
d. Had a good **bit crack** with him after the game.
e. Had a **bit walk** around their camp.
f. Went through to Seaham for a **bit wander**.
g. a **bit plodge** n'that just keeps ya nice and cool, man.

Here, *of* is absent after the noun *bit* where it would be present in SE. The SED records this phenomenon for Northumbrian locations, for example: *a bit string, a bit brown sugar, a bit feed, a bit cake, a good bit money* (Orton and Halliday 1963: 770). 'Partitive' constructions with *of* arose in the ME period, when the genitive inflection was replaced with the *of*-phrase, possibly with support from French possessive *de*, so that Old English *an bite brædess* becomes *a bit of bread* (Traugott 2010: 42). The permissibility of *of*-deletion in such constructions in NEVE is an echo of this earlier 'native' structure, which is to be found in other Germanic dialects, including Dutch (*een beetje brood*) and German (*ein bisschen Brot*). We should also note *of(a)*-deletion in non-partitive expressions in which the approximative sense of *bit* comes to the fore and it seems to be functioning as an epistemic hedge (Burke and Burridge 2023), as in (34d,e,f,g).

Also of interest is the suffix *-ie* used to form nouns from monosyllabic adjectives and nouns. The process is more common in Scots than NEVE but is perhaps worth mentioning due to its role in the formation of *Geordie* and *Smoggie* (as well as *daftie*).

3.4 Pronouns

Many English dialects demonstrate considerable variation in their pronominal systems (Trudgill and Chambers 1991; Hernández 2011; Wales 1996) and this is certainly the case with NEVE. In this section I draw on RTG to illustrate the richness of the system, covering personal pronouns, possessive determiners and pronouns, reflexives, demonstrative determiners and pronouns, indefinite pronouns, and relative and interrogative pronouns.

3.4.1 Personal pronouns

Table 3.1 *Forms of personal pronouns on RTG (standard forms in bold and more localised forms in italics; selected orthographic representations from RTG are shown in angle brackets)*

	Subject singular	Object singular	Subject plural	Object plural
First person	**I** <a, ah, aa>	**me** *us* <uz, iz, ez>	**we** <wah, wuh, wa> *us*	**us** <uz> *we* <wah, wuh, wa>
Second person	**you** <ye, ya, yer, yay, yee> *thou* <tha, thoo, thow> *thee*	**you** <ye, ya, yer, yay, yee> *thou* <thow>	**you** *yous* <youse, yuz, yez, yees, yeez, yers, yerz, yas, yiz, yays>	**you** *yous* <youse, yuz, yez, yees, yeez, yers, yerz, yas, yiz, yays>
Third person	**he, she, it**	**him, her, it**	**they**	**them**

3.4.1.1 First person subject pronouns

The RTG spellings <a>, <ah>, and <aa> suggest pronunciations such as [ɑ] and [a] for *I*.

(35) a. **a** think Henry was unreal as well but **a** still think Aguero is the best.
b. **Ah**'m not unhappy about living in Australia.

The feature has been enregistered in NEVE since at least the nineteenth century, as this entry from *NW* indicates:

> AA, AW, AH, I the pronoun of the first person. This long, broad sound is a characteristic of the dialect of the Tyneside and of South Northumberland. (Heslop 1892: 2)

Forms in *a-* probably arose when *I* [ɪ] (a development of OE *ic*) was lengthened under stress in ME, and later diphthongised – probably to [ɑɪ]. The second element was lost under lack of stress and a new form [ɑ] and later [ɑː] arose. Such forms are recorded for Northumbrian locations in SED, as well as in the other northern counties, the Midlands, and East Anglia (see *SEDDG*: 486). They are also distinctly Scottish.

In the plural, SED records *us* functioning as equivalent of SE *we* in Northumbrian locations, and also quite widely across the dialects. It is to be found (though rarely) on RTG.

(36) a. It is what it is and **us** cant change nowt.
b. A nugget I used to work with, "**Us**'ll dee that then" What?

We also sometimes encounter respellings on RTG which attempt to capture what *OED* calls a 'chiefly northern' form of the first person plural subject pronoun: *wa*.

(37) a. "**Wa** hafta play for wor pride noo lads".
     b. Oh we hate Newcastle but **wa** like brown ale.

3.4.1.2 First person object pronouns
A common colloquial use of *us* is as the equivalent of SE *me*. SED records objective singular *us* across the whole of England (*SEDDG*: 486). It usually appears in imperative constructions such as 'give **us** a kiss', sometimes with the pragmatic function of softening the force of the request. This feature is common on RTG (the broader context of the examples makes it clear that *us* has singular reference).

(38) a. Someone hoy **us** a link.
     b. mack **iz** one of them.

In NEVE, however, singular *us* is used more widely, meaning sentences like the following can also be heard, as they can in Scotland (Miller 2004: 49).

(39) a. My lass give **us** a dead arm once.
     b. Are yer gonna knack **iz** marra?
     c. some aunty bought **ez** it.

Spellings with <z> are used to reflect the widespread northern pronunciation of the pronoun, while <i> and <e> spellings represent the unstressed form. Evidence for the regional saliency of this feature can be found in SED. For example, in response to a prompt designed to elicit the order of pronouns in *given it me/me it* (Orton and Halliday 1963: 1070), eight of the nine Northumberland informants and three of the six from County Durham rejected *me* and substituted *us*. The entry for *us* in *NW* suggests this distinctive usage has been around for a while:

> US, used for *me*. "Wiv *us*" – with me. "Tiv *us*" – to me. "He gov *us* ne answer." Sometimes shortened, as, "What'll ye gi's?" (Heslop 1893: 758)

OED only refers to non-imperative *us* in relation to its use by 'a sovereign, ruler, or magnate', but *DSL* has colloquial examples spanning the mid-nineteenth century to the present day.

Another distinctive first person objective pronoun associated with NEVE is *we*. Described by Beal et al. as a limited form of pronoun-exchange (2012: 53), it is not recorded in SED, though it is attested for Northumberland in *EDD*, with the example used drawn from *NW*: 'WE, us. "Haw-way

Morphology

wi *we*.'" (Heslop 1893: 775). It is also found in Scotland. On RTG, objective *we* often favours prepositional phrases (40a,b), with spellings reflecting the unstressed form found in this position in speech. (40c) is the title of a famous Joy Division song rendered into NEVE.

(40) a. Don't know how I didn't know that story when he was with **wuh**.
    b. they're way too smart for **wah**.
    c. Luv will tear **wa** apart.

3.4.1.3 Second person subject and object pronouns

RTG also has a rich array of non-standard second person pronouns. SED records *ye* as a singular second person subjective and objective, realised as [jiː], [jɪ], and [jə] (*SEDDG*: 486). On RTG <ye>, <yee>, and <yer> are found, with <yee> and <yay> sometimes used to represent the emphatic/stressed pronunciation (see 7.2.11). Modern *ye* is derived from Old English *ge*, which was the subjective case of the second person plural pronoun. *Ye* with singular reference emerges in the Middle English period, used instead of *thou* originally as a marker of respect, deference, or formality. *Ye* develops an objective function in the later Middle English period. These examples show *ye* as singular subject (41a) and object (41b,c).

(41) a. **Ye** canna mak a savaloy out of an alsatian, man haway. ;)
    b. fuck **ye** Frank.
    c. Is that **yee** on the phone like?

Like forms of *I* in *a-*, *ye* has a Scottish flavour, and is widely attested there, as it is in varieties of Irish English.

Alternatives to *you* as a second person plural pronoun are a widespread vernacular angloversal (Kortmann 2020: 639). *Yous* is common in NEVE. It is attested across the linguistic North, as well as in American, Australian, Canadian, Irish, and New Zealand Englishes. Its 'spread has been traced to a source in Irish English (possibly calqued from Gaelic)' and it seems to be 'localized to areas that experienced high volumes of Irish immigration in the nineteenth century' (MacKenzie et al. 2022: 58). On RTG *yous* and *yees*, like *ye*, function as both subject and object (note also the variant spellings in Table 3.1).

(42) a. **Yous** need to be careful.
    b. Hope this shuts **yous** up.
    c. **Youse** will survive, just.
    d. Some of **youse** are ganning on like the mags.
    e. If **yees** take offence to that you need to get a life you sad bastards.

Beal points out that for 'some younger speakers, *yous* has been generalised as the local form, and may be used to address one person' (1993: 205).

(43) a. It must be your little hands and beady eyes that give **yous** the edge like.
b. Love **yous** too marra.

SED also records the older forms *thou* and *thee* as singular subjective and objective pronouns in NEVE, with *thou* sometimes realised as [ðuː] or [ða] (*SEDDG*: 486). Orthographic representations of these realisations occur on RTG (44). There are also examples of *thou* as a plural (44c), which is possibly an innovation through analogy with *yous*.

(44) a. Does **thoo** not sleep Hank?
b. **thou**'s fukn crackers **thou** is.
c. If **tha** ivvor comes tu Shotton I'll buy **thous** a gill.
d. You don't have to act like a scratter in a scratter shop **thee** nars.
e. '**Tha**'s Got Hair Like a Ducks Arse'.
f. I'd rather cut my tiddler off with a blunt comb than gan for a pint with **thou**.
g. I shall have a pint with **thee**.

Historically, *thee* is the objective case of *thou* but this distinction is not maintained in those northern dialects where the pronoun is still used. *Thee/thou* in NEVE is rare, and some instances on RTG involve contributors 'impersonating' people from further south in northern England, particularly from South Yorkshire, where it is an enregistered feature of the dialect (Cooper 2019: 71). Since the SED was carried out, when forms in *th-* were widely distributed across England, at least amongst older, rural speakers (*SEDDG*: 486), they have gone into steep decline. However, as the examples here show, there is enough evidence on RTG to suggest some contemporary currency in NEVE, confirming that Burbano-Elizondo's informants who 'argued that *thou* could be heard in Sunderland' (Beal et al. 2012: 54) were correct. On RTG it commonly occurs in the discourse marker 'thou knows' (3.2.1.2 and 6.3.3), which is variously rendered orthographically to capture pronunciations such as [ða naːz] and [ðiː naːz].

(45) a. Has a turkish cap **thee knas**.
b. The NHS is creaking, **tha knas**.

Heslop's remarks (1893: 727) are worth considering here:

> THOO, thou; sometimes shortened to *tu* or *ta. Thoo'll,* thou wilt. *Thoo's,* thou art or thou shalt. *Thoo* is only used by intimates, or by a superior or senior to an inferior. Used in any other way it expresses the greatest possible contempt for the person addressed.

The pragmatics of nineteenth-century usage are echoed in the RTG data, especially in relation to the expression of social solidarity (examples 44a,c,g) and contempt (44b,d,e,f).

Morphology

3.4.1.4 Third person subject and object pronouns

By and large, in both the subjective and objective, there is correspondence between SE and NEVE third person forms, though pronoun exchange sometimes occurs when the subject element consists of a pronoun conjoined with a noun. This is common in many varieties of English.

(46) a. If **him and his son** want to come and watch as fans they're more than welcome.
b. **Him and me dad** were best mates when they were younger.

In the plural, *them* is recorded in SED as a subject form in County Durham (and more widely) and also occurs on RTG.

(47) a. **Them**'s the bastards that bombed me granny.
b. Aye **them**'s the ones. ;)

Also of note is 'singular' *they*, which is rapidly increasing in all varieties of English (see Paterson 2014).

(48) a. Anyone who says **they** don't care is a joke of a fan in my opinion.
b. Who takes an AK47 when **they** go burgling.

3.4.2 Possessive determiners and pronouns

Table 3.2 *Possessive determiners and pronouns on RTG (standard forms in bold and more localised forms in italics; selected orthographic representations from RTG are shown in angle brackets)*

	Possessive determiner	Possessive pronoun
First person singular	**my** *me* <mi, ma, mah>	**mine**
First person plural	**our** *wor* <wor, wa, wuh>	**ours** *wors* <wors, worz>
Second person singular	**your** <yer, yewa> *thy* <thee>; *thous* <thoos>	**yours** <yewas> *thine*
Second person plural	**your** <yer, yewa>	**yours**
Third person singular	**his, her, its**	**his, hers, its**
Third person plural	**their**	**theirs**

3.4.2.1 First person possessive determiners

Me is used widely in NSE as a first person possessive determiner, particularly in unstressed conditions. On RTG, <me> is the typical spelling (more rarely <mi>). We also find the spelling <ma(h)>, reflecting a lower, backer vowel of the sort which according to the *OED* has been attested in northern varieties of English since at least the eighteenth century (like *a* and *ye, ma* is particularly associated with Scotland).

(49) a. **Me** car's broke.
      b. I'm just about to have **mi** tea.
      c. **Ma** Mam and Dad still live in Hendon.

Of more local salience to NEVE – though it is also found in Scottish varieties – is the plural possessive determiner *wor*.[7] In SED *wor* is attested for Northumbrian locations, but it was also recorded across the northern counties and as far south as Bedfordshire and Buckinghamshire as [wɐʁ~wər~weɹ] (*SEDDG*: 488). Due to de-rhotacisation this is now often [wə] in speech, reflected in spellings like <wa> on RTG (see 7.3.1 for a discussion of the status of /r/ in NEVE).

(50) a. Ya have to understand **wor** pride and passion.
      b. I am getting **wor** lass to drop us off afterwards.
      c. Only we could drop **wa** best player for a must win game.

In parallel with *us*, *wor* is sometimes used with singular reference. Example (50b) shows a common pattern in NEVE, where there is 'a tendency for the first person plural form to be used with reference to family members and sexual partners' (Beal et al. 2012: 53).

OED records forms in *w-* emerging in the sixteenth century in Scotland, and labels them as 'northern' by the nineteenth century. *Wor* has long had a particular cultural salience in NEVE, as is evident from its repetition in the quotation from a patriotic Northumberland song from 1824 which Heslop uses to illustrate the word: 'In defence o' **wor** country, **wor** laws, an' **wor** King, / May a Peercy still lead us to battle' (1893: 797). Its use as a badge of north east identity is evident in its appearance on signs and artefacts in the 'linguistic landscape' (see Pearce 2017), as is its occurrence in national media contexts in conjunction with north east celebrities: for example, the headline "Why-aye that was reall-aye beautiful!' weeps **Wor** Cheryl' appeared in the *Daily Mail* in 2014. However, it should be pointed out that some participants in perceptual dialectology research carried out in North East England associate *wor(s)* with Tyneside and Newcastle, suggesting that such forms are less common in the more southerly parts of the region (Pearce 2012: 14–15). These perceptions have some basis in fact: in the SED when the phrase 'with our eyes' was prompted, all but one of the Nb. informants favoured a *w-* form, while only two of the Du. informants did – most used *our* (Orton and Halliday 1963: 601). On RTG this identification of *wor* as 'a characteristic feature of present-day urban Geordie' (Wales 2006: 185) is reflected in parodic performances of 'Geordie' speech, as in this impersonation of Steve Bruce (manager of Newcastle United F.C. from 2019–2021).

---

[7] There is also sporadic use of *us* as a possessive determiner, as in 'Put hairs on **us** chist like rusty nails.'

Morphology

(51) Wa roll **wa** sleeves up dust **wa**selfs down wa go again :lol:.

3.4.2.2 First person possessive pronouns
In the first person singular, there is general correspondence with SE on RTG (i.e. *mine*), but in the plural we do see forms in *w-*.

(52) a. Got **wors** at Costco mate.
b. **wors** came today.

Wors is recorded in SED for Northumbrian locations (Orton and Halliday 1963: 1072–1073), though as is the case with *wor*, it is more common in Northumberland than Durham. Like *yous*, *wors* is a relatively late addition to the pronoun system. Heslop's earliest citation is from a song published in 1819, in which Newcastle is compared favourably with London. Indeed, the capital's streets turn out to be just 'like **wors**' (1893: 797).

3.4.2.3 Second person possessive determiners
These usually coincide with standard *your* (sometimes spelled <yer> or <ya>). But *thy* (with variants like *thee, thou* and *thoo(s)*) can also be found.

(53) a. Haway man woman man, had **ya** pash.
b. Had **thee** pash.
c. Should have known **thy** ears would prick up!
d. And wharrabout **thy** hair?
e. Ad **thee** oss. Get **thee** pipe.
f. What's **thou** name lad?
g. Mek **thoos** mind up lad.

In SED, *thy* [ðɪ~ðə] is attested for Northumbrian locations (*SEDDG*: 488).

3.4.2.4 Second person possessive pronouns
Non-standard second person singular forms are rare on RTG, though *thine* is to be found, and was recorded for Northumbrian locations in SED (*SEDDG*: 488).

(54) a. I wonder whee's shitty arse the wife there'll have to see to first, the bairn's or **thine**!
b. With an avatar like that, I'd fuckin' dread to see **thine**!
c. Back in the day, my granda met Prince Philip when he visited the Caterpillar factory, shook his hand and replied to his comment that 'you look like you've got a good job here' with 'not as good as **thine** marra'.

3.4.2.5 Third person possessive determiners and pronouns
As with the third person subject and object pronouns, there is no local morphological variation in these categories. Occasionally, respelling is used

to show the /h/-loss which sometimes occurs at the start of function words such as *his* and *her* in fast connected speech (7.3.3).

(55) a. Gary Bennett motions fer the ball, so I 'spray' a pin point pass ter **eez** feet.
b. "Aks **'er** mother for a kiss under the mistletoe".

3.4.3 Reflexive pronouns

Beal notes that in SE 'reflexives are formed by adding *self/selves* to the possessive forms of the first and second person pronouns (e.g. *myself, yourself, yourselves*), but to the objective form of the third person pronouns (e.g. *himself, herself, themselves*). Tyneside English is more consistent in this respect, adding *self/selves* to the possessive form in every case' (1993: 206). On RTG we encounter outputs of this 'levelling' process, which is widespread in non-standard English and Scots (see 'Pronouns' in SSA).

(56) a. he didn't even do it by **hisself**.
b. County Durham Mags should be ashamed of **theirselves**.

However, the full picture of reflexives in NEVE also includes variability in the reflexive suffix (Buchstaller and Corrigan 2015: 87), so that on RTG we also see *-sel(s)* and *sen(s)* alongside *-self(ves)*.

The *-self(ves)* element is OE; *-sel(s)* seems to have emerged in the sixteenth century through consonant cluster simplification, while *-sen(s)* perhaps reflects a development of a plural form in *-n* (as in Early Modern English *sellfenn*) and is recognised as dialectal by the eighteenth century. In SED the *-sel* form has wide distribution across the northern counties, the Midlands, and beyond, particularly in the first person singular (i.e. *mysel*). It is also quite common in colloquial Scottish English. Forms in *-sen* are rarer with a narrower distribution focused on Yorkshire (*SEDDG*: 488–489), where it is an enregistered feature (Cooper 2019). Both are identified as 'pan-northernisms' by Ruano-García et al. (2015: 145). The use of first person *w-* and second person *th-* forms (cf. the related simplex pronouns *wor* and *thy*) is also notable.

3.4.3.1 First person reflexives
In the first person singular, the simplex pronoun onto which the reflexive suffix is attached is *my* or *me*. SED records *mesel* [mɪsɛl] for all locations in Northumbria, Cumbria, and Lancashire, while in Yorkshire *mesen* [mɪsɛn] can be found alongside *mesel* (Orton and Halliday 1963: 1093–1097). Both are to be found on RTG, together with the much more widespread colloquial form *meself*.

(57) a. I'm ashamed of **meself**!
b. I got **myself** a glass of sauvignon blanc at halftime yesterday.

Morphology

  c. I've landed **mesel** in a bit bother with all this.
  d. I shat **mysen**.
  e. Was just going to make **mesen** a Tuna salad baguette.

As far as the first person plural is concerned, RTG contains a few reflexives based on *wor* (see 3.4.2.1).

(58) a. We dust **worselves** down.
  b. Wa dust **worsels** down.
  c. We were shitting **waselves**.
  d. We'll have to work it out for **wasels** i reckon.

In the *Basic Material*, [wasɛlz] is recorded for Nb., but not for Du., continuing the pattern found for *wor* and *wors* (Orton and Halliday 1963: 1097). We might also note *our* combining with non-standard -*sels*.

(59) a. Aye, we don't want to give **oursels** too long to hang on like.
  b. Aye theres still time to save **oursels**.

Morphologically singular forms also occur, mainly with plural reference.

(60) a. If we compare **ourself** to league one clubs we'll stay as a league one club.
  b. Getting far too ahead of **ourself**.

3.4.3.2 Second person reflexives

There is more variation in the second person on RTG than was found in SED, which only records *thysel* and *yoursel(s)* for Northumbrian locations (*SEDDG*: 488–489). The singular forms in (61) illustrate this variety.

(61) a. Have a read and educate **thyself**.
  b. Gan fist **thysel**.
  c. How's it gannin **theeself**?
  d. Get **theesel** down to the computer shop.
  e. Whey behave **thysen** this time round Joe.
  f. Don't be too hard on **yoursel**.
  g. Get **yesel** on the train like man.
  h. get **yoursen** down the match.

Plural forms in -*s* also occur.

(62) a. Be kind, be safe, look after **yoursels**.
  b. Perhaps decide between **yesels**?

3.4.3.3 Third person reflexives

Hissel(l,f), hersel(l), and *theirsels* are recorded for Northumbrian locations in SED and all are found on RTG.

(63) a. he's shot **hisself**.
 b. Tell him to get **hissel** over to Roker and sort it out.
 c. Carol has just bought **herself** a new house.
 d. how do the symptoms manifest **theirsels** there mate?
 e. They would just piss **thasels**.

Spellings in *tha-* probably reflect a reduced *their*; [ðəsɛlz] was a pronunciation recorded in SED for Northumbrian locations (Orton and Halliday 1963: 1097).

In addition, we find the reflexive suffix *-sen(s)* combining with the objective pronouns *him* and *them*, and *-sels* combining with *them*.

(64) a. unsurprisingly he drank **himsen** to death.
 b. they've really gone the full Guzman and all got **themsens** bulletproof Audis now.
 c. Smoggy bastards don't like people enjoying **themsels**.

We also see singular uses of 'plural' reflexive forms.

(65) a. Whoever that was needs to take a long hard look at **theirself**.
 b. So you are seriously commending a person for drinking **themself** to death?

3.4.4 Demonstrative determiners and pronouns

Generally, in contemporary NEVE, the demonstratives used to mark whether something is near or distant from the speaker (in Cartesian or social space) correspond to SE (e.g. *this/that, these/those*), although *them(s)* as a distal plural form (a widespread contemporary dialect feature) also occurs.

(66) a. Just say how you feel sorry for mike ashley having to put up with **them** idiots.
 b. **Thems** were the days.

In addition, we occasionally find the distals *thon* and *yon*, both of which were recorded in SED for Northumbrian locations and also widely across the northern counties (Orton and Halliday 1963: 1089).

(67) a. **Thon** shite player Maja.
 b. I started watching **thon** Paddy Conroy videos.
 c. You cool fuckers in **yon** end wouldn't be able to hear.

Morphology

Heslop records pronominal uses of *thon* and *yon* e.g. 'Whe's **thon**?' (1893: 727), but on RTG *thon* only occurs as a determiner, sometimes with plural reference as in (67b). Etymologically, *thon* seems to be an alteration of *yon*, with – according to the *OED* – the initial consonant being assimilated to *this* and *that*. *Yon* and *thon* (used interchangeably as they are on RTG) are also features of Scots dialects (McColl Millar 2007: 69), described by Murray as 'constantly used in Scotch, in referring to things remote in place or time' (see 'Demonstratives' in SSA).[8]

3.4.5 Indefinite pronouns

NEVE contrasts with SE mainly in relation to negative indefinite pronouns, because *no* as a quantifier (and *none* as its corresponding pronoun) is often pronounced [niː(n)] or [neː(n)] in NEVE, preserving earlier unrounded forms (for unrounded negative response forms, see 6.4). The spellings <nay, ney> reflect a development whereby [niː] → [neɪ] (cf. <ye> → <yay>).

(68) a. **Neebody** is going to own up.
 b. Hope **nee one** ever does a countdown to your redundancy then.
 c. Well **ney one** can accuse you of sitting on the fence.
 d. **Neen** o' this turkey shite for me.

It is worth noting formulations such as the following which combine *nee* with an expressive noun.

(69) a. **Nee fucker** gives a fuck about Bradford either so bog off.
 b. **Nee cunt** in my family looks like steve agnew marra :lol:
 c. **Nee bugger** else is allowed in.
 d. **neebugger** believes it surely?

The well-known pan-northernisms *nowt* and *owt* – alterations of *nought* and *aught* respectively (cf. Scots *nocht* and *ocht*) – are also common on RTG, typically used as the equivalent of SE *nothing* and *anything*. Indeed, *nowt* is the keyest dialect keyword in the sample corpus, while *owt* comes in at number ten (see 1.3). Also of note is the use of *summat* for *something* (a reduced form of *somewhat*).

(70) a. **Nowt** happening.
 b. **Owt** confirmed?
 c. he looked as cool as **owt**.

---

[8] Murray suggests that *thon* 'is probably a corruption of *yon*, developed by analogy of *thys, that*, to render it more significantly demonstrative. It is in regular use in all parts of Scotland, in Northumberland, about Shields, and as far south as Teesdale' (1873: 186).

d. I look sexy as **owt** in my thermal long johns and long sleeved vest.
  e. Aren't you from Whitley bay or **summat**?

In the public imagination these indefinites are strongly associated with Yorkshire dialect (Cooper 2019), though they are also common in NEVE. And the use of *as ... as owt* – the equivalent of the colloquial SE correlative construction *as ... as anything* – has a particularly strong NEVE flavour. The first *as* is typically omitted, as in (70d).

The pronoun which in SE is *one(s)* sometimes occurs as a *y-* form on RTG.

(71) a. Layers and layers for **this yin**.
  b. proper insult **that yin**.
  c. the deep fried **yins** are the best.
  d. it was 25 years ago and they were auld **yins** then.

Forms of *one* in *y-* are northern English regional and Scots (see 'One' in SSA). They date from the seventeenth century, reflecting the development of a front glide before certain vowels (Aitken and Macafee 2002).

3.4.6 Relative and interrogative pronouns

In SE, the pronouns used to introduce relative clauses are *who, which, that, whom,* and *whose*. In NEVE in relation to *who/whose* we encounter pronunciations such as [hwiː(z)] and [wiː(z)] at all Northumbrian locations (Orton and Halliday 1963: 1078–1079). These are orthographically rendered as <w(h)ee, w(h)ee(s,z)> on RTG, where they are used to represent both relative and interrogative *who* and *whose*.

(72) a. Can't remember **whee** it was exactly.
  b. I was wondering **weez** keys they were.
  c. **Whee**'s this bloke then?
  d. **whee** can afford eight kids like.
  e. **weez** daft fault was that though?
  f. "**Weez** keys are these keys".[9]

Whee is well established in nineteenth-century sources: Murray links it with Shields (1873: 91) and Heslop has an entry on it in *NW* (1893: 780).

RTG also has evidence of *thats* <thats, that's> as a genitive relative pronoun, with the *-s* possibly added to *that* by analogy with *who* and *whose*. Seppänen (1997: 153–154) reviews the history of this form, which has been noted in studies associated in particular with Scotland, though it is also

---

[9] This question is sometimes mockingly asked by Newcastle fans of Sunderland fans in the belief that *whee(s)* is a shibboleth of Sunderland speech.

Morphology 81

recorded in SED for Essex (Orton and Tilling 1971: 1327) and is widespread in colloquial spoken English.

(73) a. Bought a car off me **that's** engine was utterly fucked.
  b. It's one **thats** clients are Man Utd, Liverpool, Leeds, Marseille and few others.

Syntactic aspects of subordinate clauses are covered in 4.5.

3.5 Determiners

Determiners signal the reference of a noun. We have already considered possessive and demonstrative determiners in 3.4.2 and 3.4.4, alongside their pronominal counterparts, identifying salient forms in NEVE like *me*, *wor*, *thon*, and *yon*. In this section I focus on the morphology of the definite article and the quantifying determiners *more* and *no*.

3.5.1 Definite and indefinite articles

Definiteness or indefiniteness can be indicated by the articles *the* and *a(n)*. One of the most well-known features associated with northern dialects of English in England is the variety of forms taken by the definite article. Twelve forms are recorded in SED, not including mainstream [ðə], [ði:], and [ðɪ]. Most of them can be described as instances of 'definite article reduction' (DAR), usually represented in writing as <t'>, as in <t'pit>, first noted in the mid-seventeenth century (for an overview of the topic see Rupp and Page-Verhoeff 2005). Nineteenth-century sources point to a wide distribution of these forms across northern England; but in contemporary Britain the feature is usually associated with Yorkshire and Lancashire, though SED records some instances in Northumbrian locations. However, the further north the SED fieldworkers went, the fewer instances of DAR they found (*SEDDG*: 480). This distribution matches the pattern in the nineteenth century, with the *EDD* reporting in its entry for *the* that in Northumberland 'T'' is 'only heard in the extreme s.-west corner of the county'. While this entry does not mention County Durham, evidence from citations in other *EDD* entries suggest some usage there: for example, 'Clot them stanes into **t**'cart' (associated with south Durham). Heslop seems certain that the 'TH, in *the*' within 'Northumberland and that portion of the county of Durham lying on the right bank of the river Tyne from Wylam to Jarrow' is 'never shortened to a mere *t*'" (1892: vii, xviii), though in 'the southern part of the county of Durham … in speech a short *t'* is used for *the*' (1892: ix). This feature is represented orthographically on RTG with <t'> or <th'>.

(74) a. I did a cycle up that way **t'other** day.
 b. I can't tell the difference between one and **tother**.
 c. Get down **t'pit**.
 d. How pet, just purrit in **th'oven**.

Do these examples represent 'actual' usage or are they more performative in intent? Certainly, the spellings <t'other> and <tother> reflect attested pronunciations in North East speech, and can be found in DECTE. The other examples are jocular representations of pronunciations more typically associated with other parts of the north of England.

Interestingly, DECTE also has evidence for *tother* as a pronoun in itself, rather than DAR + *other*: *they had to do a bit fiddle and all one thing or* **the tother** (TLSG37); *watching everybody going by and all this that and* **the tother** (TLSG03). *The tother* (derived from *þe toþer*, for earlier *þet oþer/þat oþer* 'the other') occurs as early as the fourteenth century. It can also be found on RTG, and is attested for Northumberland in SED. Also, SED finds evidence of *the* appearing in contexts where it is not typically found in SE; for example, it occurs in the names of common ailments in Northumbrian locations (e.g. 'the headache', 'the toothache'), as it does before 'wife' (to mean the equivalent of 'my wife'). *The night* ('tonight'), *the morrow* ('tomorrow'), *the morn* ('tomorrow'), and *the day* ('today') are recorded in SED for the North East too (*SEDDG*: 481), and all these are attested in the *EDD* entry for *the*, as is *the both*, which *EDG* describes as general in Ireland 'and most parts' of England (Wright 1905: 260). Indeed, such non-standard usages are widespread across the linguistic North (see 'Determiners' in SSA) and all occur on RTG.

(75) a. Can't remember **the t'other**.
 b. Had my tea, had a nap and still got **the headache** off them.
 c. I've already had **the Covid** twice.
 d. Staring blankly at some bread, a tin of beans and a toaster, trying to work out how to survive without **the wife**.
 e. Cheers, I'll sleep **the neet**.
 f. Big game **the morrow** chill out have a beer pet.
 g. Hope the lads do her proud **the morn**.
 h. Used to get **the both** every year without fail.

RTG also shows some variation in relation to the indefinite article, as in these examples.

(76) a. Our lass is **a apple** fan boy.
 b. What **a interesting** programme.
 c. has **a owt** for nowt attitude.
 d. The religious can celebrate, the rest of us **get holiday** when we want.
 e. Fax machine – still have **a one** in the office that still works.

Morphology 83

In SED *a* appearing before a vowel was observed in Northumbrian locations, and was also widespread across England (76a,b,c). In addition, SED notes that the indefinite article is sometimes absent in Northumbria where it would be present in SE (76d); it also records the pronominal form *a one* (76e) (*SEDDG*: 479–480). Etymologically, the articles *a* and *an* are reduced forms of *one* (OE *aan*). According to Kurath (1952: 1), as the use of *one* as an article develops in ME, the 'variant **a** is used before words beginning with a consonant, the variant **an** before words beginning with a vowel, but not yet with the same regularity as in MnE'. This results in sentences like this one from 1450: 'I besett to Richard Clarell **a apparell** for **a auter**.' The survival of such phrases is noted by Wright (1905: 223), who remarks that 'in the dialects of Eng. the **n** in **an** has gen. disappeared before a following vowel, as **ə apl**.' (For an overview of this phenomenon, see Kjellmer 2001.)

3.5.2 Quantifying determiners

Quantifying determiners can be used to express quantity. Numerals can also act as determiners. In NEVE, *more* and *no* have distinctive forms.

On RTG, *more* as a determiner is sometimes written to indicate forms in -*ai*- and -*e*- and -*a*-, reflecting pronunciations such as [mɛː].

(77) a. Tells **mair** porkies than Boris.
b. Yiv been **mair** places than David Attenborough yea!
c. Whees got **mer** log ins than most on here?

NW records this form widely amongst its citations: '"Put **mair** coals on, the oven's getten slack"'; '"Give 'or a bit **mair** ankor"' (Heslop 1893: 652 and 1892: 14). On RTG these forms also occur when *more* is functioning as an adverb.

(78) a. is that a train line? fuck, **mair** scary than the big dipper.
b. I promise not to have **mer** than 2 more.

Historically, such forms have northern associations (*mair* is a well-known Scots feature). The northern Göttingen MS of *Cursor Mundi* certainly favours *mare* over *more*, as demonstrated in these paired examples, in which the northern versions are (a) and the midland versions are (b).

(79) a. þou folow þaim na **mare** þan þi fas, þat vnto wicked dedis gas
b. Folwe hem no **more** þen þi foos pat vnto wickede dedes gos

(80) a. Na **mare** þan wic may to gode will
b. No **more** þen euel may do good wille

No as a quantifier ('there are **no** books in the house') is a reduced form of *none*, with loss of final -*n*. As we saw in relation to indefinite pronouns, in

NEVE the pronunciation of *no* often preserves an earlier unrounded vowel, resulting in spellings like <nee>, <nae>, <ney>, or <nay>.

(81) a. I wad have **nee** reason to go into town for owt.
      b. **nee** beer in it tho, ive got neen in.
      c. **Nae** money, **nae** scouts, **nae** knowledge or idea.
      d. young lad, **ney** bairns, **ney** responsibilities, just hobbies.
      e. aye **nay** bother.

Nee has a long history in the north. For example, it occurs in northern versions of *Cursor Mundi*; and *neen* also appears in Chaucer's *Canterbury Tales* (c.1390): 'By goddes sale, it sal **neen** other bee'. This line from the *Reeve's Tale* is given to Aleyn, a student at Cambridge University who is from 'fer in the north'.

3.6 Adjectives

SED records doubly (or even triply) marked comparative and superlative forms of adjectives across the whole of England (*SEDDG*: 485). Some (lexically restricted) examples can be found on RTG.

(82) a. things can only get **worser**.
      b. Apple bores and real ale bores are **worserer**.
      c. Who's your **bestest** bud on here?
      d. But according to Marco he's one of the **worstest** players to play in the premier league.
      e. That would be the **most bestest** thing ever in the world ever.

There is nothing particularly 'North East' about these somewhat jocular formations, though we do find on RTG some adjectives derived from participles with distinctive non-standard forms, as exemplified here (see 3.2.1).

(83) a. We dont buy **frozzen** stuff either.
      b. looks a **brocken** man there walking off.

Adjectival *frozzen* and *brocken* are recorded in *EDD*.

3.7 Adverbs

In many varieties of English, adverbs can share the same form as the adjective. There is evidence for this vernacular angloversal on RTG.

(84) a. I think she hurt him **bad** like.
      b. Have done some **real** stupid things.

Morphology

    c. **Near** scored off another defensive mistake by us mind.
    d. Meant to be one coat, but with 18ltrs will **easy** Dee a couple.

Additionally, some adverbs have different forms from those found in SE, or do not occur in the standard. The main items of interest here are the degree adverbs *canny* and *geet* and the stance adverbs *maybes* and *probablies*. We should also note the additive adverb *and all*, the locative adverbs *down street* and *aheight*, and the temporal adverb *before long*.

3.7.1 Degree adverbs

3.7.1.1 Canny

Canny is one of the most well-known shibboleths of North East English, and its role as a regional cultural keyword has long been acknowledged (see Pearce 2013: 568–572). Here I focus on *canny* as an adverb of degree. While *canny* as an adjective probably originated in the sixteenth century, lexicographical evidence for adverbial *canny* suggests that this is a late eighteenth-century innovation. Jamieson mentions it in passing in the 1808 edition of his Scottish etymological dictionary. *EDD* records *canny* as an adverb, with its earliest citation drawn from a poem by Robert Burns: 'Speak her fair, / An' straik her **cannie** wi' the hair' (1786). Such adverbial uses are found on RTG.

(85)   a. He played **canny**. Not class and not poor.
       b. He did **canny** in a position he wasn't used to.

The most interesting twentieth-century development in NEVE is the expansion of the function of *canny* to become a degree adverb. According to Biber et al., degree adverbs – which can be amplifiers or downtoners – describe 'the extent to which a characteristic holds'. Amplifiers increase the intensity of the gradable adjective they precede, indicating degrees on a scale. Conversely, downtoners 'scale down the effect of the modified item' (1999: 554–555). The earliest evidence I have found for *canny* as a degree adverb is in *EDD*, which gives this (undated) instance from Westmorland: 'We are canny near home'. The meaning here is glossed as 'fairly, tolerably', which suggests it has been interpreted as a downtoner (home is fairly near). However, this example illustrates the problems associated with the interpretation of *canny* as a degree adverb, since the speaker could be indicating extreme closeness to home (they might be 'very' near home), which would make *canny* an amplifier in this case. What a speaker/writer intends and what a hearer/reader infers is dependent on context. For example, the surrounding co-text might indicate whether the quality of the adjective is being reinforced or attenuated in some way; also, speaker intonation might be important. Do we gloss *canny* in (86a) as 'very', 'really', or 'quite', for example? Perhaps in (86b,c) *canny* is more obviously an amplifier (emphatic clause-final *like* perhaps points us towards this interpretation), though we cannot be certain, especially in the absence of the prosodic cues we would have in speech.

(86) a. Had it from Aldi before and it was **canny** nice.
 b. The churches in Peterlee are **canny** good like.
 c. Think it's **canny** smart me like.

In many instances where *canny* is functioning as an amplifier, the quality which is intensified generally has a positive semantic value (e.g. 'nice', 'good', 'smart'). Given the positive aura which surrounds *canny* as an adjective in NEVE, this is perhaps to be expected. However, *canny* as a degree adverb is undergoing a further development.

(87) a. I live in the metropolis of Crook, yeah it's **canny** shite.
 b. they do look **canny** awful like!
 c. Felt **canny** stupid about that one like.

The fact that in contemporary North East English something (or someone) can be 'canny shite', as well as 'canny nice' suggests the word is undergoing a process of delexicalisation: over time its lexical content has been reduced 'so that it comes to fulfil a particular grammatical function ... but has little or no independent meaning' (Morley and Partington 2009: 155). In other words, in some cases *canny* is simply performing the functions of intensification or emphasis when it precedes an adjective. Of course, this process is common throughout the history of English. When used as amplifiers, downtoners, and emphasisers, words like *pretty*, *fairly*, *terribly*, *bloody*, and *fucking* bear little, if any, trace of their full semantic value. The introduction of *canny* into the system of degree adverbs in North East English reflects how innovative speakers can be in this area of language (see Childs 2016 for the semantic-syntactic distribution of *canny* as an intensifier in NEVE).

3.7.1.2 Geet

This innovatory tendency can also be seen in relation to the intensifier *geet* (variously spelled <geet, git> and more rarely <gid>) which is typically used to amplify/intensify the meaning of the following adjectival head, performing an analogous function to items such as 'really', 'very', 'completely', and so on (its role as a discourse marker and quotative is covered in 6.3.2). Often, the adjectival heads occurring with *geet* convey general evaluation (both positive and negative), though it can also intensify adjectives from a wide range of semantic domains, as demonstrated in these RTG examples.

(88) a. Julio's my favourite because hes **geet** canny.
 b. Everyone joined in and I felt **geet** good and that.
 c. Seen it, not **git** bad, but not **git** good either, alreet – ish.

Morphology

    d. I can remember a baboon stuck in a tiny cage, looked **git** sad.
    e. I remember they served lager in them **git** heavy dimpled glasses.
    f. love this song. **gid** easy to play on the guitar.

As with more widespread degree adverbs like 'very' and 'really', *geet* can be used to modify other adverbs (89), as well as verbs capable of showing degrees of activity or intensity (90).

(89) a. Love my BMW and drive it **git** fast without indicating.
      b. Heard a lad (**git** loudly) telling his pals about him and his lass.

(90) a. I'd **git** kiss her like.
      b. This lad kicked me in the fanny once and it **git** knacked for ages.

We also find instances of *geet* functioning as an adjective intensifier, sometimes to indicate large size or extent (91a), or to convey general evaluative or emotive meaning denoting judgement or emphasis (91b).

(91) a. My fatha with his **git** mutton chops was mistaken for Jimmy Monty.
      b. My mate in school used to think he was mint 'cos he'd wander about dein that one, the **git** gonk that he was.

Etymologically, *geet* is complex. The examples in (91) suggest a derivation from a broadly northern form of *great* (reflected in vernacular spellings such as <grit, greet>, which are both present on RTG), with the loss of /r/ perhaps resulting from 'burr retraction' (7.3.1). The examples in (88), (89), and (90), however, are perhaps more convincingly linked to a form nowadays usually regarded as Scots, for which Heslop has this entry: 'GAY, GAE, GEY, rather, somewhat, very; or added to emphasize. "He's *gay* aad." "Yor a *gay* lang time i' comin"' (1893: 320). Possible reasons for the replacement of *gey* by *geet* in NEVE are outlined in Pearce (2011).[10]

3.7.1.3 Other attested intensifiers in NEVE

As well as *geet* and *canny*, there are several other vernacular intensifiers to be found in NEVE, reflecting the 'fevered invention' (Bolinger 1972) associated with this aspect of language use, a creativity 'driven by speakers' desires to be original, demonstrate verbal skills and to capture attention' (Tagliamonte 2012: 334). Tagliamonte goes on to suggest that 'intensifiers by their very nature cannot have staying power since their impact is only as good as their novelty. Overuse, diffused use, and long-time use will lead to a diminishment in the intensifier's ability to boost and intensify.' However, some of the most characteristically 'North East' intensifiers do display

---

[10] A long vowel in *geet/git* is perceptually associated with Tyneside and the north of the region, while a short vowel is associated with County Durham and the south.

considerable staying power and geographical range. This can be seen in the cases of *dead*, *proper*, and *pure*.

Dead as an adverb is attested in *EDD*: 'Very, exceedingly, completely. In gen. colloq. use.' It was recorded as having wide geographical distribution across Britain, as it still does. The earliest unambiguous *OED* citation is from 1857, in the work of an American author. Adverbial *proper* is also attested in *EDD*: 'Thoroughly, completely; exceedingly, very; freq. used before an *adj.* as an intensitive.' It is recorded in SED too, but in both sources no particular link with North East England is noted (*SEDDG*: 114). The earliest unambiguous *OED* citation is from an 1838 work by a Nova Scotian. *Pure* is recorded as an adverb in *EDD* and SED. The examples provided by *EDD* are from across England, but it is not attested for Scotland, which is perhaps surprising, given the strong evidence for *pure* as an intensifier there (the earliest *DSL* citation is 1979, which seems oddly late). The earliest unambiguous *OED* citation is from an English novel published in 1810.

Like *geet*, in NEVE *dead*, *proper*, and *pure* can be used to amplify/intensify the meaning of the following adjectival head.

(92) a. i'm **dead** healthy.
 b. It is **proper** shite but I'll probably watch it again.
 c. Honeyman being captain on a game like today was **pure** embarrassing.

They can also modify other adverbs, and verbs showing degrees of activity or intensity.

(93) a. a bloke went **dead** fast and got a spotty top for doing well in the mountains.
 b. Watching him now for Betis he's playing **proper** high up the pitch.
 c. Aye, he's **proper** disappointed me tonight like.
 d. she's **pure** running her hands through cowell's hair.

Like *geet*, *proper* and *pure* can also function as adjective intensifiers.

(94) a. Blackpool v PNE is a **proppa** nawty derby I've heard.
 b. Canelo is a **pure** beast mind.

As with *canny* as an intensifier, *dead*, *proper*, and *pure* have undergone semantic leeching, so that *dead* can be used to convey positive and neutral meanings, while *proper* and *pure* can be used in neutral and negative contexts.

Hellish, which is typically an adjective used to describe something or someone very good or excellent (see 5.2), can also function as an intensifier.

(95) a. I understand you get great seats but it seems **hellish** expensive.
 b. The original double maxim brewed by Vaux's was a **hellish** good beer.

Morphology

EDD records *hellish* as an intensifier for Yorkshire and Worcestershire (cf. North American *hella*, which occurs once on RTG).

The use of *over* where SE typically has *too* is also noteworthy (for a discussion of the form *ower*, see 3.8.3).

(96) a. McGeadies the same but it's **ower** late for him to change.
b. Not **ower** keen on snakes and lizards either.

This usage is recorded in SED for the northern counties and is in *NW* (Heslop 1893: 517).

3.7.2 Other adverb types

Maybe and *probably* are the two commonest stance adverbs occurring in conversation (Biber et al. 1999: 869). Both have a vernacular variant with an -*s* morpheme and both can be found on RTG, often spelled in ways which represent pronunciations in connected speech.

(97) a. **Maybes** I'm just a miserable twat?
b. I'm ganna put some of his tunes together soon and **mebees** Youtube them.
c. **Problees** end up at QPR like.
d. **prollies** end up scrapping and sparking each other out there mate.

EDD records *maybes* for Northumbrian locations, though the earliest lexicological reference is in Brockett (1825). It is also found in Scotland. *Probablys/probablies* is not recorded in nineteenth-century sources or SED, though it is unlikely to be a recent innovation since *likelys* is in *EDD* for Scotland and Yorkshire, as is *hardleys* for Northumberland, Scotland, Cumberland, and Yorkshire, and *oftens* in Northumberland, Durham, Westmorland, Cumberland, Yorkshire, and Lincolnshire. *Anyways* and *noways* are also recorded widely in EDD. All appear on RTG.

(98) a. im more than **likelys** massively down.
b. It's been pointed out at work (constantly) that I pluralise words inappropriately, I'll say **mebbees** instead of maybe and more than **likelys**.
c. i was mortal drunk could **hardlies** stand up myself.
d. a mag that **oftens** hangs out with us.
e. He can't drive **anyways**.
f. being poor as a kid there was f***ing **neeways** we could afford it.

Maybes, probablies, likelys, oftens, anyways/noways, and *hardlies* – the latter of which Brockett (1829: 147) describes as 'universal among the vulgar' – contain what Roger Lass poetically calls 'the ghosts of old morphology'

(1997: 307). In PDE there are several adverbs such as *nowadays, unawares, once, whence, always, besides, perhaps, whereabouts* which incorporate a 'ghost' adverbial -s morpheme which is no longer productive (Brinton 2012: 153).

A variant of *maybe(s)* is *mevvy(s)*, which is given as a headword in *NW* (Heslop 1893: 476). Ellis records [ˈmɛviː] as 'commoner' than [ˈmɛbiː] in Newcastle (1889: 664). Indeed, Pease (1899: 10–11) describes 'constant use of "mevvies"' as one of the ways a 'true Northumbrian is in ... danger of betraying his origins'. It appears on RTG.

(99) a. **Mevvies** this Nobel laureate thowt he'd dee a tribute.
      b. **Mevvies** fewer visits, but make mare of 'em?

In colloquial English, the additive adverb 'and all' sometimes occurs clause-finally, performing functions for which SE typically uses *too, as well*, and *also*. In the written representation of some varieties of English it is often rendered elliptically or as a single word (*OED* lists *an a, an aw, anaw, an all, anall, enal*, etc.). The favoured non-standard spelling on RTG is <anarl> (in this form it is one of the ten keyest dialect items in the sample corpus).

(100) a. The mojitos are to die for **anarl**.
       b. the venue at Spennymoor was canny **anarl**.

OED describes 'and all' as '*colloquial* and *regional* (chiefly *Scottish*)'. In Scots orthography, the <ll> is often left out to reflect pronunciation, as in this example from the *EDD*: 'Woo'd and married **an' a**''. In written NEVE, the spelling <anarl> reflects a pronunciation along the lines of [əˈnaːl]. The *EDD*'s entry on AND ALL, *adv*. suggests that as well as having an additive function, as in (100), it can also be used as a stance adverb, conveying various kinds of emphasis. This is also the case in contemporary NEVE. For example, in (101a) the poster is apparently exasperated because a recent purchase has been rendered unusable after the closure of the local swimming pool due to COVID-19, and in (101b) *anarl* is used to emphasise the culinary value of home-made kebab meat, while acknowledging that this might not be a widely held view.

(101) a. Just bought a snorkel **anarl**.
       b. I make me own kebab meat, lush it is **anarl**.

There is a similarly Scottish flavour to the temporal adverb *before long*, meaning 'soon'.

(102) a. EastEnders will be cancelled **before long**.
       b. They'll be back in the Championship **afore long**.

Morphology

c. So summat might gan off **afore lang**.

Finally, two locatives are worth noting. *Aheight* (a reduced form of 'on height') was once widely found (it occurs in *King Lear*, for example) but is now largely limited to North East England, where it is often used figuratively, as in (103b). The geographical distribution of *down street* has narrowed even further than *aheight*. *EDD* records it for Cornwall and Wiltshire, as well as Durham and Cumberland, defining it as 'the lower part of a town' (presumably analogous to 'down-town'). In contemporary NEVE, the phrase seems only to be known and used in relation to the town of South Shields.

(103) a. Hoof the bastard up **a height**.
     b. If we were playing the mags tomorrow I'd be up **a height** now.
     c. Our lass calls us 'Doll' but she is from Shields and also says daft things like '**down street**' if she is going into Shields centre.
     d. I once saw a lad in his mid 20s **downstreet** in Shields in full Sunderland kit while doing some shopping, socks the lot :eek: :lol:

3.8 Prepositions (form)

In this section I consider instances where the form of certain prepositions in NEVE differs from those in SE. For the function of prepositions, see 4.4.

3.8.1 *To*

The spellings <ti, te, tee> are common on RTG, representing pronunciations of *to* – such as [tɪ], [ti] or [tiː] – which arose through what is sometimes called 'Northern Fronting' (see the discussion of *do* in 3.2.2).

(104) a. it gans back **ti** wor Civil Waar.
     b. Met Quinny, who said 'fair play **te** ye!'
     c. Am garna mak em an offer ee cannit say nar **tee** like.

The pronunciations reflected in these spellings are common in northern varieties and were recorded widely in SED and *EDD*. RTG also has examples of fronted forms of *to* with the addition of -*v*.

(105) a. Beat yer **tiv** it.
     b. Or 1977 if you prefer to gan **tiv** Abigail's party.
     c. Tony Davidson needs to get **intiv** it, ha ha.

The phonological process behind *tiv* is discussed in 7.4.2.

The spellings <te> and <ter> can also be found, presumably suggesting unstressed [tə], found widely in colloquial speech.

(106) I was picturing the boxer garn toe **ter** toe with the gull.

3.8.2 *Between, before, beside, behind*

These prepositions have variants with an *a-* prefix: *atween, aside, afore, ahint* (cf. German *hinter*). They are recorded with quite a wide distribution in SED, but with a northern focus. *Afore* and *(a)tween* are more common than *aside* and *ahint* on RTG.

(107) a. that was **atween** the three of us.
 b. good bit banter there **tween** me n thee.
 c. **Aside** a big pile of mowed grass cuttings at the corner of the Bowling green.
 d. I'll look forward to a few pints over the town, **afore** the game.
 e. away for a knee trembler **ahint** the trees.

According to *OED*, the *a-* prefix here represents a development of the *on-*prefix (with loss of [n] in unstressed positions) combined with *a* as a preposition used to express position, motion, time, as in words like *abed* and *ashore* (cf. *aheight*).

3.8.3 Other prepositions

Atop (as an alternative to *on top of (the)* or *above*) is also found on RTG.

(108) a. He's just had his 30th can of Red Bull and is **atop** the Post Office tower, shirtless, roaring at passing aircraft like King Kong.
 b. That new footy ground **atop** the pit.

This preposition is not recorded in SED, but *EDD* notes a wide distribution amongst the dialects.

Over is commonly spelled <ower> or <owa> on RTG to capture a northern pronunciation which was recorded in SED and typically transcribed as [aʊə] or [ɔʊə] (*SEDDG*: 283–284). Pronunciations where the fricative in *over* is elided have a long history, and were recorded in ME.

(109) a. Leaning **ower** the counter to nick a sausage when she went out back.
 b. I'd gan **owa** his heed & ask ter speak ter the branch manager.

For adverbial uses of *over*, see 3.7.1.3.

3.9 Conclusion

This chapter has shown that the morphological diversity of NEVE is well-represented on RTG. While features such as the levelling and regularisation of verb paradigms can be found across all non-standard varieties of English, RTG also contains verb forms associated with the vernacular linguistic North, with some (e.g. *gan, knaa,* and *mak*) having particular salience in North East England. RTG also reveals a system of pronouns containing some forms which contrast with those found in SE, offering evidence for the survival of second person and demonstrative pronouns in *th-*, and a wider range of reflexive suffixes, demonstratives, interrogatives, and indefinite pronouns than is typically mentioned in descriptions of the dialect. We also find evidence of the development of new intensifiers, like *canny* and *geet*, and instances of adverbs derived with the *-s* morpheme (beyond the well-known *maybes/mebbies*). Prepositions do not usually receive much attention in studies of NEVE, and some formal contrasts with SE as revealed in RTG posts were set out in this chapter (e.g. *atween, tiv*); functional contrasts are covered in the next chapter, where my description of grammatical diversity in NEVE moves from morphology to syntax.

CHAPTER 4

Syntax

Kids these days dinnat nar they're born.

In this chapter I identify syntactic features on RTG which contrast with those typically found in Standard English. I consider non-standard patterns of agreement between verbs and their subjects, modal verbs, negation, prepositions, and subordinate clauses.

4.1 Agreement

The grammatical phenomenon in which one item in a sentence requires a second item to appear in a particular form is known as 'agreement'. The RTG examples in (1) exemplify non-standard patterns.

(1) a. But that's why **people was** showing frustration.
     b. I commute just under **ten mile** a day.

SE requires *people* to agree with *were* (rather than *was*) and *ten* to agree with *miles* (rather than *mile*). The patterns of agreement in (1a,b) are grammatical in NEVE but not in SE. The kind of agreement in measure phrases illustrated in (1b) is dealt with in 3.3; in this section I focus on subject-verb agreement.

4.1.1 Lexical verbs (present tense)

In lexical verbs in SE, subject-verb agreement in the present tense is restricted to the third person singular, which takes an -s ending, e.g. *she says, she goes*. Everywhere else the verb is bare, e.g. *I say, I go* (Tagliamonte 2013: 65). In NEVE we sometimes encounter different patterns of person and number agreement.

The examples in (2) reflect a pattern which is widespread in contemporary English dialects, in which first person pronouns are used with -s

Syntax

endings, typically in the context of narration of past events and especially when speech or thought is being reported (Rupp and Britain 2019: 80–83).

(2)   a. **I drinks** pints of water.
        b. **I says** come in, tak a seat.
        c. **I gans** aye fully expecting her to get bored of it.
        d. 'So, **ah gets** in the taxi and **says** "Waterloo"'.
        e. **We says** do we sound like we come from Huddersfield.

Examples of this pattern in NW are *aa gets*, *aa says*, and *aa gans*. In relation to the latter, Heslop remarks that it is often used in describing a past event in narrative (1893: 315).

Second person -*s* endings are recorded for Northumbria in SED (*SEDDG*: 492), but only when the subject pronoun is *thou*, as in the somewhat fossilised *thou knows* (see 3.2.1.2 and 6.3.3). They are rare on RTG.

(3)   a. **You seems** to think it was never intended.
        b. everything **you says** is always laughable and shite.
        c. **You knows** what I am thinking about.
        d. There are some rough bastards in East Herrington **tha knars**.
        e. Anar **thou knars**.

As far as the third person plural is concerned, some of the examples in (4) potentially represent the application of a much-studied phenomenon known as the 'Northern Subject Rule' (NSR), whereby 'every verb in the present tense can take an *s*-ending ... unless its subject is an immediately adjacent simple pronoun' (Kortmann 2008: 482).

(4)   a. **Some people thinks** he is worthy to start a rebuild.
        b. I watch it cos **the bairns likes** it.
        c. Is it me as well, or do **all these scouse players says** they won't talk to The Sun.
        d. **Google and the postie sez** ...
        e. neeone was complaining and **they says** ah well then, do as you please.
        f. **They knows** the rules.
        g. Lets hope **they gets** a chance.

However, these examples would suggest that if the rule is still in operation for some speakers of NEVE it is in decline, and used variably by individuals, since simple pronouns can also be found adjacent to verbs with the -*s* morpheme, as in (4e,f,g). The claim in Beal et al. that the rule is 'largely observed' in North East England is possibly an overstatement, given its rarity on RTG (2012: 50). Historical evidence from SED also shows the -*s* morpheme occurring with pronouns: **they keeps** *chickens;* **thou seems**

(*SEDDG*: 492–493). Indeed, sentences like 'they knows the rules' and 'they keeps chickens' in North East England could simply reflect the general fact that subject-verb agreement varies extensively both regionally and socially; indeed, paradigm regularisation tending towards the extended use of the -*s* suffix has historically been common in many northern dialects of English (Siemund 2020: 620). For example, Murray, who is widely credited as having first proposed the NSR nevertheless cites Atkinson's 1868 work on the dialect of Cleveland (the eastern part of Yorkshire's historic North Riding), in which the paradigm of *gan* is given as 'Ah gans, thou gans, he gans, we gans, you gans, they gans' (1873: 214).

4.1.2 Present tense of *be*

In SE in the present tense of the verb *be* there are three forms: *I* **am**, *you/ we/they* **are**, *he/she/it* **is**. In NEVE we find a similar generalisation of the singular third person form as we see with lexical verbs, resulting in the following non-standard patterns which have been exemplified with RTG data.

(5) First person singular and plural + *is*
   a. **Ah's** not scared of it.
   b. i think **I's** getting awld.
   c. **Ah's** gannin' to the Pembleton Arms.
   d. **We is** ganin up in the wurld.
   e. **We is** shit.

(6) Second person + *is*
   a. Nar, **thou's** getting Kane.
   b. **thoo is** fukn mad **thoo is**.

I + *is* (typically in the form *I's*) is recorded for Northumbrian locations in SED, and Wright notes that across the north '*is* is often used for *am*' (1905: 297). *I* + *is* and *thou* + *is* are to be found in *NW* (e.g. '**Ah's** aal reet'; '**Thou's** lyin like a hog'). *I* + *is* has a long history as a marked northern form. In *The Reeve's Tale* (written c.1392–1395), Chaucer incorporated it into the speech of the Cambridge students from the north who trick the greedy miller: 'I is but an ape', says John. The southern reeve uses 'ik am'.

4.1.3 *Was-/were*-levelling

In SE, past tense forms of *be* follow the singular-plural opposition, except for the second person singular (*you were*). But 'regional varieties' sometimes 'manifest the analogical extension of one form into the domain of the other' (Siemund 2020: 622). This '*was-/were*-levelling' or 'generalisation' can be found on RTG.

Syntax

(7) a. **You was** mouthing off again.
 b. **You was** going to get 10m for this player and 15m for that player.
 c. Didn't realise **we was** on the same plane.
 d. When **we was** good – whenever that was.
 e. that's what my mam said **they was**.

(8) a. Aye when **I were** a lad you could get an original Van Goff for a glass of absinthe.
 b. When **I were** a bairn we'd hoy a shirt down the mine shaft and a new striker would pop out.
 c. Mind **she were** fond of a drop or three.

It seems that in NSE generally, *was*-levelling is commoner than *were*-levelling, and this is the case in NEVE, where the examples in (7) are more natural and widespread than those in (8). This reflects a historical pattern where in the northernmost counties levelling tended to be in the direction of *was* rather than *were*, while the main area of *were*-levelling was further south in northern England. Indeed, due to its strong associations with Yorkshire, Lancashire, and Derbyshire (Pietsch 2005, in Rupp and Britain 2019: 174–175) *were*-levelling typically occurs as a stylistic device on RTG, humorously evoking nostalgia for an idealised northern past (8a,b). But we also need to take into account what Pietsch refers to as *was/weren't* realignment: an 'innovative pattern where the *was-were* contrast is realigned according to clause polarity, with positive *was* versus negative *weren't*' (2012: 356–357).

(9) a. Pity **it weren't** mine.
 b. **She weren't** best pleased.

4.2 Modal verbs

Formally, in NEVE the central modal verbs *can, could, may, might, must, shall, should, will, would* are the same as in SE. However, usage and distribution of these forms differs in certain respects from SE, to the extent that some regard the system as closer to that of Scots than it is to Standard English and English dialects in the south and midlands (Beal et al. 2012: 65). The main contrasts with SE are demonstrated below in relation to *shall, must, would*, and 'double modals'. The discussion focuses mainly on modal verbs in clauses with positive polarity (see 4.3.1 for the enclitic negation of modal verbs).

4.2.1 *Shall, must, would*

Beal claims, based on an analysis of NECTE data that *shall* is 'hardly used at all in the North-east' (2008: 386), a characteristic NEVE shares with Scots

(Miller 1993: 116–117) and Irish English (Hickey 2007: 396). In English generally, it is also the rarest of the central modals (Biber et al. 1999: 486) and has been in decline throughout the twentieth century (Mair 2006: 101–102), particularly in declaratives where it now has a rather formal quality. In PDE it is mostly to be found in first person interrogatives, as in (10a). But in NEVE, *will* is also acceptable in this context (10b).

(10) a. What **shall** I do now?
b. What **will** I do tonight after work. Suggestions please.

In relation to *must*, SE and NEVE generally coincide in clauses with positive polarity, where it is used with the meaning of obligation (11a) or to express a conclusion (11b). Beal et al. also note that in contrast to SE *must not* can be used to express conclusions (11c) as well as obligations (2012: 67).

(11) a. Bruce **must** apologise.
b. Bruce **must** be running out of patience.
c. Thought I'd replied to this yesterday but it **mustn't** have worked.

In terms of the expression of obligation, Beal et al. also record a distinctive usage in relation to the semi-modal *have got to*. In SE the negative *haven't got to* means 'not obliged to' (12a); in NEVE it can also be used to mean 'obliged not to' (12b).

(12) a. at least I **haven't got to** worry about it for another 5 year.
b. Only right, we **haven't got to** upset toonies who shop there.

Finally, we might note the respelling <wad> for *would*, which is common on RTG, and has historical pedigree, appearing in the work of Burns, for example, as in this well-known couplet: 'O **wad** some Pow'r the giftie gie us / To see oursels as others see us!' The spelling reflects a pronunciation with an unrounded vowel, recorded in *EDG* for Northumberland and County Durham (Wright 1905: 688) and still widespread in Scotland.

(13) a. Oh yes I **wad**.
b. I **wad** have nee reason to go into town for owt.

Heslop has *wad* for *would* as a headword in *NW* (1893: 761) and it occurs in several citations (e.g. 'Aw wad div owt aa could').

4.2.2 'Double modals'

According to Hickey (2014: 196), 'double modals' (that is, two modal verbs appearing in a single verb phrase) occur in varieties that have historically had a Scots input, so they are found in the southern United States as well as across the linguistic North.[1] Beal et al. suggest double modals are permissible in NEVE 'so long as the second modal is *can* or *could*' (2012: 68). Evidence from RTG, however, would suggest more permutations are possible.

(14) a. I think that **might could** be it.
      b. i reckon we **might could** struggle.
      c. Kent-Mackem **would might** be a bit of a clue for them.
      d. Or maybe it **should might** inspire him to say right I'll fucking show you lot.

There is considerable scholarly debate about the origins of double modals. The main argument is over whether they should be seen as remnants of the earlier system in English (lasting until the transition from Middle English to Early Modern English) in which two-modal sequences were permissible, or as a later innovation in Scots and related dialects of the far north of England (see Schneider 2004: 286). Whatever the origin, by the nineteenth century they are firmly established in northern British varieties, as attested in *EDD* (Fennell and Butters 1996). Since then, however, 'double modals' have declined sharply in British English. It appears that they are making their last stand in England in the North East. Beal et al. (2012: 68) claim that this construction is 'now very rare in Tyneside and apparently unknown in Sunderland or Middlesbrough'. However, the feature's sporadic appearance on RTG suggests that its demise is not imminent.

4.3 Negation

As Britain points out (2010: 44), negation is a 'site of considerable diversity' in dialect syntax. Of particular interest in NEVE are the variants of negated forms when they are attached to the auxiliary/operator as a clitic, multiple negation, and non-standard *never*. I also consider the use of uncontracted negatives in interrogatives.

4.3.1 Enclitic negation of *do*

In NEVE, *-n't* (a reduced form of *not*) can be added to finite forms of the three primary auxiliary verbs, as it can in SE (e.g. *isn't, hasn't, doesn't*).

---

[1] In the southern USA the main source of Scots influence were 'Scotch-Irish' immigrants from Ulster (Montgomery 2017). The international range of double modals is demonstrated by *The Simpsons*' Cletus Spuckler. Referring to a pair of hobnail boots he found dangling from an overhead cable, the show's favourite hillbilly stereotype tells his partner Brandine, 'You **might could** wear these to yer job interview' (Brandine is auditioning to be a bar dancer and refuses Cletus's offer on the grounds they might 'scuff up the topless dancin' runway'). For more on double modals in American English, see Grieve et al.'s innovative study of twitter data (2015).

In NEVE, the main dialectological interest here is that vernacular forms of *do* often have an unrounded vowel where the SE vowel is typically rounded, and sometimes combine with a hiatus breaker (see 3.2.2 and 7.4.2). The following RTG examples are annotated with county labels to show attestation in SED (Orton and Halliday 1963: 806–807 and 1036–1037).

(15) [dɪ] + *-n't* (Du.); [dɪz] + *-n't* (Nb. and Du.)
 a. I **dint** even kna what song ya on about ya daft twat.
 b. This marriage **disnt** last long neither.

(16) [dɪ] + hiatus breaker [v] + *-n't* (Nb. and Du.)
 a. **Divvent** shoot the messenger please.
 b. **Divven't** need a rudder ... got feet like f*ckin' flippers, man.

In addition, these unrounded forms combine with a set of negative enclitics (traditionally written as *-nat/-nit* and *-na/-nae/-nee*) which don't occur in SE.

(17) [dɪ] + *-(n)nat/-(n)it* (Du.)
 a. Hendersons **dinnat** dee savoury dips either, criminal.

 [dɪ] + *-(n)na* (Nb. and Dur.)
 b. Ah **dinna** think Pugwesh is gannin like.

 [dɪ] + *-(n)nae*
 c. **Dinnae** like rum, you filthy pirate.

4.3.2 Enclitic negation of modal verbs

These vernacular enclitic negatives are also added to modal verbs, exemplified below in relation to *will* and *can*. The NS forms in the RTG examples in (18) are annotated to show their attestation in SED (Orton and Halliday 1963: 1019 and 1032).

(18) *will/can* + *-(n)nat/-(n)it* (Nb. and Du.)
 a. We **winnat** win.
 b. Ive wanted to get my lip done for ages but work **winnit** lerriz.
 c. Love them me but **cannat** buy them down here.
 d. **Cannit** wait for tomorrow like.

 can + *-(n)na* (Nb. and Du.)
 e. yer **canna** gan rang with these.

 can + *-(n)nae*
 f. I **cannae** believe that he's gone.

Syntax

In these enclitic forms the spelling <na> probably represents [nə], while <nee> represents [niː]. <nae>, which is a common orthographic representation in Scots, probably does duty for [nə] or [niː]. Where do the -na types come from? Jespersen (1917, in Anderwald 2002: 54) states that '*na* was very frequent in OE and later as a rival of *not*, and has prevailed in Scotch [*sic*] and the northern dialects, where it is attached to auxiliaries in the same way as -*n't* in the South: *canna, dinna*, etc.' It could therefore be claimed that this clitic represents the preservation of a form which once prevailed across the linguistic North but is now in decline in England. For example, SED identifies Northumberland, County Durham, and Cumberland as the northern strongholds of -*na* as a negator of auxiliary verbs, with some evidence of usage in other northern English counties, including Lancashire, Cheshire, and Derbyshire (*SEDDG*: 502). *NW* has a separate entry for *canna*, with the date of the citation indicating its long-standing presence in NEVE.

> CANNA, cannot. "Ye *canna* say them nay, Mr. Mayor." *Quayside Ditty*, 1816. (Heslop 1892: 129)

How do we account for forms in -*at* and -*it*? The -*t* could have been added to -*na* by analogy with -*n't*, possibly reflecting the influence of the Standard and the acquisition of literacy. They might also represent the 'survival' of *nat* (albeit in enclitic form), which like *not* is a reduced form of *nought/naught*. While evidence from Middle English texts suggests that *not* was commoner during this period than *nat* (and was eventually adopted as the standard form), *nat* is found well into the Early Modern period, sometimes co-existing in the same text as *not*, as in this passage from *The boke named the Gouernour, deuysed by syr Thomas Elyot knight* (1531).

> Wherfore it maye **not** be of any wyse man denyed, but that Cosmographie is to all noble men, **nat** onely pleasaunt but profitable also, and wonderfull necessary.

4.3.3 Multiple negation

The use of two or more negative forms in a single clause is a widespread feature of vernacular English, so much so that it has been described as a vernacular angloversal (Kortmann 2020: 639).

(19) a. I **dint** want **nee** screaming kids!
 b. **Never** saw **nowt**.

Multiple negation was once 'routine in all varieties of English, before becoming socially unacceptable in the emerging standard dialect in Britain between the sixteenth and eighteenth centuries' (Penhallurick 2018: 204). But, as Elizabeth Wright points out, 'in the dialects the old pleonastic negatives remain, as: He nivver said nowt neeaways ti neean on em; Neeabody's neea bisniss ti thraw nowt inti neeabody's gardin; I deean't want nobbut yan' (1913: 156–157).

The status of multiple negation as a feature of social stratification is well known in sociolinguistics, but is there any evidence to suggest a regional distribution? Beal et al. (2012: 59–60) report findings from the Survey of British Dialect Grammar (Cheshire et al. 1993) of multiple negation being more common in the south than in the north of England, a distribution confirmed by Anderwald's analysis of BNC data (2002). However, there is nothing particularly distinctive from a syntactic perspective about multiple negation in NEVE.

4.3.4 *Never*

Never as a preverbal past tense negator with definite time reference is, like multiple negation, among Kortmann's vernacular angloversals. The following paired sentences from RTG are more or less synonymous, except that *never* has a discourse function of foregrounding what is being negated.

(20) a. I **never** went on Saturday.
  b. I didn't go on Saturday.

  a. Pity the ref **never** saw it.
  b. Ref didn't see it.

While this use of *never* was not a target in the SED it is recorded in relation to negative forms of past tense *do* (*SEDDG*: 498). It is also present in *EDD*, and *OED* has evidence for this usage dating back to the Middle English period.

4.3.5 Negative interrogatives

In SE, *yes-no* questions with negative polarity (e.g. 'Isn't she coming?') and negative question tags ('She's coming, isn't she?') typically have a contracted negator. NEVE is unusual because even in informal situations we find uncontracted negatives (Beal and Corrigan 2005).

(21) a. **Is she not** new?
  b. **Do they not** pay wages like?
  c. **Can we not** just go back to basics and play simple 4 4 f*cking 2.
  d. PSG fan **is he not**?
  e. Yes, so their scouting department will be "watching" all of their loan players **will they not**?

They can also be found in some *wh-* questions, though in these cases the full form is perhaps less marked.

Syntax

(22) a. Why **is she not** keen on taking the vaccine?
     b. Why **can we not** park near the SOL?

The canonical structure of tag questions in PDE is shown in these RTG examples.

(23) a. That's just wrong though **isn't it**?
     b. we all support the same team **don't we**?
     c. people will be offended on his behalf though **won't they**.
     d. It's not rocket science **is it**?
     e. But we don't exactly have the power to put it right, **do we**?
     f. McGeady won't be fit **will he**?

Negative tags are added to positive statements, seeking confirmation for a positive proposition, as in examples (23a,b,c); positive tags are added to negative statements, signalling that the speaker is seeking confirmation for a negative proposition, as in (23d,e,f). Furthermore, negative tags are almost always contracted. But in NEVE, in addition to the 'standard' structures we also find uncontracted tags (21d,e), and 'double' negative tags, consisting of auxiliary + *n't* + subject + *not*.

(24) He'd want to be first choice **wouldn't he not**.

Examples like (24) are rare on RTG, as are instances of a further pattern identified by Beal in which a negative clause is followed by auxiliary + subject + *not* (e.g. *She can't come, can she not*) and auxiliary + *n't* + subject + *not* (e.g. *She can't come, can't she not*). For more on the pragmatics of these constructions, see Beal (2004: 124–125).[2] Similar patterns can be found in Scots and Scottish English.

4.4 Prepositions (function)

In 3.8 I considered prepositions in NEVE that differ formally from those found in SE. Here I focus on the syntactic functions of *off* and *off of* (in relation to agency, source, and goal), and *of* and *on* (in relation to time) which they do not perform in SE. There are some parallels here with the prepositional system of Scots (Miller 1993: 131–132).

In SE, *by* is routinely used to express agency in passive constructions (e.g. *England were beaten **by** the Aussies*), but in NEVE (in certain contexts where

---

[2] In relation to contractions more generally, some observers (e.g. Beal and Corrigan 2005: 148–151) have noted a tendency in NEVE to contract auxiliaries rather than negatives, so that, for example 'he will not → he'll not' (rather than 'he won't') and 'she is not → she's not' (rather than 'she isn't').

the semantic 'patient' is undergoing a violent act – literally or figuratively) *off* can also be used for this function (rarely, *off of* can be found). *Off* is more likely in *get*-passives than *be*-passives.

(25)   a. England got beat **off** the Aussies at Twickenham in the final.
      b. we were beat **off** a far better team.
      c. I remember playing on the pit heaps, coming home filthy and getting knacked **off** my parents for it.
      d. saw an ald man get hit **off** a bus in durham.
      e. I won't miss watching us get beat **off of** the big teams.

In NEVE *off* can also be used to indicate the source of something received by a beneficiary (as can *off of*).[3] In SE this is typically indicated by *from*, as in *I got a present* from *my mother*.

(26)   a. I got Fortnite pyjamas **off** me Mam.
      b. just bought it **off of** eBay.

This usage is noted by Heslop (1893: 509).

> OFF, used in the sense of *from*. "Aa'l borrow'd *off* ye." Often duplicated with *of* as *off-of*. "The hat blew *off-of* his heed."

In addition, *off* can occur in some contexts where *on* would be more usual in SE. This is particularly the case where the semantic 'goal' is causing pain, injury, or damage.

(27)   a. I smashed my toe **off** the kitchen table.
      b. the other week I fell forward and hit me head **off** the shower screen.

It is also used in prepositional phrases where SE would typically have *at*, as demonstrated in these paired RTG examples.

(28)   a. I once threw a burger **off** Freddy Kanoute's head.
      b. someone threw a burger **at** me.

While the prepositions *off* and *at* are performing similar functions in (28), it should be noted that in NEVE to say that you have thrown a burger *at* someone does not necessarily mean you hit the target, whereas to say you have thrown a burger *off* someone does.

---

[3] *Off of* also has a wide distribution in *EDD*, from Scotland ('I wiz noor **aff o'** ma feet sin 'e mornin') to Devon ('The cup fell **off of** his handle'). Wakelin (1972: 118) claims that, 'as is well-known', *off of* 'is a feature which occurs throughout the country', supporting his assertion with reference to SED data.

EDD records *off* indicating source in the sense of 'from', 'of', 'out of', citing for Northumberland the example from Heslop above, and a line from a 'Border Ballad' published in the 1840s: 'Or mischiefe **off** our kye or sheepe.' But this usage is recorded across the north and midlands, as well as in Scotland (see 'Prepositions' in SSA).

In SE, *on* or *in* is used in constructions which indicate the time period (i.e. the name of the day or part thereof) during which an event takes place, especially if the event is repeated or occurs regularly, as in 'I practise **on** a Saturday/Saturdays'; 'I practise **in** the evening(s)'. In NEVE, *of* can occur in both these contexts.

(29) a. I'd rather just go to the boozer **of** a Saturday.
 b. Good memories of bunking off college **of** an afternoon to play pool and eat hot beef dip and chips.
 c. Nowt beats walking up the steps and seeing the grass under the flood lights **of** an evening.

This usage does not appear in SED, though it is recorded with wide distribution in *EDD*. The phrase *of an evening* is on the border line between colloquial SE and NSE.

We might also note *on a(n)* where SE typically prefers *in the*.

(30) a. Our lass leaves the lamp on in the kitchen all the time **on an** evening.
 b. I've never felt hungry early **on a** morning.

This usage is perhaps only marginally dialectal.

Finally in relation to the function of prepositions we observe a localised usage of *across* in the prepositional phrase 'across the doors', meaning 'out (of) doors', used particularly in the context of being housebound due to illness or some other form of constraint (including – in the case of (31b) – a global pandemic).

(31) a. In his papers I found he had donated, on one occasion, £200 to Children in Need despite being poor, living with threadbare carpets and hardly going **across the doors**.
 b. I haven't been **across the doors** for months.

EDD links '*to get across the doors*, to be able to get out of doors after illness' with east Durham.[4]

---

[4] Sometimes prepositions are absent when one might be expected, as in a local use of *belong/belang* – also found in Scotland – to mean 'come from' or 'reside at': 'I belong Thorney Close' (RTG). According to Palgrave 'a man, on being asked where he "belongs," says, "I belong Hetton," meaning his home, or place of birth, according to circumstances' (1896: 3).

4.5 Subordinate clauses

In this section I consider non-standard patterns of subordination, focusing on relative, complement, and adverbial clauses.

4.5.1 Relative clauses

This type of subordinate clause adds information about who or what is being talked about in the main clause and is typically introduced with a relative pronoun or adverb, as in these RTG examples.

(32) a. I was a miner **who went on strike for a whole year in 1984–1985**.
b. Well he had red stains on his shoes **which left nice footprints down the corridor**.
c. At Farringdon we had a Biology teacher **whose gob wobbled** when she spoke – Wobblygob.

Two other kinds of relative clause found in PDE are *that* and the 'zero' (Ø) relative pronoun.

(33) a. her dad was a miner **that went to war at 35**.
b. She took inspiration from the books **Ø she loved as a child**.

Which is used when the antecedent is a non-human creature or an inanimate entity or idea; *that* is used with human, non-human animate, and inanimate antecedents. *Who* is used when its antecedent is human or has quasi-human characteristics, while *whose* is used when the pronoun is in a genitive relationship with its antecedent (see 3.4.6 for NEVE forms of *who* and *whose*). Omission of the relative pronoun (as in 33b) can only occur with certain types of 'restrictive' relative clause when the antecedent is *not* the subject.

The system is complex, with a complicated history (see Tagliamonte 2013: 94–105 and Beal 2010: 43–47). Research on British dialects has revealed considerable regional variation, including the omission of *wh-* relatives even when the antecedent is the subject. For example, in the SED participants were given the prompt 'If I didn't know what a cowman is, you would tell me: He is the man ... looks after the cows.' As well as the more standard *who* and *that*, the survey recorded 'He is the man Ø looks after the cows', and use of *as* ('He is the man *as* looks after the cows'), *at* ('He is the man *at* looks after the cows'), and *what* ('He is the man *what* looks after the cows') as relativisers (*SEDDG*: 489–490). In Nb. and Du., SED records *that* and *at* as the favoured relativisers. Predictably, RTG has plenty of examples of semi-standard *that*, but none of *at*, a form which is recessive (Beal 2010: 46).

A question mark hangs over the use of relativiser *what* in NEVE. It occurs on RTG, but infrequently.

Syntax

(34) a. Fearne Cotton and that bloke **what was on radio 1 at nights a few years back**.
b. George Clarke – architect gadgie **what grew up in Roker Avenue**.
c. They also have a song on FIFA15 and are hotly tipped by Zane Lowe (the prick **what he is**).

Historically, the *what*-relativiser has been regarded as a southern feature (Kortmann 2008: 491), but one which is potentially spreading northwards (Cheshire et al. 1993: 68). However, as Beal et al. point out 'although relative *what* is attested in North-Eastern varieties, it is still not used as frequently here as further south' (2012: 55). The RTG examples suggest that use of *what* might be associated with environments where the context is somewhat disparaging towards the referent of the antecedent noun.

4.5.2 Complement and adverbial clauses

This section focuses mainly on non-standard manifestations of complement and adverbial *to*-clauses and *ed*-clauses.

To-clauses are non-finite subordinate clauses with a variety of roles. They are used to complete the meaning of the verb, adjective, or noun in the main clause (e.g. *I want **to go home***), but they can also introduce an adverbial clause (e.g. *I want to go home **to sleep***). In some English dialects, *for to* can introduce an adverbial clause, particularly one of purpose. Some instances of this structure can be found on RTG.

(35) a. Apparently the FA Board are meeting tomorrow *for to* **hear the recommendation**.
b. I can't find any numbers *for to* **call them**.

Tagliamonte (2013: 116) states that 'the use of *for to* as an infinitival marker is fairly widely reported ... where it is considered a preservation of a historical complement structure' (for example, Chaucer's pilgrims are headed to Canterbury from 'every shires ende' in England, 'the holy blissful martir **for to** seke'). It is attested for Scots and Irish dialects – indeed, Miller calls it 'a great shibboleth' of broad Scots (1993: 131) – and SED records '**for to** see (the doctor)' across England, including all six northern counties except Westmorland (*SEDDG*: 504). However, its rarity on RTG suggests it is a recessive feature in NEVE.

After verbs of necessity like *need* and *want* we sometimes see patterns of complementation on RTG which contrast with those found in SE.

(36) a. Struggled to read this, screen desperately **needs cleaned**.
b. bed sheets **need cleaned**.
c. I'm not kidding the op **wants slapped** with a cringe stick, that's embarrassing.

    d. Nice cross, but Jacobson **wants punched** in the face for letting Carroll go there.

A more SE pattern here would be to use an *ing*-clause ('needs cleaning') or passive construction ('needs to be cleaned'). This feature is also found in Irish and Scottish English, and some varieties in North America, possibly as a relic of Ulster Scots speech transported there from the eighteenth century (Hickey 2014: 334). Sometimes *need* and *want* can occur with a prepositional adverb as complement, conveying a sense of motion.

(37) a. Clearly he **wants away**.
    b. Sterling **needs away** like.
    c. His reputation was shot, his pocket was taking a hit and he **wanted** and **needed out**.

Additional non-standard forms of subordination found in NEVE include *so as* and *whiles*. In SE the complex subordinator *so that* is sometimes used to introduce adverbial clauses of purpose. *OED* records *so as* performing the same function, a usage it labels as 'dialect'. It is not recorded in SED, though it does occur in several *EDD* citations, showing wide geographical distribution. On RTG we find both full and contracted forms.

(38) a. just trying to establish all the facts **so as** I can judge the factuality of statements made.
    b. Just **so's** I know what to watch.
    c. trying to kneel down **so's** they can reach the water.

So as/so's is the remnant of a wider dialectal use of *as* as a subordinator.

In the context of subordinate clauses, we should also note the occurrence of the subordinator *whiles*. It is rare on RTG, but where it is found it performs the same function as the SE conjunction *while*.

(39) a. I try to fall asleep **whiles** it's going on.
    b. People who buy nachos to eat **whiles** watching a film should have nacho cheese poured over them.

Whiles is not recorded in SED, but Heslop has an entry for *whiles* as an adverb (1893: 782). There are no instances of *whiles* as a conjunction in *NW*, but in *EDD* it is attested for locations in the midlands and the south, and its history is a long one, with the earliest *OED* citation from the thirteenth century. (For more on the adverbial *-s* ending, see 3.7.2.)

4.6 Conclusion

In this chapter I have shown how RTG can be used to explore the full range of non-standard syntax in NEVE. Some of the features covered, such as the verbal ending -s in the first person narration of past events, *was*-levelling and *was/were* realignment, multiple negation, past tense *never*, and relativiser *what*, occur widely in non-standard varieties in the British Isles. Others, such as *I + is*, *wad* for *would*, double modals, enclitic negation with *-na*, uncontracted tags, *-ed* participle complementation with *need* and *want*, are more localised and characteristic, shared only with other dialects in the vernacular linguistic North (or in North American varieties with significant inputs from them). Some of the NS morphosyntactic features presented in this and the previous chapter have been recorded in both southern Scotland and across the northern counties of England, revealing the significance of a 'greater Northumbria', stretching back to the Anglo-Saxon period and persisting into the present day (e.g. verb forms like *brocken* and *hing*; unrounded forms of *do*; *I* as [ɑ~a]; singular non-imperative *us*; cluster simplification in *-self*). Those with shorter attested histories nevertheless reflect multiplex and sustained interactions between southern Scotland and the far northern English counties (e.g. *ahint*, adverbs formed in *-s*, forms of *one* in *y-*). Some also reflect the commonalities that parts of the region have with the 'Great Scandinavian Belt' (Samuels 1985) – the Norse-influenced territories further south (e.g. *I + is*, pronominal forms in *th-*, and the reflexive suffix *-sen*). And some, if not unique to North East England, have a particular cultural salience there, such as *wor* and *yous* or *mak* and *tak*.

As we saw in some of the examples in Chapters 3 and 4, on RTG non-standard morphosyntax can be deployed in 'high performance' dialect stylisations and is occasionally the subject of metalinguistic commentary. However, many of the examples seem to reflect the posters' informal, everyday linguistic behaviour, as they transfer and adapt facets of their spoken vernacular style to the written mode. In contrast, the topic of the next chapter is lexis, an aspect of language more subject to conscious selection and manipulation than the more ingrained morphosyntactic features discussed so far.

CHAPTER 5

The dialect lexicon

> Ploating – now there's a cracking old word.

It would interest the author of the epigraph to know that *ploating* is indeed a dialect word with considerable pedigree in North East England (though it is a newcomer compared with some). According to *OED*, the verb *ploat* – which it describes as *English regional* (chiefly *northern*) – has two sources: one is Dutch *ploten* 'to pluck'; the other is from Scots *plot* meaning 'to scorch or burn; to make too hot, to overheat' (unlike *ploat*, the origin of *plot* in this sense is unknown). The earliest *OED* citation for *ploat* is 1757, and it first appears in a dictionary in 1825 (Brockett's *Glossary of North Country Words*), while *plot*'s earliest citation is from 1606. The *EDD* entry for *plot* (to which readers are directed from *ploat*) includes variants like *ploat*, *plooat*, *plooit*, *plote*, *plout*, and *plowt*, and gives a distribution across Scotland and northern England (Northumberland, County Durham, Westmorland, Cumberland, and Yorkshire). It lists several senses concerning high temperature (particularly in relation to liquids, but also general heat, burning, and scorching) as well as ones relating to the plucking of feathers (figuratively extended to 'fleece, rob, plunder … cheat') – thus reflecting the word's 'double' etymology. The final sense given is another figurative extension: 'to scold'. *Ploat* also features in SED. It is elicited by the question 'What do you say you do when you strip the feathers off a dead chicken?' and is recorded for all six northern counties except Lancashire, with an interviewee from County Durham describing *ploat* as 'older' than the 'more genteel' *pluck* (Orton and Halliday 1963: 408). By the time of the *Voices* survey, it is only recorded for North East England, elicited by the prompt TO HIT HARD, with participants in Longbenton suggesting it was 'used in past' and offering *I'll ploat you if you're naughty* as an example (Robinson 2021: 303).

Ploat, with its long, well-attested history is clearly a central member of a subset of the English lexicon which I refer to as 'Traditional Dialect Lexis', or TDL (Pearce 2020). This chapter focuses mainly on words found on RTG belonging to this group. More precisely, if a word (or non-standard

The dialect lexicon 111

usage of an otherwise standard form) was recorded in *EDD* or SED for any Northumbrian location (that is, any location in the historical counties of Northumberland or County Durham) it is regarded as a traditional North East dialect word.[1] I do not claim to have located all items falling within these parameters on RTG. The words recorded here should therefore be treated as a sample of a larger set of unknown size.

The chapter is organised as follows. In 5.1 the sample is presented in the form of a set of semantic fields and discussed from the perspectives of currency, meaning, and usage. I show how such a resource can complement more conventionally sourced lexicographical and survey-based data (such as that collected in *EDD*, SED, and *Voices*), offering additional insights into lexical maintenance and loss in NEVE. In 5.2 I consider 'non-traditional' dialect lexis: words and phrases on RTG which – though geographically focused – were coined later or overlooked, so do not appear in *EDD* or SED, though many are recorded in later lexicographical works, such as Bill Griffiths' *A Dictionary of North East Dialect* (*DNED*).

5.1 Traditional dialect lexis on RTG

The TDL element of NEVE is by definition geographically restricted. Dialect lexis acquires its regional distribution in one of two main ways. First, some English words (or senses of words) seem always to have been 'local'. This is perhaps most clearly seen in items which have Norse origins and entered English in areas of Scandinavian settlement and adjacent territories, as was the case with words such as *bait, kist, lop, lass, marrow, poke*. Later arrivals in the linguistic North might be traced to interactions across the North Sea between speakers of English, Dutch, German, Danish, and cognate languages, e.g., *blare, bowk, cavel, clag, femmer, gissy, haar, howk, hoy, keek, ket, mizzle, ploat, poke, skimmer*. We might also include in this category TDL which came into northern speech through Angloromani – for example, *deek, gadgie, shan*, and possibly *pagger*. Second, many words which are now localised were once found more widely, but eventually became dialectal because they were confined to the colloquial English of a particular region and not adopted into Standard English, as in these NEVE words with Old English origins: *bairn,*

---

[1] 'Recorded in *EDD* or SED' should be interpreted quite broadly. For example, if a lexical item is *not* recorded in *EDD* for Northumberland or County Durham but *is* recorded for Scotland and/or adjacent areas in England (e.g. Yorkshire, Cumberland) it is regarded as a lexicographical oversight and has been included in the sample (marked *). Occasionally, an item is included because it appears in an *EDD* citation, even though it is not listed as a headword. If it is missing from *EDD* but is mentioned in a relevant EDS publication, such as Heslop's *Northumberland Words*, it is also included (as are words recorded in SED but not *EDD*). Regarding orthography, as we saw with *ploat* many TDL words have variant spellings. I generally use *EDD* or *OED* citation forms, although spellings on RTG sometimes diverge from these.

brock, burn, gan, lather, neb, sackless, and *spelk*. Anglo-Norman/Old French is also the source of words which were once more widely dispersed, such as *bonny, bray, foisty, poke*, and *poss*, as well as items which seem always to have had northern associations, such as *creel, fash, rammel*, and *stour*.

The difficulty of establishing etymologies was raised in relation to *ploat*; it is also illustrated by *poke* ('a bag, sack'), to which it is possible to ascribe three different origins. Was it brought by the Vikings or is it a later import from Anglo-Norman/Old French or Dutch? Durkin devotes six and a half pages to this problem in *The Oxford Guide to Etymology* (2009: 62–68). *Pagger* also shows the often complex and uncertain etymologies of some dialect lexis. In this form it does not occur in *EDD*, but I have categorised it as TDL because it is used as a synonym for 'exhausted' by a single informant from Yorkshire in SED (Orton and Halliday 1963: 695). Is *pagger* related to *peg*, which we do find in *EDD*, meaning 'a blow or thump with the fist, esp. in boxing; stroke', 'to hammer; to beat; to thump with the knuckles'? *DSL* defines *peg* as 'to whack, beat, belabour', and records the derived noun *pegger* to refer to a shower of rain. Ultimately, these senses of the verb *peg* (borrowed from the Middle Dutch noun *pegge*) – including meanings related to exhaustion and death, as in 'peg out' – are figurative extensions of its basic meaning, which is to fasten or fix with a peg. But it is not clear how we get from *peg* to *pagger*. A possible explanation is that *pagger* is derived from *peg* with reinforcement from a non-Germanic source. In his lexicon of Angloromani (2010: 176–217), Matras gives European Romani *phager-* ('break') as the etymon of Angloromani *pagger*, meaning 'break', 'fight' and 'hit'.

(1) a. I may give you a shout in a few months when mine [a car] **paggers** ;).
 b. The seat is normally **paggered** after about 2 weeks.
 c. they're full of **paggered** furniture.
 d. Seen one [a barn owl] having a **pagger** with a seagull once.
 e. I saw the mother of all wild west style **paggas** in there late one Christmas Eve night.
 f. I remember once when he'd been **paggered** off someone in a cage fight.

As with *peg*, *pagger* can be semantically extended to convey meanings related to tiredness, as in the SED example and in the RTG posts (2a,b); also 'drunk' (2c), or generally incapacitated (2d).

(2) a. Sweating like a pregnant nun. He was f***ing **paggered**.
 b. Our dogs are **paggered** just walking in the heat.
 c. there's millions of git strong stouts to get me **paggered** on.
 d. Bloody hell he looks **paggered** even sitting next to Ronnie Wood.[2]

[2] We also find a few instances of *pag(ged)* with a similar meaning to *pagger(ed)*, but whether this is a development of *peg* or a back-formation from *pagger* is not clear: 'He was **pagged** as soon as the bell sounded'. Interestingly, Angloromani is sometimes referred to by Romanichals as *pogadi chib* ('broken language').

5.1.1 Semantic fields

In this section I have categorised the TDL sample into eleven semantic (or 'lexical') fields. Because there is no 'agreed method for determining what constitutes a lexical field … each scholar must draw their own boundaries and establish their own criteria' (Jackson 2002: 146). My approach is based on the lexical taxonomies used in *The Scots Thesaurus* (Macleod et al. 1990), which also focuses on traditional dialect lexis, though on a national rather than regional scale. By presenting the lexicon according to these criteria, rather than as an undifferentiated list, readers can get a sense of which areas of meaning are 'over-' and 'under-lexicalised' with TDL on RTG; and – since some items can appear at more than one location in the taxonomy – this format gives an indication of the extent of polysemy and general 'semantic complexity' to be found in TDL (Markus 2020), issues which will be considered further below. To give an indication of the broader northern distribution of these items, superscript *DSL* and *CUD* are used to indicate that a word is recorded in *Dictionaries of the Scots Language* and *A Concise Ulster Dictionary* respectively.

In the sample, the house and its environs are represented, together with the everyday activities that take place there, like cooking, eating, and cleaning. We see dialect words for quotidian features in the vernacular landscape and some of the plants and animals inhabiting it. The weather and other aspects of the environment also feature. But the most extensive set of terms relates to people. There are words for items of clothing and other accessories, body types, parts of the body, bodily functions, states, afflictions, and behaviours. We see words used to label or describe people and their relationships with each other, including the way they communicate. Energetic physical action is also represented, particularly when it is associated with violence, as is the world of work and recreation.

A. Wild animals

Traditional dialect lexis associated with creatures in the wild.

(i)   **Birds**: *cuddy-duck, jacky^{DSL}, linty$^{DSL+CUD}$, maggie^{DSL}, skem, spug(gy)$^{DSL+CUD}$, steg$^{DSL+CUD}$, throstle$^{DSL+CUD}$*
(ii) **Mammals**: *brock$^{DSL+CUD}$*
(iii) **Invertebrates**: *bummler^{DSL}, clegg$^{DSL+CUD}$, logger, lop*

B. Domestic animals

Words for livestock.

(i)   **Pigs**: *gissy^{DSL}*
(ii) **Horses, donkeys**: *cuddy$^{DSL+CUD}$, gallower$^{DSL+CUD}$*
(iii) **Domestic birds**: *banty$^{DSL+CUD}$, chucky-hen*$^{*DSL+CUD}$, skem, steg*

C. Plants

Terms for plant-life (including fruit and vegetables).

(i) **Flowering plants**: *docken*$^{DSL+CUD}$, *pittle(y) bed*
(ii) **Grasses and sedges**: *bent*$^{DSL+CUD}$
(iii) **Fruit**: *brambles*$^{DSL+CUD}$, *gowk*
(iv) **Vegetables**: *carlings*^{DSL}, *chatties/chetties*^{*CUD}, *scallions*$^{DSL+CUD}$, *taities/tatties*$^{DSL+CUD}$

D. Environment

Terms associated with landforms, features, and use; the weather and general environmental qualities (e.g. clean and dirty).

(i) **Land**
   a. Forms, features and use: *bank*^{DSL}, *bent(s)*$^{DSL+CUD}$, *chare*, *dene*^{CUD}, *gill*^{DSL}, *heugh*$^{DSL+CUD}$, *law(e)*^{DSL}, *lea(s)*$^{DSL+CUD}$, *loan(ing)*$^{DSL+CUD}$, *nook*$^{DSL+CUD}$, *steel*, *trod*, *wynd*^{DSL}
   b. Rocks, soil, mud: *claggy*$^{DSL+CUD}$, *clarty*$^{DSL+CUD}$, *clem*, *hack(y)*, *sleck*
(ii) **Weather**
   a. Rain, mist, snow, frost: *fret*, *haar*^{DSL}, *mizzle*^{CUD}, *ploating*^{CUD}, *stotting*, *teeming*$^{DSL+CUD}$
   b. Thunder and lightning: *brattle*$^{DSL+CUD}$
   c. Temperature: *mafting*, *nithering*^{DSL}
(iii) **General environmental qualities**
   a. Dirt(y): *hack(y)*, *stour*$^{DSL+CUD}$
   b. Clean: *skimmer(ing)*^{DSL}
   c. Crowded: *throng/thrang*$^{DSL+CUD}$, *whick (with)*^{DSL}
   d. Stuffy/stuffy and smelly: *foisty*$^{DSL+CUD}$, *stife*^{DSL}
   e. Unpleasant in smell and/or taste: *lifting*, *rank*, *reasty*^{DSL}
   f. Rubbish/waste: *ket*^{DSL}, *rammel*

E. Water, sea, ships

The sea, inland waters, ships, and fishing.

(i) **Water, sea**
   a. Water, liquids: *drawked*$^{DSL+CUD}$, *teem*$^{DSL+CUD}$
   b. Rivers, ponds, lakes: *beck*, *burn*$^{DSL+CUD}$, *cundy*^{DSL}, *sleck*
   c. Sea(s) and seashore: *bent(s)*^{DSL}, *plodge*^{DSL}
(ii) **Ships, shipping**
   a. Ships, boats, sailing: *coble*^{DSL}, *foy-boat*, *keel*, *keelboat*
   b. Ships, navigation: *groin/groyne*, *staith(e)*^{DSL}
   c. Sailors: *keelmen*

The dialect lexicon

(iii) **Fishing**
    a. Sea fishing: *creel*$^{DSL+CUD}$, *willok*$^{DSL+CUD}$
    b. Fishing boats: *coble*^{DSL}

F. Life cycle, family

Life stages and family relationships.

(i) **Childhood**: *bairn*$^{DSL+CUD}$, *wean*$^{DSL+CUD}$
(ii) **Youth, adolescence**: *lad*$^{DSL+CUD}$, *lass*$^{DSL+CUD}$
(iii) **Adulthood** (male): *folk*$^{DSL+CUD}$, *gadgie*^{DSL}, *lad*$^{DSL+CUD}$, *marra*$^{DSL+CUD}$
(iv) **Adulthood** (female): *buer/bewer*, *lass*$^{DSL+CUD}$, *wifey*$^{DSL+CUD}$
(v) **Old age**: *dothery*^{CUD}, *gadgie*^{DSL}, *ganny*
(vi) **Family relationships**: *da*$^{DSL+CUD}$, *ganny*, *lad*$^{DSL+CUD}$, *lass*$^{DSL+CUD}$, *ma*^{CUD}, *mam*^{DSL}, *son(ner)*, *the mrs*, *the wife*, *wed(ded)*
(vii) **Terms of address**: *hinny*, *man*, *marra*, *pet*, *son*

G. Physical states

Types and conditions of human bodies.

(i) **Physical types/appearance**
    a. Attractive: *bobby-dazzler**$^{DSL+CUD}$, *bonny*$^{DSL+CUD}$, *canny*$^{DSL+CUD}$, *smart-looking*
    b. Unattractive: *clip**$^{DSL+CUD}$, *springe(d)*^{CUD}
    c. Fat and thin: *scrat*$^{DSL+CUD}$, *scratty**, *scrunt*$^{DSL+CUD}$, *spelk*^{DSL}
    d. Physical deformities: *glee-eyed*$^{DSL+CUD}$, *scrat*$^{DSL+CUD}$, *scratty**, *scrunt*$^{DSL+CUD}$
    e. Naked: *scud(dy)*$^{DSL+CUD}$
(ii) **Parts of the body**
    a. Face, head: *chollers*$^{DSL+CUD}$, *gizzard*, *lug-hole*^{DSL}, *lugs*$^{DSL+CUD}$, *napper*^{CUD}, *neb*$^{DSL+CUD}$, *pyet*^{DSL}, *sneck*, *snitch*, *thrapple*$^{DSL+CUD}$
    b. Hair: *baldy*
    c. Eyes, sight: *deek**^{DSL}, *gawk/gawp*$^{DSL+CUD}$, *glee-eyed*$^{DSL+CUD}$, *gleg*$^{DSL+CUD}$, *keek*$^{DSL+CUD}$, *skeg*
    d. Hands, arms: *cuddy-handed*^{CUD}, *cuddy-wifter*, *oxter*$^{DSL+CUD}$, *w(h)ick*^{DSL}
    e. Feet, legs: *honkers/hunkers*$^{DSL+CUD}$
    f. Skin: *blebs*$^{DSL+CUD}$, *plook*$^{DSL+CUD}$, *scrat*$^{DSL+CUD}$
    g. Stomach: *kite*$^{DSL+CUD}$, *lisk*$^{DSL+CUD}$
    h. Genitals: *clems*, *cobs*, *stones*
(iii) **Sensations**: *drawk*$^{DSL+CUD}$, *lathered*, *mafted*, *nithered*^{DSL}, *scumfished*^{DSL}
(iv) **Breathing**: *blowing*$^{DSL+CUD}$
(v) **Sleeping, rest, waking**: *rax*$^{DSL+CUD}$
(vi) **Tiredness, exhaustion**: *blowing*$^{DSL+CUD}$, *jiggered*, *paggered*
(vii) **Eating, drinking**: *clamming*, *stowed*^{DSL}

(viii) **Excretion, body fluids**: *bowk*[DSL+CUD], *cockle*, *dottles*[DSL+CUD], *howk*, *pish*[DSL+CUD], *pittle*, *rift*[DSL+CUD], *slaver/slavver*[DSL+CUD], *skitters*[DSL+CUD]
(ix) **Activity, movement**: *bat**[DSL+CUD], *bray*[DSL], *clash*[DSL+CUD], *clip*[DSL+CUD], *dunch*[DSL+CUD], *fetch*[DSL+CUD], *fettle*[DSL+CUD], *gan*[DSL+CUD], *graft*, *hing*[DSL+CUD], *howk*[DSL+CUD], *hoy*[DSL], *jarp*, *kep*[DSL+CUD], *knool*[DSL], *leather*[DSL+CUD], *loup*[DSL+CUD], *pagger*, *pelt*[DSL+CUD], *ploat*[DSL+CUD], *plodge*[DSL], *poss*[DSL+CUD], *rax*[DSL+CUD], *rive*[DSL+CUD], *scud*[DSL+CUD], *skelp*[DSL+CUD], *stot*[DSL+CUD], *tappy-lappy*[DSL+CUD], *twank*, *welt*[DSL+CUD], *yark*[DSL+CUD]
(x) **Good health**: *canny*[DSL+CUD], *champion*, *clever*[DSL+CUD], *good fettle*[DSL+CUD]
(xi) **Bad health**: *bad*[DSL+CUD], *bad fettle*[DSL+CUD], *cockly**[DSL], *femmer*
(xii) **Insanity, mental handicap**: *radgy*[DSL], *daftie*, *doil*[DSL+CUD]
(xiii) **Sanity**: *canny*[DSL+CUD]
(xiv) **Injuries**: *spelk*[DSL]

H. Food and drink

Foodstuffs and their preparation and consumption.

(i) **Food**: *bagie*, *bait*, *bullets*, *fadge*[DSL+CUD], *ket(s)*, *pan-hagerty*[DSL], *pease-pudding*[DSL], *scran*[DSL+CUD], *stotty (cake)*, *willok*[DSL+CUD]
(ii) **Drink**: *scad*[DSL+CUD], *Spanish water*
(iii) **Processes**: *kizzened*, *shive*[DSL+CUD], *teem*[DSL+CUD]
(iv) **Consumption**: *scran*[DSL], *sup*[DSL+CUD], *swally*[DSL]
(v) **Kitchen equipment**: *dishclout*[DSL+CUD], *gully*[DSL+CUD]

I. Trades and occupations

Working life, hobbies and recreations.

(i) **Vehicles, tools, equipment**: *bogie*[DSL+CUD], *mash-hammer*[DSL], *mell*[DSL+CUD]
(ii) **Conditions of work**: *back-shift*, *cavel*, *graft*, *kenner*, *lowse*, *ten o'clock*
(iii) **People**: *gaffer*, *marrow/marra*[DSL+CUD]
(iv) **Mining**: *baff*, *goaf*, *hew*[DSL+CUD], *hogger*[DSL]
(v) **Farming (livestock)**: *banty*[DSL+CUD], *cuddy*[DSL+CUD], *gallower*[DSL+CUD], *gissy*[DSL], *chucky-hen**[DSL+CUD]
(vi) **Farming (animal husbandry)**: *blinders*[DSL], *byre*[DSL+CUD], *cree*, *creel*[DSL+CUD], *ducket*[DSL+CUD], *hen-cree*, *pig-cree*, *ploat*[DSL]
(vii) **Joinery**: *lat*[DSL+CUD]
(viii) **Knitting, crochet**: *proggy mat*
(ix) **Pigeon-keeping**: *cree*[DSL+CUD], *ducket*[DSL+CUD], *hant(ed)*[DSL+CUD]
(x) **Children's games and toys**: *ally*[CUD], *bogie*, *crake*[DSL+CUD], *fog*, *halfer(s)*[DSL+CUD], *keppy-ball*, *liggy*, *penker*, *shuggy*[DSL+CUD], *skinch*, *wag*
(xi) **Festivals and celebrations**: *guising*[DSL], *hoppings*, *pace eggs*[DSL]

The dialect lexicon

J. Building(s), architecture

The built environment.

(i) **Structure and parts of buildings**
   a. Roofs: *chimley*$^{DSL+CUD}$
   b. Doors, gates: *sneck*$^{DSL+CUD}$, *snib*$^{DSL+CUD}$
   c. Rooms and their contents: *bleezer, cracket*$^{DSL+CUD}$, *crib*^{DSL}, *kist*$^{DSL+CUD}$, *netty*

(ii) **Buildings**: *but and ben*$^{DSL+CUD}$, *byre*$^{DSL+CUD}$

(iii) **Household items**: *poke*$^{DSL+CUD}$, *vine*^{DSL}

(iv) **Gardens**: *hogger, rickle*$^{DSL+CUD}$

K. Character, emotions, social behaviour

Aspects of human personality, appearance, behaviour, and emotions.

(i) **Intelligence**: *canny*$^{DSL+CUD}$

(ii) **Stupidity**: *feckless*$^{DSL+CUD}$, *fond*$^{DSL+CUD}$, *glaiky*$^{DSL+CUD}$, *sackless*^{DSL}

(iii) **Character types**: *canny(-lad), radg(y)*^{DSL}, *scratter, scunner*$^{DSL+CUD}$

(iv) **Personal values and behaviour**: *canny*$^{DSL+CUD}$, *pawky/parky*$^{DSL+CUD}$

(v) **Social behaviour**
   a. Drink: *mortal*^{DSL}, *palatic*$^{DSL+CUD}$, *swallowed*^{DSL}
   b. Chitchat: *blather/blether*$^{DSL+CUD}$, *crack*$^{DSL+CUD}$, *mither, noration*$^{DSL+CUD}$, *pash*^{DSL}, *twine (on)*^{CUD}, *slaver/slavver*$^{DSL+CUD}$, *twist*$^{DSL+CUD}$, *yammer*$^{DSL+CUD}$, *yarp*
   c. Nosiness: *nebby*$^{DSL+CUD}$, *keek*$^{DSL+CUD}$
   d. Being hampered: *fash*$^{DSL+CUD}$, *knacky*$^{DSL+CUD}$, *stowed*^{DSL}, *throng/thrang*$^{DSL+CUD}$, *whick (with)*^{DSL}

(vi) **Clothing and accessories**: *breeks*$^{DSL+CUD}$, *claes*$^{DSL+CUD}$, *galluses*$^{DSL+CUD}$, *gansey*$^{DSL+CUD}$, *hoggers*$^{DSL+CUD}$

(vii) **Emotions, states, evaluations**
   a. Anxiety, care: *tew(ed)*$^{DSL+CUD}$
   b. Anger: *radgy*^{DSL}
   c. Fear, disgust: *scunnered*$^{DSL+CUD}$
   d. Sorrow, tears: *blare*^{CUD}, *bubble*$^{DSL+CUD}$, *greet*$^{DSL+CUD}$
   e. Complaining: *beal*^{DSL}
   f. Something/someone good: *topper*

5.1.2 Currency, meaning, and usage

For some, a lexicon like this will index a 'northern' English working-class sociocultural milieu. A world of cramped domestic spaces set in marginal, de-industrialised landscapes, plagued by inclement weather and populated by a folk admiring of physical toughness and humour, with a matter-of-fact attitude to the body, its processes, and the traumas to which hard manual labour makes it vulnerable. But lexical inventories categorised *etically* by semantic domain offer only a partial, high-altitude prospect of the territory. A corpus is not simply a wordlist: a large-scale collection of vernacular multi-party interactions such as RTG allows for nuanced, high-resolution understandings of the meanings and contexts of use of dialect words, revealing a degree of semantic complexity which is not usually remarked on in studies of dialect lexis. Additionally, sites like RTG can help counter what Caroline Macafee – reflecting on her role as editor of *A Concise Ulster Dictionary* (1996) – has called 'one of the most frustrating and intractable problems in the study of traditional dialects' – the problem of *currency*. Does 'anyone out there' still *use* 'the words and phrases that we document in the dialect dictionaries?' (Macafee 1991: 71). The questionnaire format of large-scale dialect studies can sometimes result in 'a skewing towards passive knowledge' (Wales 2006: 196). In contrast, RTG offers insights into questions of currency and usage, because it provides contextualised examples of dialect lexis 'in the wild' (as well as unprompted metalinguistic commentary).

In relation to what RTG data might be able to tell us about currency, meaning, and usage, we can return to the example we began the chapter with. We saw how the two largest-scale dialect surveys of the twentieth and twenty-first centuries – SED and *Voices* – treat *ploat*. SED records only its narrow agricultural meaning, while in *Voices* it appears as a response to the prompts TO HIT HARD and TO RAIN HEAVILY (spelled <plote>). Both surveys record brief comments from informants about the word's association with the past. While a comparison of these two data sets reveals something about the narrowing geographical distribution of the word in the course of the twentieth century, the methods used in these surveys mean we glean from them only limited information about this word. In contrast, RTG reveals layers of meaning and usage. For example, in (3) we see *ploat* as a topic of metalinguistic discussion, with the semantic complexity noted in (3a) discussed in (3b–e).

(3)   a. it appears **ploat** has a bunch of meanings.
       b. The word '**ploat**' originally meant to pluck the feathers from a dead fowl, or remove the hair from a pig's carcase by pouring water onto it.
       c. **Ploat** – to thump (although it originally meant to pluck a bird).
       d. My dad said **ploat** used to mean pluck (as in plucking a chicken).
       e. **plote** – pluck or bring down.

Although the word's agricultural usage is known to some, this element of meaning is associated with the past. Such a loss of sense is not surprising, given that few people in North East England now work in any branch of agriculture, or are involved in raising poultry (see 5.1.3). But what can RTG tell us about current usage and recent developments? In (4) we see

The dialect lexicon

instances of *ploat* in actual use on RTG, showing that meanings associated with punishment, recrimination, and violence – a very early figurative extension which goes back to the nineteenth century at least – are common (4a–d).

(4) a. The bloke in the car in front of me got out and was trying to **ploat** him.
b. He shook his head then **ploted** the lads lights out.
c. the **ploating** of his lifetime.
d. he has a mush that needs a good old **plowting**.
e. At least the mags are getting **ploated**.
f. **Ploating** doon here in sr5.
g. It's **ploating** doon and looks like it will all day.

RTG evidence reveals further figurative usages. In (4e) *ploated* is what happens to a sports team suffering a heavy beating; and in (4f,g) *ploating* means 'raining heavily', following a common metaphoric pattern in which verbs of violent and/or energetic activity are used to describe heavy precipitation. *A Thesaurus of English Dialect and Slang* (Robinson 2021: 184–190), which collates the lexical data set of *Voices*, records a number of items that follow this pattern, some of which are widespread (e.g. *belt, chuck, hammer, pelt, scythe, throw*) and some of which are more geographically restricted (e.g. *hoy, plote* [sic], *sling, stot*).

An interesting question raised by the examples in (4) is does the TDL here reflect the posters' everyday vocabulary use, or is it a self-conscious part of dialect stylisation? Some TDL is often used unselfconsciously and 'naturally'. In the examples in (5), for instance, *bairn, canny, spelk, gan, hoy, bait,* and *graft* are used in ways that suggest they are likely to be part of these posters' active vocabulary in most informal contexts when talking about domestic, everyday concerns.

(5) a. **Bairn** trains with Cramlington United.
b. I have a small **spelk** in my finger.
c. **Gans canny** with crab sticks on a sarnie.
d. it needs to be cooked for longer, not **hoyed** in the bin.
e. Had them for me **bait** in **graft** a few times.

Such items appear to be holding their own against more standard quasi-synonyms on RTG. For example, in the 10-million-word sample corpus, frequencies of *bairn(s)* and *child(ren)* were roughly equal (though standard-colloquial *kid(s)* was more frequent than both), and *hoy, hoys, hoyed,* and *hoying* occur 44 times compared with 35 times for *chuck, chucks, chucked,* and *chucking*. They seem to be part of a regional 'standard vernacular' lexis in the North East, certainly in informal contexts like RTG.

As we saw in 1.2, this unmarked presentation of TDL contrasts with its performative applications. Performative discourse is 'characterized by orientation to an audience, attention to the form and materiality' of language, and reflexivity (Androutsopoulos 2013: 53). Since lexis is arguably the linguistic level most open to 'conscious modification and manipulation' (Sandow and Robinson 2018: 335), and since words live a 'socially charged life' (Bakhtin 1981: 293) dialect lexis can have an important role in the indexing of social meanings, stances, personal characteristics, persona styles, speaker characteristics, and social types. RTG is full of cultural performances such as jokes, anecdotes, and reminiscences, in which the poetic function of language has prominence 'and considerations of 'style' become particularly salient' (Coupland 2007: 147). For example, it is notable that many of the surviving traditional dialect words can encode 'high-affect'; that is, they can be used expressively to convey 'feelings, moods, dispositions and attitudes towards the propositional content of the message and the communicative context' (Besnier 1990: 419). Such items are valuable resources in the representational spaces of Web 2.0, where participants often express emotional states and opinions in highly charged and occasionally intemperate discussion and debate. High-affect is seen particularly in the way people are described and categorised using TDL. For example, they are often presented in unflattering terms, and their actions and attitudes assessed negatively.

(6) a. Got some **sneck** on him like.
 b. With them swimmers of yours and the **kite** to match, you must be Henry VIII.
 c. just some **radgy** gobshite on a train.
 d. I can just about guarantee there will be some **sackless** arsehole feeding them Pringles.
 e. A load of loud, shouty, fish lipped **bewers**.

We also see TDL used to denote acts of communication. Sometimes the contributions of others are represented critically, often as a line of attack in an argument.

(7) a. don't **beel** like a pissy knackered bairn.
 b. People on here **twisting** like babies.
 c. you're **twining** about a few lads getting paid twenty quid for doing more than eleven twats doing nowt and getting paid sixty grand.
 d. If it stops him **greeting** about it and hitting the bottle it'll pay for itself.
 e. How man, had yer **pash** ;).

More broadly, high-affect is conveyed through words describing the action of hitting something/someone.

(8) a. Aye, grabbing their faces like they've been **ploated**.
 b. None of us ever **howked** a horsey.

The dialect lexicon 121

    c. If the bairn mentions the Mags in our house I **skelp** his arse.
    d. A got **possed** of me mam.
    e. **Scud** the scruffy bastard all ower.
    f. a boy wanders in and **brays** 3 lads with a bat.
    g. safc lad on crutchs inside ground got **batted** on head off copper on horse.
    h. I can remember a threat from my grandmother that if I didn't behave I was gonna get **clashed**.
    i. Don't tell me to shut up or I'll be sending a Shields face round to give you a f***ing **clip**.
    j. The Newcastle mob got **leathered** by the East Durham lads.
    k. I seen Ernie get a **paggering** outside there once.
    l. he went off it, went back to the barbers & **ploated** the lad who cut it.
    m. I got a right **skelping** and my father wouldn't talk to me for a fortnight.
    n. Got **stotted** twice on the heed the bastards.
    o. innocent folk getting **welted**, gangs and weapons being used?
    p. got sent down for **yarking** some bloke in a pub in Morpeth with a pool cue.

In these instances, the TDL could have been replaced by mainstream English words such as *nose* (for *sneck*), *belly* (for *kite*), *angry* (for *radgy*), *complain/moan* (for *beel*), *punched* (for *howked*), *beating* (for *skelping*), and so on. However, presumably in these cases the TDL was chosen for its expressive power.

One stylistic practice in which TDL is often deployed is the representation of speech and thought, where participants bring the voices of others to life.

(9)   a. aye, they'll be "**Gannin** doon tha metroooo to get the metroooo to Scumdaland to watch wor team play the dorty makums."
    b. "Eeeh open the window it's **maften** in here!"
    c. "I was using the front page of the Echo as a **bleazer** but it took ahad, man!"
    d. "I could set **tatties** behind yer **lugs**."
    e. "This winnut buy the **bairn** a new frock."

As exemplified here, the motivations behind giving voice to others are various. For example, participants sometimes offer affectionate and often nostalgic reconstructions of the speech styles of friends and relatives. But other representations are far less affectionate, often employing hyperdialectisms to construct caricatures of the social or cultural 'other', such as supporters of Newcastle United (Sunderland's arch-rivals), 'charvers', and so on (see 1.2).

To produce cultural performances like these, participants require considerable metalinguistic knowledge. In such displays, knowledge of and receptivity towards sociolinguistic variation is implicit. But there are also instances where participants overtly display their understandings and attitudes, as we saw in relation to *ploat*. These displays take a variety of forms, ranging from simple glosses to highly technical explanations. The following examples are illustrative of the wealth of material on RTG.

(10) a. There was some old bloke **howking** (coughing) his guts up outside when I drove past.
b. I think we've established that it's "**crack**" and not "craic" although I respect the rights of those who prefer to use the faux Gaelic version.
c. Anyone who spells **crack** as craic is clearly a fucking bellend.
d. **Gully** – the geet big sharp knife yer nana used to keep in the scullery drawer.
e. **Kite** is your belly.
f. Giz a **deek** – yeah kids at school all said this. Not me … I was rather more refined.
g. **Stotting** means like banging. You can **stott** a ball or have a **stotting** headache.[3]
h. Grew up with **marra** being used in Sacriston, same as **fettle**. Every other word me grandad said was **fettle**, had many different meanings.
i. **Mafted** as in hot. Only recently heard it and had no idea what it meant.
j. I had never heard nor used the term "**scratter**" til I seen it on here and now it's part of my day to day vocabulary.
k. **bleb**'s a crackin word imo mate.
l. My nana used to always say she was **stowed** (full) after eating something.
m. I still say I'm **stowed**-out when I'm full.
n. Me Da and me stepma call each other **hin** (eurrgh).
o. **Hoggers** means pants or trousers round Easington way.
p. "**Bairn**" is nothing whatsoever to do with Danes or Vikings, who had virtually no influence on our dialect. It's from the Anglo Saxon "bearn".
q. I live in Oxford and no one has heard of the word "**bairn**" apart from me family (all from Sunderland).

These examples reveal that metalinguistic commentary on RTG about TDL is rich and various. It is also often dynamically constructed in argument and debate. We observe discussions about etymologies; a word's status as standard or non-standard, dialect or slang; its currency and geographical and social distribution. Semantic and pragmatic discussions consider word meaning, meaning change, and semasiological variation. Some comments aspire to objectivity, while others are highly evaluative. But they all suggest a considerable degree of 'sociolinguistic receptivity' on the part of the writer: an interest in linguistic variation which is often accompanied by

---

[3] This poster does not mention that to have a 'stot(t) on' is to be in a state of tumescence, a metaphorical extension also found on RTG: 'Got a weird **stot on** for Everton you like.'

The dialect lexicon

positive regard towards dialects, a knowledge and appreciation of linguistic differences, and some understanding of linguistic concepts (Benson and Risdal 2018). In addition, some metalinguistic commentary indicates that RTG is the site of a folk-language revitalisation project, as exemplified in (10j). Several posts follow this pattern, with a participant stating a gap in their knowledge ('I had never heard nor used the term') then acknowledging the role of RTG in filling that gap ('til I seen it on here') and sometimes claiming, as a result of this exposure, that the term has become part of their active vocabulary ('now it's part of my day to day vocabulary'). Some participants also refer to their own revitalisation efforts in the real world: 'I've been single-handedly bringing that word back recently. Got loads of people saying it now like.'

5.1.3 Survival and loss

Some of the meta-discourse in the previous section broaches a subject that has also received attention from dialectologists: the survival and loss of traditional dialect lexis. In an important study published at the end of the last century, Upton and Widdowson compared SED data (collected mainly in the 1950s from older conservative rural speakers) with data from the Atlas Linguarum Europae (ALE) project (collected between 1976 and 1980 from a comparable stratum of informants), concluding somewhat starkly that 'there is no doubt that the regional dialect lexicon is being eroded, and across its full range rather than simply in the more specialised fields of usage' (1999: 22).[4] Projects focused on North East England have come to similar conclusions. For example, Simmelbauer's lexical recognition survey in Northumberland found that some of the 101 traditional dialect words she examined 'were still widely known, several were known by very few or no subjects, and knowledge of others varied according to the age and/or gender and/or location of the informants' (Beal 2010: 64). A similar method was used in Burbano-Elizondo's study in Tyne and Wear, which tested informants' knowledge of twenty-one traditional dialect words taken from everyday semantic domains. She concluded that in general these words 'were not as widespread among my informants as they had been in earlier studies' (2003: 36). Simmelbauer and Burbano-Elizondo used a similar approach to the lexical questionnaire component of the Tyneside Linguistic Survey (see 2.2.5) which was administered to forty-nine participants in the late 1960s and early 1970s. It tested the recognition and use of

---

[4] Lexical 'erosion' can occur when changing patterns of social life (such as the post-war decline of agriculture, fisheries, mining, and heavy manufacturing in the UK) mean that certain words (or word meanings) become redundant. Erosion is also a consequence of speakers of different dialects coming into contact, as linguistic features which are more 'local' (and/or less widespread) tend to be discarded in favour of those which are more widely understood (Beal 2010: 73).

the following items: *bairn, bait, beck, bonny, boody, bray, bullets, clamming, clarts, coin, cree, dunch, fettle, gully, howk, hoy, ken, kep, knooled, lowe, mell, mense, nebber, parky, poorly, stot, varnigh*. In Beal et al.'s analysis of the survey data, the following words were described as 'known and used fairly widely': *bonny, bairn, parky, cree, bait, fettle, clamming, bray, bullets*; at the other end of the scale were items which were 'neither known to nor used by the majority of participants': *aside, howk, coin, boody, mense, mell, varnigh, knooled, lowe* (2012: 84). With the exceptions of *boody, coin, lowe*, and *mense*, all can be found on RTG, though on the site and in NEVE generally words such as *bairn* and *bait* have much wider currency than words like *knooled* and *mell* (as they had at the time of the TLS). While it seems reasonable to conclude from studies such as those cited that dialect lexis is in decline, evidence from RTG suggests the picture might be more complex. Indeed, Widdowson himself offered a slightly less pessimistic view of the findings of the 1999 study a few years later, acknowledging that while there were

> substantial losses in dialect vocabulary across the country, notably in the more specialised fields of usage such as that of older traditional aspects of agriculture, animal husbandry, and rural life in general ... the diversity of regional dialect vocabulary in less specialised fields such as domestic life and work was seen to have remained remarkably resilient in times of rapid linguistic and social change. (Green and Widdowson 2003: 22)

As well as the semantic domain of a word influencing its chances of survival, it might also be related to its semantic and pragmatic 'potential' (Pearce 2020: 14–15). Even words that were once strongly associated with specialist domains have a chance of surviving if their meanings can be extended. This was noted for *ploat* and can also be seen with *howk* – a word elicited in SED for Northumbrian locations in relation to digging and the feeding behaviour of pigs. But as the examples in (11) show, its current meaning potential/semantic range is much wider.

(11) a. Going to get one of those cotton bud things and **howk** some out.
 b. It is about a bloke who has a big yeti and they go somewhere with some little bears and **howk** some people in white suits.
 c. City will **howk** them at least 3 nowt.
 d. Did you get **howked** out mate?
 e. Dry on kitchen towel then **howk** onto bread of choice.
 f. I'm not joking, she's just **howked** up.

While *howk* in (11a) corresponds broadly with the SED meaning, (11b and c) exemplify typical current usage in NEVE, where it is a synonym of *hit* and *beat* (both in the physical sense and in relation to victory in competition).

The dialect lexicon

It should be noted that this broader meaning is not a recent innovation – one of the senses of the verb *howk* in *EDD* is 'to punish', with the noun *howking* defined as 'punishment, a beating, thrashing'. However, (11d,e,f) might indeed represent a more recent development of meaning: here *howk* is a synonym of *throw*. The survival of other traditional dialect words might also be ascribed to their wider meaning potential, as can be seen with *steg*, *neb*, *chollers*, *dottles*, and *lifting*. *Steg* is used figuratively on RTG as a mildly offensive term for a messy or unattractive person and never in relation to geese (it is derived from Old Norse *steggi*, meaning male bird); *neb* is used not for a bird's bill but as a nominal and verbal synonym for *nose* – but only in the extended sense of being 'nosey'. On RTG *chollers* is used for the jowls of dogs and humans, but not the wattles of domestic fowls. *Dottles* describes human excrement in a particular form rather than sheep dung. And while the meaning of *lifting* seems to have broadened out from insect infestations to crowding in general ('place was **lifting** with our lads'), it has also been extended to bad smells ('Real life offshore is full of boro riggers talking bollocks while everyone is doing **lifting** farts'); unpleasant food ('one had tomato sauce instead of béchamel, was **lifting**'); uncleanliness ('**Lifting** them like. Why don't you keep them clean?'); and general negative evaluation ('His highlights reel is **lifting**'). These examples perhaps indicate that while the contexts relevant for the use of the narrower, specialised meanings of such words have declined, their extended meanings have been preserved and built on.

5.2 'Non-traditional' dialect lexis on RTG

As Wales points out 'the inevitability of language change means that [dialect] words must come and go, as in the Standard, as new objects, pastimes, etc. appear or disappear, and cultural practices change' (2006: 195). In dialect lexis we therefore should expect gains as well as losses, renewal as well as attrition.

What are the sources of lexical innovation in NEVE? In (12) we see examples of words at the informal end of the stylistic continuum which differ from the lexis discussed so far in that they have appeared more recently and are more widely distributed.

(12) a. Always thought he was a **cracking** player.
   b. We were then escorted up to the ground by the **Feds**.
   c. Was surprised to see the beard and general **hench** appearance.
   d. light up a **blunt** and it's as if you're there.
   e. They're all at ours **rinsing** the feeders dry.
   f. Then I'll start doing the online learning **shizzle**.
   g. This world is pure mad, when a copper goes **tooled up** to a club.
   h. Why do **chavs** set off fireworks on Halloween instead of 5th November?

i. They have **narks** everywhere.
j. The ending with the **rozzers** turning up was bollocks.
k. Liar, nee **lush** lasses got in there.
l. A right **minger** and a **fruit loop** nee chance that factory boss fancies her.
m. He was **mint**.
n. Used to be fairly healthy but **swear down** the bairn brings so much shit home from nursery.
o. He's an absolute **melt** can't stand the bloke.
p. Bitter as a lemon that **muppet**.
q. You f***ing **window licker**.
r. You know exactly what im on about you sad fat **meff**.
s. Some gadgie Len ain't he?! f***ing **looper** :lol:
t. They can see straight into my **gaff** from theirs.

Innovative, colloquial vocabulary such as this – which is sometimes labelled (not always helpfully) as 'slang' – tends to originate in youthful, often non-mainstream social groups and to be associated with certain semantic domains and pragmatic functions (Green 2016). For example, this stratum of the lexicon is rich in derogatory and offensive terms (e.g. *melt*, *meff*), and words and phrases associated with marginalised people and 'deviant' areas of social life (e.g. *chav*, *blunt*, *nark*). Taboo items also proliferate in the highly informal context of RTG, hence the abundance of terms associated with genitalia and breasts.

(13) a. Peterlee is the genital wart on the north east's otherwise glorious **minge**.
b. **Mott** like a Gorilla's wig.
c. It's teaming with grade A posh Yorkshire **clunge**.
d. Canny **chebs**.[5]
e. Canny **norks** on some of them.
f. I saw his **meat and two veg** once at a Seaburn Roadshow in the 80s.
g. Everyone gets a **boner** over teams with big budgets in small leagues.
h. Stop being a **knob**.
i. What a **helmet** this bloke is.
j. Would bet my **nads** it'll be neither of them two.
k. Got it on the second guess, suck me **plums**. :lol:

---

[5] Are *chebs* breasts or penises? In a thread entitled *Controversial cheb debate* several posters make the point that while *chebs* for 'breasts' is general slang, *cheb* for 'penis' is unique to the North East. It is possible the latter derives from *cheb(b)le*, which represents a localised pronunciation of 'table', as confirmed by this poster who avers – and they are not alone – that *cheb* is a clipping from the local expression 'he's gorra cock on him like a chebble leg'. See 7.3.5 for the phonology behind this pronunciation.

The dialect lexicon 127

Note the metonymy in (13c), and slang words for male genitalia deployed abusively (13h,i,k). Synecdoches in which a word for female genitalia is used to mean 'women' are rife in misogynistic discourse, but terms for male genitalia are rarely used in this way.

While lexis like this is widely dispersed, some 'slang' items have acquired a regional flavouring. For example, *lush* as a synonym of 'attractive' is heard across the UK but is particularly prevalent in Wales and North East England; *minger* as a synonym of 'unattractive' is popular in South Wales, the north west of England, Scotland, and North East England (*Voices*; see also Robinson 2021).[6] Thus, 'slang' can sometimes be difficult to distinguish from dialect lexis. This can be seen in relation to words that have come into English through the language of Romani people. As we saw earlier in the chapter, a few words of TDL in NEVE originate with this widely dispersed ethnic group (e.g. *deek, gadgie*), but we also find Romani words that do not fall into the category of TDL (that is, they do not appear in *EDD* or SED for Northumbrian locations). Some of these have a national distribution and can be categorised as slang, rather than dialect. In (12) we have already encountered *chav* < Romani *čhavo* (unmarried Romani male or male child), *nark* < Angloromani *nok* (nose), and *minge* < Angloromani *mindj* <European Romani *mindž* (the female pudendum), to which we can add items like the ones exemplified in (14).

(14) a. I joined the CS after hearing how **cushty** it is.
 b. I look like a **divvy**.
 c. I hope they get **mullered**.
 d. There was a **mush** down roker called bottle, right looper in his day.
 e. 32k is a lot of **wonga** for a golf like!
 f. Just been on the phone to a **bewer** who asked if I was Irish or Scottish.
 g. Backed England against Ireland. Never again. Lost me 50 **bar** the useless wankers.

But some Angloromani-derived words on RTG have a more limited geographical range.

(15) a. Scotch pie, peas, chips and gravy....**bari**.
 b. A thick **charver**.
 c. Has he **chored** some more wine to quaff on his way to work?
 d. What a prize **doylem** you are man.
 e. your crack is **ladgeful**.
 f. it all boils down to how much **lowie** is thrown their way.

---

[6] In NEVE, *lush* is often used to describe food. Alongside home-made kebab meat (see 3.7.2), other concoctions described as 'lush' on RTG include cheese and honey sprinkled with instant coffee and a chicken and mushroom pot noodle poured over a packet of chip shop chips seasoned with salt, vinegar, soy sauce, and pepper.

g. Lad just come in my office reckons he has refused to train and **nashed** off back to France.
h. stay the night in Orlando and go out on the **peev**.

The northern distribution of these items is confirmed by their appearance in *DNED* (*barry, charver, lowie, nash, peev*) and *DSL* (*barrie, chore, lowie, nash*). They can be categorised as part of the dialect lexicon of NEVE, rather than general slang.[7]

Romani is not the only source of non-traditional dialect lexis in NEVE. We also encounter a strand consisting of 'native' items that were possibly coined locally during the twentieth and twenty-first centuries (or perhaps they originated earlier and were overlooked by lexicographers). A selection of these is exemplified in (16), where most of the highlighted words are recorded in *DNED*, but do not appear in *EDD* or SED.

(16) a. Me dad had one other day said it was **belter**.
b. Was it [a fox] doing a **chod**?
c. He'll have to be git fit to push the bike & chew **chuddy** at the same time like.
d. I used to **doll off** school and knock about the old railway lines as a kid.
e. That yoofs **dut** on the right is quite apt also.
f. me **gegs** have steamed up.
g. Give those rose tinted **geps** a wipe.
h. you taking the mickey out of my jam jar bottom **glegs** like?
i. The **gowy** was crap iirc but the cards are probably worth a fortune now.
j. No mate, it was a **hellish** goal. Absolutely class.[8]
k. Most players can't function without a good **hockle** every ten seconds.
l. He's a **knacker** like.
m. That's not that **micey** fella with the baseball cap is it?
n. **Narkies** take 30 mins.
o. **Panackelty** is a thing of beauty when done properly.
p. climbing a tree to find out the nest had been **puggied**.
q. yer skinny little **rarf**.
r. Down Roker now, bit **rawty** like.
s. I remember having to have a **sandshoe** 'bag' at junior school which hung on the coat pegs.
t. Get loads of **shnide** claes.
u. the microwave job might work for mashed **snadger** but it's nee good when roasting it.

---

[7] Matras (2010: 190) suggests two sources for *doylem*: Angloromani *dinilo* ('fool') and Yiddish *goylem* ('fool'). Or it could be an alteration of *doyle* (see 'G. Physical states, (xii)' above), from Scots *doilt* (which shares the same OE source as *dull*).
[8] Here, *hellish* is an adjective meaning 'very good, excellent'. For its use as an intensifier see 3.7.1.3.

The dialect lexicon 129

    v. Kwik Save in Chester Le Street for **tabs** and cuppas.
    w. Prawn mayo, on a **wass** seeded bun, pure lush like!
    x. Those Nike kits were **waxa**.
    y. Bloke was a right **worky ticket**.

5.3 Conclusion

The examples in (16) demonstrate that where lexis is concerned, RTG can be seen as a vast, unruly 'monitor' corpus: an unparalleled means of tracking lexical innovation in NEVE.[9] But as this chapter has revealed, the site can also offer fresh perspectives on traditional dialect lexis, enabling us to see long-standing local words as part of the living vernacular of a region and not merely as decontextualised items on a static list with only historical interest. RTG shows us that 'old' words can be a valuable resource in the construction of dynamic discourses of place, affiliation, and identity. Furthermore, data from the site reveal the poetics of TDL: how it can be deployed performatively to produce a range of rhetorical and stylistic effects. The salience of TDL for some posters means it can also become the topic of meta-discursive practices; indeed, sometimes whole threads with titles like *Phrases you heard years ago, but still use today* and *Exclusively Mackem and Geordie words* are devoted to discussions about the sociolinguistics and pragmatics of dialect words and expressions, their meanings, histories, and symbolic values. And while conversations about TDL on RTG do often evoke ideas of 'loss' (reflecting the inescapable fact that as times change so does language), examination of usage on RTG suggests these 'losses' are nuanced: for example, traditional dialect words can remain current if they are available for semantic extension – either literally or figuratively – as in the case of *ploat, hoy, stot,* and *howk*.

---

[9] Some of these innovations have established etymologies; some do not. For example, *glegs, gegs,* and *geps* for 'spectacles' all probably derive from the TDL word *gleg* ('glance'), while *schnide/shnide* represents a NEVE development of the general slang term *snide* for 'fake, counterfeit'. *Knacker* ('fool, contemptible person') probably derives from two related colloquial items: *knack(er)*, meaning to injure, and *knacker(s)*, a synonym for testicle(s). The origins of items such as *wass* ('big') and *dut* ('hat') are more difficult to determine.

CHAPTER 6

Discourse-pragmatic features

> Eeeeeee a was there tonight hinny pet.

As we saw in the preceding three chapters, RTG provides a wealth of information about the pool of vernacular grammatical and lexical features which north easterners can dip into when communicating with each other in informal contexts – either as part of their everyday unconscious linguistic behaviour or in more carefully considered dialect stylisations. The high levels of interactivity on the site (see 1.1.1) and the emphasis on the expression of feelings and attitudes (see 1.1.2) mean that RTG is inevitably a rich repository of 'discourse-pragmatic features': morphosyntactic constructions and lexical items which – while syntactically optional and/or peripheral, and with little referential meaning, nevertheless – 'perform a range of interpersonal and/or textual functions in discourse' (Pichler 2016: 3). Their optionality is demonstrated in the chapter epigraph: if *eeeeeee*, *hinny*, and *pet* are removed the utterance remains grammatical and the propositional content is unchanged.

Since discourse-pragmatic features form a large and heterogeneous class, my approach is selective, with an emphasis on items which – formally or functionally – have a particular salience in North East England. The chapter is organised as follows. In 6.1 I consider interjections (e.g. *Eeeeeee!!*), while vocatives (e.g. *hinny*), greetings, and attention signals (e.g. *areet, hew*) are the focus of 6.2. In 6.3 I turn to discourse markers/particles and quotatives (e.g. *BE + geet*). Response forms (e.g. *aye*) are covered in 6.4, and in 6.5 I consider what Tagliamonte calls 'expressions': phrases or clauses sometimes referred to as 'turns of phrase' or 'formulaic utterances' (2013: 161–162). In 6.6 I look at some 'disruptions' of typical word order associated with interactive discourse, focusing mainly on right dislocation (e.g. *Love working from home me*).

This chapter will demonstrate how such features can give 'significant clues as to dialect origins of speakers' (Wales 2006: 190–191). In recent years there has been an 'upsurge' in sociolinguistic research 'investigating

Discourse-pragmatic features

patterns of variation and change in discourse-pragmatic features' (see Pichler 2016: 1–2 for an overview). And the growing interest of dialectologists is reflected in the fact that almost every volume in the authoritative 'Dialects of English' series (EUP/De Gruyter Mouton, ongoing from 2007) has a chapter (or part of a chapter) dedicated to the subject.

6.1 Interjections

Interjections have an exclamatory function, typically expressing emotion, and are therefore 'a natural element of dialect speech' (Markus 2014: 116). RTG is full of interjections. Some – such as *wow* and *oops* –are found in many parts of the English-speaking world and have become lexicalised (1a,b); some –like *eurghh* – are idiosyncratic nonce formations (1c), and some are regionally-restricted, as in the case of *ee* (1d).

(1)   a. **Wow**, I seen him at Seaham Hall last night.
        b. **oops** youve had a mare there mate.
        c. I was like "**Eurghh**, mam!"
        d. **Eee** you're dead clever you.

In this section I will focus on the kind of localised forms exemplified in (1d).

The interjection pronounced [iː] and typically spelled <ee> is an example – like *wow*, *oops*, and *eurghh* – of what Culpeper and Kytö (2010) call 'pragmatic noise': semi-natural vocalisms used to express pragmatic meaning/discourse function. Although it was defined in *NW* as 'an expression of delight or wonderment' (Heslop 1892: 263), in current NEVE its pragmatic range is much wider – as it almost certainly was in Heslop's time. Indeed, Palgrave notes that this 'true North-country exclamation' is 'capable of various meanings, according to intonation and context' (1896: 15). *OED* classifies *ee* as *English regional (northern)* and suggests that it is chiefly used in speech or represented speech 'to express a range of emotions or responses, both positive (pleasure, eagerness, surprise, etc.) and negative (doubt, consternation, dismay, etc.)'. Posters on RTG sometimes use respelling to capture the full meaning potential of this form.

(2)   a. **Ee** I was creased the other day watching Come Dine With Me Couples.
        b. **Eee** man, it's ten o'clock and not a bairn's been weshed.
        c. **Eeee**, you're good at this.
        d. **Eeeee** well fuck me.
        e. **Eeeeee**!! I never knew that!
        f. **Eeeeeee** a was there tonight hinny pet.
        g. **Eeya** man!
        h. **eeeeeehhhhhhhhhhhh**!

The examples in (2) do indeed range widely across the emotional continuum. Heslop includes *ee* (spelled <eee>) in an extraordinary list of items under the heading of EXCLAMATIONS (1892: 268–270). Most of these are no longer to be heard (e.g. 'smash me hoggers!'; 'boodyankers!'; 'od's fish!') but some are still current, including *how!/ha(o)way* and *hadaway!*

First recorded by Brockett in 1825, *hadaway*, apparently derived from *hold* + *away*, is described by Heslop as 'equivalent to *begone*', or as an 'exhortation of encouragement, equal to "go on," "hold on"' (1893: 352). Both meanings are preserved on RTG, though the first predominates, particularly in figurative use to convey disapproval of a belief or opinion.

(3) a. **Hadaway** man she's lush!
     b. **Hadaway** and shite man.
     c. **Hadaway** and bollocks man.
     d. "Areet pet, **hadaway** in inside".

Related to *hadaway* is *howay/haway*, which combines *how* + *way*. Heslop claims '*howay* is equivalent to *come*' (1893: 352), though the exhortation *come on* is closer in meaning. Like *come on* it can be used to signal disapprobation and exasperation (often in combination with *man*), as well as enthusiasm and encouragement.

(4) a. **Haway** the Lads.
     b. **Haway** then predictions for tomorrow?
     c. **Haway** Ross sort it out.
     d. **Haway** man, get a grip.
     e. **Howay** man is this you?

(4a) is chanted by fans regularly during Sunderland games, while 'Howay the Lads' is similarly popular amongst followers of Newcastle United. The variation in spelling reflects a widespread perceptual association of *howay* with Newcastle and *haway* with Sunderland (see Pearce 2012: 16), a contrast recognised in the *OED*. It's also noteworthy that *how!* by itself can have a disapprobatory function (the respelling <hew> is discussed in 6.2).

(5) a. **How** man. I'm a Geordie and proud.
     b. **Hew** marra you better watch your tone and language.
     c. My 5 year old grandson has taken to shouting '**How** man!' at his little sister when she irritates him.

As well as <howay/haway>, other orthographic variants include <ho'way> and <ha'way>, with the latter used in the spelling out of the phrase with white seats against a background of red seats at the Stadium of Light. The sociolinguist Julia Snell has written a fascinating article which explores how *howay* – often with no initial glottal – is deployed strategically in the

Discourse-pragmatic features

discourse of children on Teesside to construct a particular kind of working-class identity (Snell 2017).

Finally, we observe the use of curtailed oaths starting with *by*. Such euphemistic exclamations can be heard across the north of England (one possible full form – itself containing a euphemism for *hell* – is shown in (6d)).

(6)   a. **By**, there's a blast from the past.
        b. **By** you've got a canny memory for a man of your age mind.
        c. **By** it's gonna be a busy week when I get back to work.
        d. **By heck** it's windy out there.

6.2 Vocatives, greetings, and attention signals

Vocatives are noun phrases used by a speaker or writer to refer directly to the person addressed. Of particular importance in the highly sociable context of RTG are 'familiarisers', those vocatives which help build solidarity and camaraderie; in addition, some vocatives are 'endearments', positing a relationship of regard and affection between the addresser and the addressee (Leech 2014: 172). NEVE speakers can draw on a set of vocatives shared with other varieties of English (containing such items as *bud(dy)*, *folks*, *man*, *son*, *love*, *darling*, *fellow*, *mum*, *dad*, *pal*, *mate*, and *guys*); additionally, they can use more localised terms, some of which are exemplified below.

(7)   Endearments
        a. You are more than welcome **hinny**.
        b. Just hang on in there **pet**.
        c. Nee one asked yay (just joking **petal**).
        d. There you go **flower**.

(8)   Family terms
        "**Mam**, I want some new toys!"

(9)   Familiarisers
        a. You're gonna be in football paradise soon **marra**.
        b. Careful **bonny lad**.
        c. Chin up **sonner**.
        d. Chin up, **fella**.
        e. Watch and learn **kidda**, watch and learn.

I will demonstrate some of the discourse-pragmatic functions of vocatives in NEVE with reference to *man, marrow, bonny lad, lass, kidder, hinny, pet,* and *mam*.

Man has been used widely as a vocative in English since the OE period, but its prominent clause-final use in NEVE has particular dialect interest. *EDD* suggests *man* is a 'familiar term of address to a person of either sex or of any age; often used at the end of a sentence to give it special emphasis'. As can be seen on RTG, the 'special emphasis' conveyed by terminal *man* in NEVE is typically annoyance, impatience, and exasperation.

(10) a. What a bellend **man**.
      b. What a complete clownshoe **man**.
      c. Don't do that **man**!
      c. Mav and Goose were in the Navy **man** woman **man**!

OED suggests that *man* used to address a person emphatically – usually a man but sometimes a woman or child – is 'now somewhat *archaic*'. However, this is not the case in North East England, where it is current and common.

In contrast to *man*, the most distinctively localised vocative forms can be used in more affiliative and positive contexts.

(11) a. Sounds good **marra**.
      b. Cheers **marra**. Made my day that.
      c. Happy birthday **bonny lad**.
      d. You're welcome **bonny lad**.
      e. Keep it up **bonny lass**.
      f. Yer doin' well **kidder**.
      g. I said "don't let him get to you **kidder**".
      h. Couldn't have put it better mesel **hinny**.
      i. Morning **pet** great news.

Marrow is defined by Brockett as 'a fellow, companion, or associate; an equal, a similar' (1825: 133). For 'MARROW, MARRA', Heslop (1893: 467) has 'a comrade, a close friend, a workfellow, one of a pair of things, an equal' (note that he also records the spelling <marra> which now prevails in written NEVE and which in this form is the third keyest dialect item in the RTG sample corpus, behind *nowt* and *canny*). The etymology of the word is uncertain, though *OED* suggests it could be a borrowing from early Scandinavian. *EDD* notes that it was in 'general dialect use' in County Durham and Northumberland – as we might expect – but also in Cumberland, Westmorland, Yorkshire, Lancashire, and Shropshire. It was also recorded for Scotland and Northern Ireland. While *marrow* does occur nominally on RTG, as in (12a), it is also widely used as a vocative familiariser (12b,c), evoking solidarity, comradeship, and *marradharma*.[1]

---

[1] A compound coined by the County Durham poet William Martin (1925–2010) to describe the unique spiritual force animating North East life and culture (Jackson 2019: 2). *Marra Familia* is the title of a 1993 collection of Martin's verse.

(12) a. I was once stitched up by me **marras** and had to dee it on karaoke.
 b. Hew **marra**, Chester is next to Wales.
 c. Good luck **marra**.

Such affiliative usages of vocative *marrow* are also recorded in citations in *NW* (Heslop 1893: 389, 769; 1892: 253).

(13) a. How there, **marra**?
 b. "Ye'll he' yor wark-set there, **marra**, aa think."
 c. "Oh! **marrow**, oh! **marrow**, where hast thou been?"

The quotation in (13c) is from 'The Collier's Rant', a song first published in the 1700s. *Marrow* has been an enregistered feature of North East dialect since at least the nineteenth century. In 1878, a joke appeared in several British newspapers, including the *Blackburn Standard*, the *Kilburn Times*, the *Banbury Advertiser*, and the *Merthyr Telegraph*. It tells of an encounter between two Northumberland miners and a meteor, and includes the line 'How, marra, whaat's that?'

Bonny lad(s)/lass(es) is similarly emblematic of North East dialect. While the historical associations of *bonny* with Scotland are very strong (the unofficial slogan of the nation is, after all 'Bonny Scotland'), the word, meaning 'beautiful', 'handsome', and generally pleasant to behold, was once also widely used across England (it is in Shakespeare and the Brontës, as well as Dunbar and Burns). Indeed, one of the most famous speakers of Yorkshire dialect in English literature, Joseph the servant in Emily Brontë's *Wuthering Heights* (1847) refers ironically to the psychopathic Heathcliff as 'yon bonny lad'. *EDD* gives its nineteenth-century distribution as Scotland, Ireland, and all northern English counties, together with some midland and southern counties, including Leicestershire, Sussex, Hampshire, and the Isle of Wight. Today however, in England it is generally restricted to northern dialects. On RTG it can be found as an adjective modifying a range of nouns (though it is mainly people who are bonny or who have bonny characteristics).

(14) a. You need to stop your drink man, in what world has he got a **bonny** face?
 b. Shes a **bonny** dog.
 c. He has a **bonny** wife mind.
 d. Looks a **bonny** place Edmonton.
 e. Some **bonny** big houses off up the lanes.

EDD also records a wide distribution for *lad*, but unlike *bonny* and *lass* it has retained its general colloquial status across the British Isles (*OED* describes *lass* as 'the ordinary word' for 'girl' in 'northern and north midland dialects', whereas in the southern counties 'it has little or no popular currency'). The combinations *bonny lad* and *bonny lass* are first recorded in the seventeenth century, and early on they were used as vocatives, as in these lines from a Restoration ballad set in Scotland and printed between 1682–1691: 'Bonny Lass I love thee well / bonny Lad I love thee better'. Earlier still we find non-vocative occurrences of these phrases, including in the poem 'News from Newcastle' (printed for the first time in 1651 and ascribed to John Cleveland): 'The northern lad his bonny lass throws down / And gives her a black bag for a green gown'. Here, in this poem which consists of 'a wonderfully convoluted set of conceits in praise of coal' (Myers 1995: 17), a bonny lass and her lad are very much associated with the north.

Hinny and *kidder* are variants of *honey* and *kid* (cf. *son → sonner*). *Hinny* (sometimes shortened to *hin*) is traditional, and in *EDD* is recorded for Scotland and the north of England in the entry on *honey*; Palgrave gives *hinny* headword status and describes it as an endearment equivalent to 'my dear' (1896: 25). *Kidder* is of a similar vintage but is less salient in the region (it is also found elsewhere in the linguistic North as a general term of address). Evidence for its use in the North East in the late nineteenth and early twentieth centuries can be found in the catchphrase of the great Newcastle-born music-hall comedian Jimmy Learmouth: 'Hallo, kidders! How's yor luck?', an expression based on a colloquial North East greeting, and the epigraph of the roman à clef *Kiddar's Luck* (1951) by Jack Common.[2] Like *kidder*, *pet* is also found further afield than the North East, but is perhaps more 'widely familiar as a marker of north-eastern identity in contemporary British culture' than *kidder*, as its use in the title of the popular 1980s television series *Auf Wiedersehen, Pet* (see 2.3) would seem to imply (Durkin 2015: 319–320).

One vocative attracts particular metalinguistic attention on RTG.

(15) a. It's **Mam** man.
 b. **Mam**, mar or mother. Mum is for southern shandy drinkers.

Several threads on the site consider the 'correct' term of address for female parents. For example, *Anyone from the north east who says 'Mum' should be shot* consists of 169 turns posted by 49 different contributors (see Pearce 2015b). The northern distribution of this form is clear from the lexicographical evidence.[3]

Vocatives like *marra*, *mam*, and *mate* are often used to attract attention; they can also be used in greetings, as in 'Good morning, **mate**'. In NEVE a

---

[2] In this 'seminal text of Geordie culture' (Colls and Lancaster 2005c: 187), Common's first person account of the childhood and adolescence of William Kiddar is a thinly veiled autobiography, recounting a working-class upbringing in Heaton, Tyneside in the early years of the twentieth century.

[3] In the RTG sample corpus *mam* occurs 53.7 times per-million words and *mum* just 13.9 times.

Discourse-pragmatic features

couple of greeting formulas have dialect interest: *how* and *all right*. NW records 'how!' as a greeting, 'used alone, or in the very common salutation "*How* there, marra?" or "*How* there, lads?"' (1893: 389). The respellings in (16) indicate either an [uː] vowel or a diphthong, perhaps in the region of [əu].

(16) a. **How** marra. How's things?
    b. **Hoo** Birch Lad!
    c. **hoo** there bally lad, still mad?
    d. **Hew** Ravers and Electro music heeds.
    e. **hew** lad, whats that owa there in tha field?

The monophthong preserves the vowel found in OE *hū*.[4] In contrast with *how*, the greeting *all right* is widespread in colloquial British English, but in NEVE it usually takes the form *areet* or *alreet*.[5] The spelling <ee> represents the survival of an earlier widespread pronunciation for words such as *right* and *night* (see 7.2.4).

(17) a. **Areet** marra.
    b. **Alreet** mate.

6.3 Discourse markers/particles and quotatives

Discourse markers/particles are short words or fixed phrases which perform functions related mainly to structuring and organising spoken language and are only loosely attached to the clause. Many are common across most varieties of English, while some have a regional distribution (in terms of use, if not in terms of form).

6.3.1 *Like*

One of the most extensively studied discourse markers in English is *like*. These examples from RTG show it being used in ways which have been attested in many Anglophone contexts.

(18) a. If you go to the Corn Dolly there's **like** a back lane opposite.
    b. You have to **like** read the threads though.

---

[4] We might compare *how* with Old English *hwæt* (the opening injunction of the verse epic *Beowulf*) which is sometimes described as having similar pragmatic force to *what!*, *listen!*, or *hey!* in PDE, though this interpretation is not without its critics (see Walkden 2013).

[5] Like *all right*, *areet/alreet* is not only a greeting, it can also be used as an adjective: 'We'll be **alreet** the nars'.

c. I was **like** "nah ya alreet mate" and headed towards my car.
   d. I was **like** how did he even get them in there.

In (18a,b) *like* is a 'focuser', pointing out important information in the ongoing discourse. In (18c,d) *BE* + *like* introduces quoted speech and thought.

   A more regionally marked usage is clause-final *like*, which Beeching describes as 'the traditional realisation of *like* [as a discourse marker] in the UK ... associated with northern speakers' (2016: 139). Terminal *like* is multi-functional. For instance, it seems that in (19a,b) *like* is being used to add emphasis. Beal describes this as its most 'traditional function' in NEVE, pointing out that it can also be used in interrogatives, 'where it often conveys a sense of interest or surprise' (2004: 136), as in examples (19c,d).

(19) a. Suppose there's a bit of music snobbery going on **like**.
   b. Gorillas are class **like**.
   c. Are people not proud to wear the red n white stripes to the match **like**?
   d. Have we figured out if Wee Phillie is a bit of a hypocrite yet **like**?

Terminal *like* is also used in NEVE (as it is in Scotland) to counter 'potential inferences, objections or doubts'. Miller and Weinert, in their study of Scottish student dialogues gloss this function as 'clearing up misunderstanding' (1995: 389). On RTG we also see evidence of this.

(20) a. He's still a twat **like**.
   b. I'm not gay **like** think my boyfriend may be though.

Beeching wonders – prompted by findings from her study of BNC data – if terminal *like* is 'dying out and associated only with elderly speakers and thus considered old-fashioned and anachronistic', or if it is 'being maintained as a badge of regional and/or working-class identities' (2016: 140). She decides that BNC evidence points her towards the former conclusion, but its use on RTG suggests this feature is far from moribund.

   Vernacular *like* has a long history in the UK, dating back to at least 1840 (D'Arcy 2007, in Beeching 2016: 126). *EDD* provides examples which seem strikingly modern. These are recorded for Yorkshire.

(21) a. He would not go **like** through that.
   b. They are **like** against one another, as it is.
   c. It was there, **like**.

6.3.2 *Geet*

While *like* is a widespread feature of colloquial English, the discourse marker *geet* is limited to NEVE (its more common role as an intensifier,

Discourse-pragmatic features

together with its history and development is covered in 3.7.1.2). The pair of RTG examples in (22) shows that *geet* performs a similar focusing function to *like* (the spellings <git, gid> reflect a pronunciation with a shorter vowel to be found in the south of the region). However, it should be stressed that on RTG, *like* as a discourse marker is much commoner than *geet*.

(22) a. I'm sure when you get these transplants you are meant to leave the head untouched for **git** ages.
b. My Nan wouldn't speak to me for **like** weeks after.

Like *BE* + *like*, *BE* + *geet* can be used to introduce quoted speech and thought.

(23) a. I was **gid** THIS f***ing LAPTOP!
b. I was **gid** wtf.
c. He was **gid** "nor I'm not going out".

As Trousdale points out, 'the recycling of geet allows the more general quotative construction *BE X 'QUOTE'* to acquire a more 'local' indexicality' (2013: 73).

6.3.3 *Thou knows*

On RTG the discourse marker 'thou knows' (variously rendered orthographically to capture pronunciations such as [ðə'na:z] and [ðr'na:z]) is broadly synonymous with the much more common 'you know', though the deployment of a rare second person subject pronoun (see 3.4.1.3) makes it more stylistically marked than the more common NEVE variant [jə'na:] (see 3.2.1.2). It typically occurs clause-finally.

(24) a. Gorra degree **tha knas**.
b. ah's not daft **tha knas**.
c. He's a toon fan **tha nars**.
d. Aye it's weird **tha knars**.
e. it'll rot your teeth **thee knars**.

This feature has a long North East history. For example, it appears (in the form *thou knaws*) in *The Pitman's Pay* (1826–1830), a long poem by Thomas Wilson about the lives of Gateshead pitmen and their families which – according to Ellis – is 'the classic work' in the 'Pitman's dialect' (1889: 639).

6.3.4 Clause-final *mind* and *but*

We have already seen how NEVE is unusual amongst varieties of English in that *like* can be used clause-finally to add emphasis and to clear up possible misunderstandings or misinterpretations (6.3.1). In this position we also find *mind* and *but* performing a variety of roles.

In some circumstances, clause-final *mind* and the more widespread and unmarked *mind you* seem to function in a roughly equivalent way, similar to terminal *though*.

(25) a. I'd love to see the breakdown of all of them **mind you**.
b. I have some sympathy for them **mind**.
c. I do still enjoy watching them **though**.

In these RTG examples, *mind you*, *mind*, and *though* could be used interchangeably to produce a similar pragmatic effect. Similar, but not equivalent. For example, *mind* in (25b) arguably has a more emphatic quality than *though* in (25c). This is due to one of the senses of the verb *mind*, from which the discourse marker *mind* is derived, being to 'take care' or 'pay attention'. In the following examples there is a quality to *mind* not shared with *mind you* or *though*.

(26) a. Be careful **mind** this clownshoe means business on Sunday :lol:
b. Warning tho – my Despies/JD mix is not fer the faint hearted and will get you ratted very quickly **mind**.
c. Not allowed to say that **mind**.

Here *mind* is appended to a piece of advice (26a), a warning (26b), and a prohibition (26c). *NW* has historical evidence of terminal *mind* being used in similar directive contexts.

(27) a. "The top's varry tendert **mind**." (Heslop 1893: 723)
b. "Yese come when aa tell ye, **mind**." (805)
c. "Ye'll brick yor neck, **mind**." (Heslop 1892: 99)
d. "If ye gan, bring'z a fairin hyem, **mind**!" (273)

Terminal *mind* is widespread in colloquial speech across the UK. For example, the linguistic descriptions of the *Voices* recordings (see 2.2.4) show it being used in Cornwall, Devon, Bristol, Gloucestershire, and Coventry, as well as North East England. Clause-final *but*, however, is a rarer phenomenon (although it is found in Australian English and American English, as well as varieties of English in Ireland, Scotland, and the north of England). Terminal *but* typically has a concessive quality, and like terminal *mind* can often be paraphrased with *though* (although the situation is complex – see for example Hancil 2018). We also find terminal *but* appearing alongside *though* to increase the pragmatic force of the concession.

(28) a. I never watched it **but**.
b. Nice ground **though but**.

Discourse-pragmatic features 141

    c. Still a f***ing amazing goal **though but**.
    d. Was an awful lot of real ale twats in there **though but**.
    e. Not for me at all **but though**.

Terminal *but* can also occur with terminal *mind* and *mind though*.

(29) a. not sure what they could have done about that **but mind**.
      b. I agree about the manners **but mind**.
      c. They do, **mind though but**!

6.4 Response forms

When SED informants were prompted for positive response forms, *aye* was the most commonly occurring form in Northumbria, sometimes in the phrase 'why aye' (Orton and Halliday 1963: 965–966). *Aye* is first attested in English in the sixteenth century. Its origins are uncertain, though the fact that it is first spelled <I> suggests it could derive from the pronoun *I* used as an expression of assent in response to a question.[6] Brockett describes *aye* as 'perhaps more characteristic of a Northern dialect than any other word that could be named, as it is nearly universal and uniform' (1825: 63–64). The form remains in widespread use in northern England, the north of Ireland, and Scotland and it is certainly characteristic of RTG, lying sixth amongst the ten keyest dialect terms in the sample corpus (see 1.3).

(30) a. **Aye**, Blyth and Sedgefield are on the list too.
      b. **Aye** I would, why wouldn't you?
      c. **Aye**, I think it's open at the minute.
      d. last few places I've left I've asked if they'd have me back, feels canny good when they say **why aye**.
      e. Courteeners better than New Order, **why aye man!** :lol:
      f. Imagine being proud of being taken over by a murderous regime. 'Wuv got was club back'...**aye right**.
      g. In Shields they sell "Pain Au Chocolat" and people eat them while sitting at pavement cafes drinking their coffee – **Aye right**.
      h. Tunnels from Hylton Castle to the coast? **Aye reet**. :lol:

Why aye has become a stereotype of NEVE, with strong perceptual links to Newcastle, although it 'lubricate[s] the flow of discourse' (Wales 2010: 76) across the region. It can be used as an enthusiastic positive response, roughly equivalent to 'of course!'; it can also be deployed sarcastically, as in

---

[6] OED offers three further possibilities: a borrowing from Frisian *ay/ajj* (colloquial 'yes') in the context of trade or seafaring; a combination of the interjection *ah* plus *yea*; a semantic development of *ay* meaning 'ever'.

(30e). A similarly disdainful pragmatic force is wielded by *aye right* (30f,g,h) which can be used to convey doubt or disbelief about the truth value of a statement. It is found across the linguistic North and mentioned in the entry for *aye* in *DSL*.[7]

Where negative response forms are concerned, NEVE generally coincides with SE *no*. But sometimes forms in *-a*, variously spelled <na, nah, nar> etc., appear on RTG, reflecting pronunciations such as [na ~ naː], which are attested in SED for Northumbria (Orton and Halliday 1963: 966). This is an older, northern form (*no* emerged in Middle English because of the rounding of Old English long ā in southern and midland dialects, while northern dialects preserved the OE form *na*).

(31) a. I'll be honest i nearly said '**na**, forget that'.
 b. **Nah**, never heard any Mackem say that like.
 c. Am garna mak em an offer ee cannit say **nar** tee like.[8]

NW attests to the presence of this form: 'NA, no (*negative adverb*). The *a* very short, as in *cat, pat, hat*, etc. "Are ye gan win us?" "Na"' (Heslop 1893: 491). Occasionally, [neɪ] occurs as a negative response form, represented on RTG as <nay> (see 3.4.5).

6.5 Expressions

In 1.1.1 we saw how, because of its pseudo-live nature, RTG – like phonic conversation – contains 'ready-made' word sequences, easily recoverable from memory. Some of these are 'lexical bundles' – non-idiomatic frequently occurring lexical sequences, like *I don't know why*; *I thought that was*; other multi-word expressions are more formulaic and 'fixed' in nature, such as the verbal routines used to launch utterances ('like I say'), greetings ('good morning'), and discourse markers ('you know'). We also find relatively fixed multi-word expressions variously known as sayings, adages, maxims, proverbs, and so on.

(32) a. **You can lead a horse to water but you can't make it drink**, as they say.

---

[7] The significance of *(why) aye* in North East culture is reflected in the title of two songs by local artists: 'Why Aye Man' by Mark Knopfler (2002) and 'Aye' by Sam Fender (2021).

[8] (31c) is from a thread entitled *Film quotes changed into Mackem speech*. Cineastes will recognise this as a NEVE version of the well-known line mumbled by Marlon Brando in *The Godfather*: 'I'm gonna make him an offer he can't refuse.' The thread is a repository of classics which includes 'Where we garn ya dinnit need roads'; 'Aye Luke I'm ya fatha', and 'Lerrit gan, lerrit gan, canna howld it bak nee ma' (not from 'Frozzen' but from the Durham version, 'Nithered').

b. **Not got two pennies to rub together** but all drink Kestrel Super and smoke.
c. Saw the final score and **you could have knocked me down with a feather**.

The sayings used by the RTG posters in (32) are widely known in Anglophone cultures. But others are regionally restricted. For example, the following examples from RTG are associated with the linguistic North, while some are more localised to the North East.

(33) a. setting off soon for me Sunday dinner **I could eat a scabby hoss**.
b. Well I'll go to **the foot of our stairs**!
c. Do you think you're on **your gannie's yacht**?
d. **Shy bairns get nowt** syndrome?
e. Clock in, spray paint a door, have some bait, **get wrang** for going for a slash, paint another door, go home, hate your life.
f. My sister reckons he looks like a **wrang un**.
g. "sitting there **like a tin of milk**".
h. I'm very much for rehabilitation and don't get **up a height** when prisoners get released.
i. "We're **all together like the folk of Shields**".
j. **There's a rabbit off** somewhere with the ownership of our club.
k. Basically some edgy Preston fan was **acting himself** and chucked a bottle into our end.
l. I get it working eventually everytime but what a **clart on**.

The examples in (33) hint at the abundance of expressions in NEVE, and only a few can be discussed here. 'I could eat a horse' is widespread, but 'scabby' horses (and particularly 'hosses') are perhaps more likely to be evoked in the north of England as a cure for hunger than elsewhere. 'I'll go to the foot of our stairs' as an expression of surprise is northern and midlands (Green and Widdowson 2003: 166). Its origins are obscure – the earliest example I have found is in a 1937 short story published in the *Birmingham Weekly Mercury*, but it was clearly in circulation before then. 'Where do you think you are – your g(r)anny's yacht?' is used when someone – particularly a child – has made an extravagant demand or is behaving in a superior manner. Anecdotal evidence suggests it is used in Scotland and Ireland as well as North East England, though the only instance of it in the BNA is in a story about two young men stealing a rowing boat in Gateshead in 1977 (when apprehended by the police and asked what they were doing, one of them replied, 'I'm on my granny's yacht'). Clearly, these lads were not suffering from the 'syndrome' referred to in (33d). 'Shy bairns get nowt' – roughly equivalent to 'if you don't ask, you don't get' – has been making North East introverts feel bad about themselves for generations and regularly appears on mugs, tea towels, posters, and so on as an element of the commodified linguistic landscape (see Chapter 2). *Wrang/wrong* occurs in two well-known NEVE expressions: *get wrang/wrong* and *wrang/wrong 'un*. The former means to be told off or chastised, as in (33e), a parody of the voice-over from the famous opening sequence of the film *Trainspotting*, intended to encapsulate the dispiriting essence of shift work on the production line at a local car factory. *EDD* reveals a 'northern' distribution for this phrase up to c.1900 (Scotland, Northumberland, Yorkshire, and Lancashire) and it appears in a citation in *NW*: "Ye'll get wrang if ye mill wi'd" (Heslop 1893: 473). *Wrang/wrong 'un* refers to a criminally deviant person (33f); perhaps this is a metaphorical extension of the word's earliest recorded meaning (crooked, misshapen).

6.6 Dislocation

The planning pressures associated with 'live' interaction mean that conversational utterances tend to be structured differently from typical written sentences. For example, they are often 'composite' in nature, consisting of a 'body' which can be preceded by a 'preface' and/or followed by a 'tag'. Such composite structures are also found in the pseudo-live context of RTG (see also 1.1.1).

(35) a. **Newcastle**, they go for fat and whiney [NP preface]
 b. **Shearer**, he's a good pundit [NP preface]
 c. **Steve Bruce** he's got a big fat head [NP preface]

(36) a. No right and wrong here **marra** [vocative tag]
 b. He's an idiot **that boy** [NP tag]
 c. They sound like proper hard bastards **them**, **like** [pronoun tag + discourse marker]

Typically, in left dislocation 'a noun phrase is positioned initially and a reinforcing pronoun stands "proxy" for it in the relevant position in the sentence' (Quirk et al. 1985: 1310), resulting in constructions like those in (35). The propositional content of these sentences could be conveyed more typically by 'Newcastle go for fat and whiney', 'Shearer is a good pundit', and 'Steve Bruce has got a big fat head'. The discourse function of left dislocation is topicalisation, announcing the status of the fronted element as theme. The earliest reference to this feature in the dialectological literature appears in *EDG*, where Wright notes 'a tendency to introduce a redundant personal pronoun after a noun when emphasis is required'. He gives the example *Mr. Smith, he came to my house*, suggesting that this 'redundant' pronoun is 'especially frequent after a proper name' (Wright 1905: 270).[9]

---

[9] A famous literary example is the epigraph to T. S. Eliot's great modernist poem 'The Hollow Men' (a quotation from Joseph Conrad's *Heart of Darkness*): "Mistah Kurtz – he dead".

Discourse-pragmatic features

It has no particular significance for NEVE; as Wright himself states, it is a feature of all Scottish and English dialects.

Right dislocation is of more interest from a dialectological perspective. Formally, it involves detaching a noun phrase and moving it to the end of the clause (as a 'tag') with its 'place' being taken at the start of the clause by a pronoun. For example, *That boy's an idiot* → *He's an idiot that boy* (37a). This is an example of the 'canonical' right dislocation form (Durham 2011), used for retrospective clarification and disambiguation of the referent of the initial pronoun. There is also an 'expanded' form where the operator of the clause is also reiterated (37b, c and d), sometimes before the NP tag in the right dislocation, as in (37e and f).

(37) a. He's an idiot **that boy**.
 b. horrible little shit **he is**.
 c. thou's fukn crackers **thou is**.
 d. Utter sad bastards **they are**.
 e. He's a good lad **is Chris**.
 f. Good bloke **is Yanni** mind.

Heslop includes right dislocation – with and without the operator – in his description of the dialect (1892: xxi).

> Another tendency is that of placing the subject of a sentence at the end of a phrase. "He'd getten a sair tumm'le, Jack had." "They've come oot o' skyul, the bairns hez." "Th'or myestly a' that colour, wor coos."

We also see structures in which the whole 'detached' NP element consists of an object pronoun, as in (38).

(38) a. Proper gobshite **you**.
 b. Ooohhh you git manly bastard **you**!
 c. He's an idiot **him** like sorry.
 d. Wrang'un **him** like!
 e. He's an absolute prize bellend **him**.
 f. He's a little bell end **him** mind.
 g. Ah love owt like this, **me**.
 h. I love carpets, **me**.[10]

In these cases of pronoun 'repetition', the function is not clarification or disambiguation but reinforcement, emphasis, and evaluation. The earliest reference to this use of pronoun tags is in *EDG*, where Wright notes that 'in the northern dialects the personal pronoun is often repeated in recriminatory talk, as *thou great lout, thou*' (1905: 270). On RTG, pronoun-only NP tags are

---

[10] This frank confession is the slogan of a North East firm of flooring specialists.

often used in contexts of negative evaluation, as in most of the examples in (38). The significance of pronoun tags in English in the north of England is revealed in a study of schoolchildren in Bolton and Middlesbrough (Moore and Snell 2011), which shows how they are used not only to mark emphasis or provide clarification but also to perform a wide range of interpersonal functions concerned mainly with positioning speakers within the social group and forging and maintaining social bonds.

6.7 Conclusion

This chapter has shown how the interactive and expressive nature of RTG is demonstrated particularly vividly in the array of locally inflected speech-like discourse features to be found amongst its threads. Emotional states and responses are conveyed through interjections which have been attested in the dialect since the late eighteenth century, while affiliation and camaraderie is engineered through local terms of address and greetings formulae. RTG also contains vernacular discourse markers, some uniquely North East in form (e.g. *geet* as a focuser and quotative), while others such as *like* are well known across the Anglophone world, but in NEVE have distinctive functions or positions in the clause. RTG is also a repository of sayings and proverbs, sometimes reached for by posters as a shorthand way of conveying an idea or feeling. Various disruptions of typical word order of the kind found in spontaneous speech, some with a definite local flavour, also help to evoke the experience of listening to NEVE. Indeed, as has been demonstrated in many of the examples in this and preceding chapters, some contributors to RTG are even prepared to experiment with orthography to add an 'auditory' dimension to their posts, a subject to which the final chapter of this book is devoted.

CHAPTER 7

The soundscape

Dee ya leyk ta eyt biff borgaz wa bitrut on ya murta burt?

This question appears in a thread about options for fast food in Sunderland, in response to a contributor who jokingly suggests 'Jawdee borgah'. Of course, it is not a real request for information. The purpose (<porpuss>?) of the query – and the answer which it prompts ('Wey aye, on me porpal turbur murta burt') – is 'performative'. As we saw in Chapter 1, in response to communicative context, speakers and writers use the semiotic resources at their disposal to range across a stylistic continuum, with 'mundane performance' – or *styling* – at one end and 'high performance' at the other. Quotidian, everyday performances are responses to contextual factors such as genre (people speak and write differently when they are passing on a recipe compared with when they are reviewing a film, for example), while 'high performance' is a more elaborate and knowing act of *stylisation*, sometimes involving extravagant identity play (Mortensen et al. 2017; Coupland 2007). High performance is perhaps most obvious when speakers or writers use 'dialect stylisation' (Coupland 2001) to reproduce the words and voices of specific individuals or of personas representative of a wider social group. We have encountered dialect stylisation in many of the examples in this book, but posters are perhaps at their most creative when attempting to convey information about the sound component of NEVE, as in the exchange above. In this chapter I focus on the ways in which North East England's linguistic soundscape is represented on RTG. While respelling of the kind displayed in the epigraph will be at the heart of this analysis, it is not the only way information about 'local' sounds of speech – both segmental and suprasegmental – is conveyed by posters; in addition, RTG is a rich source of metalinguistic commentary on accent, a source on which I draw throughout the chapter. But I begin by making some general remarks on the nature of the orthographic creativity to be found on the site (7.1), before discussing RTG's representation of the linguistic soundscape of NEVE in relation to vowels (7.2), consonants (7.3), connected speech processes (7.4), and suprasegmental features (7.5).

7.1 What gets respelled on RTG and why?

In Chapter 1 we saw how orthographic creativity is rife on RTG. There I argued that these innovations were evidence of the vernacularity of the site (helping to justify its suitability for sociodialectological study). Performance features associated with producing language in real time give rise to allegro spelling (*whatcha*); the expression of feelings and attitude can result in spellings designed to convey, for instance, heightened emotional states (*fuuuuuck*); and the overarching informality of the site is also evident in eye dialect (*choons*) and dialect spellings (*poond*).

Respellings designed to give information about localised accent features – labelled 'regiolectal spelling' by Androutsopoulos (2000) – will inevitably be the main focus of this chapter, but we should not automatically discount other types of respelling. Even when they seem to provide little phonological information about accent, as in the case of <Jawdee> for *Geordie*, respellings sometimes draw attention to pronunciations which differ in some way from the mainstream (Honeybone 2020: 219–220). The contrast between eye dialect and regiolectal spelling is set out below, illustrated with examples from the start of this chapter (I also discuss eye dialect in 1.1.3 in relation to the general informal vernacularity of the site).

1. <Jawdee> appears to be eye dialect. This sequence of letters could just as easily represent a mainstream pronunciation of the word as a NEVE one. Indeed, most north easterners would say [ˈdʒɔːdi], as would many speakers of non-rhotic varieties of British English. The spelling choice here does not, therefore, provide any obvious information about accent. However, it is possible that the <aw> in the spelling could be designed to show that some people in the region have a more rounded vowel – such as [ɒː] – in this word, especially in emphatic speech, while the <ee> might reflect a particularly tense realisation of the happY vowel (see 7.2.19).
2. In contrast, the spelling of the vowel in the stressed syllable of *burger(s)* is intended to provide phonological information, making it an instance of regiolectal spelling. The vowel is represented by <or>, which most speakers of English in England would associate with a [ɔː]-type vowel, as in *for* or *store*. And indeed, some NEVE speakers do have [ɔː] in words in the NURSE lexical set (see 7.2.10).
3. A further instance of regiolectal spelling is evident when <ur> is used to represent the vowels in *boat* and in the first syllable of *motor*. In mainstream English this spelling is often used in words with an [əː]-like vowel, like *curse* or *fur*. In NEVE, there is considerable variation in the GOAT set, to which *motor* and *boat* belong (Beal et al. 2012: 31). While [əː] is not one of these recorded variants, the attested vowels [ɵː], [øː], and [œː] could all logically be represented with <ur> (see 7.2.2).
4. The spelling of the vowel in the second syllables of *burger(s)* and *motor* –

The soundscape

    <ah>, <az>, and <a> – reflects a widespread NEVE pronunciation in which the lettER/commA vowel is in the region of [ɐ] rather than the more typical schwa (see 7.2.18).
5. Eye dialect and regiolectal spelling can combine in the same word-representation. This is the case in <borgaz>, where the <z> is a phonetically 'better' fit for the -s morpheme than the standard spelling, although it provides no information about accent.

A lot of information can be conveyed by such respellings. Clearly, features of a NEVE accent – particularly the vowel phonology – are prominent, but in relation to <Jawdee> we also see the possibility of articulatory setting being represented. While no comprehensive study of NEVE voice quality has been completed, studies of urban Scottish speech – with which NEVE has some commonalities – suggest that marked tenseness, lip-rounding, and protrusion is associated with male working-class speakers (see Stuart-Smith 1999).

Allegro and expressive spelling is also a source of information about the NEVE soundscape. While certain allegro spellings on RTG associated with deletion, insertion, modification, and reduction are found in informal written representations of most varieties of English (e.g. *gonna*), some have a distinctively local flavour. This can perhaps be seen most clearly in 'T-to-R' (introduced in 1.1.1) – a topic which I return to in 7.4. Expressive spelling can also provide insights into the sonic experience of NEVE. As with allegro spelling, some are 'universal', while others have a more limited geographical salience. Most strikingly, expressive spelling can be combined with regiolectal spelling.

(1)   a. I'm gonna get a panic alarm for me **hoooose**.
       b. How do I get to ya **hooooose**?
       c. Saying is it a Wendy **hooooose**.
       d. Bali in the **hooooooose**!

In (1), the posters have broken the rules of conventional orthography to produce hyperdialectal representations of the [uː]-type vowel often heard in words in the MOUTH lexical set in North East England (see 7.2.1).

It seems reasonable to assume that the more salient a particular sound is, the more likely it is that words in which the sound occurs will be respelled. An additional factor contributing to the likelihood of respelling is the extent to which a particular linguistic form has been enregistered as part of a 'reified' dialect (see Chapter 2). Both influences can be seen in some of the orthographic innovations presented so far in this chapter. For example, research has shown that an [ɔː]-type vowel in NURSE words, captured in respellings like *borgaz* and *borgah* is associated with speakers from Tyneside, rather than other parts of North East England (Wells 1982: 374; Beal et al. 2012: 32), and on RTG such spellings often appear in parodic representations of people from that part of the region. The vowel is also enregistered as part of Newcastle dialect, appearing regularly in published dialect writing from the city, such as the *Viz* magazine comic strip 'Biffa Bacon', which chronicles the adventures of Newcastle's 'fightiest family'. In 2009 *Viz* published an advertising feature in a national newspaper in the form of a strip in which Biffa's father ('fatha') sees his son reading *The Guardian* and punches him in the face, exclaiming 'Y'dorty fuckin' porvort!'

Additional factors constraining regiolectal spelling relate to the competence and motivation of the writer and the limitations and affordances of the orthographic system itself. Someone with a more developed ability to perceive phonological distinctions and a better understanding of the 'deep orthography' of the English spelling system (Honeybone 2020: 225) will presumably be better at the task (and more motivated to attempt it) than someone with less skill and knowledge. Writers will also take different positions in relation to what Honeybone calls the 'maximalist-minimalist orthographic axis' (Honeybone 2020: 222). The maximalist position will be adopted by someone wishing to 'emphasise the differences between the variety represented and Standard/Reference English ... which could lead to a large number of respellings, of both the "eye dialect" and "phonologically motivated" kind' (Honeybone 2020: 222). In the context of RTG, the writer might also want to emphasise a distinction between, say, a mainstream North East accent (see 2.1) and a North East accent deemed to deviate in some way from that mainstream. The chapter epigraph is an example of 'maximal' accent representation (only one of the thirteen words is spelled 'correctly'), whereas some of the examples in (1) are quite 'minimal' – (1c) and (1d) only contain one respelling each. Using <oo> (and <ooo>, etc.) for [uː], as in the examples in (1) is an unambiguous strategy, since the digraph <oo> often performs this function in standard orthography. Similarly, <or> for [ɔː] is relatively transparent for most speakers of non-rhotic varieties of English. However, not all NEVE sounds are as straightforwardly capturable as this. For example, as far as I can tell no attempt has been made to represent the variability in the KIT vowel which has been noted in some studies of Tyneside English (Jones-Sargent 1983; Amand 2019). As for consonants, many people from the North East of England glottally reinforce the voiceless stops /p t k/ when they occur between sonorants in words like *jumper*, *better*, and *tricky*. This is difficult to represent orthographically and does not appear on RTG. Neither do we see attempts to capture the 'clear' /l/ which often (and unusually amongst accents of English) occurs in all environments in NEVE (see 7.3 for a discussion of how NEVE consonantal features are represented on RTG).

7.2 Vowels

In the chapter epigraph all the respellings are associated with vowel sounds. This is not surprising since – as has long been recognised – 'the

The soundscape

points which distinguish from each other ... the English of Dorset, of Norfolk, of Yorkshire, of Cumberland, the Lowland tongue of Teviotdale, of Ayr, of Fife, and of Aberdeen, are, not indeed exclusively, but at least, to a very great extent, *vowel differences*' (Murray 1873: 93). Respelling on RTG can offer insights into perceptions of vowel variation in NEVE, and in the sub-sections that follow I categorise these spellings according to Wells's lexical sets (1982), giving the typical NEVE vowel(s) associated with each set and local variants.

7.2.1 MOUTH

Table 7.1 *NEVE variants and respellings of the* MOUTH *vowel*

'Typical' NEVE vowel(s)	Local vowel variant(s)	Example RTG respelling(s)
[aʊ > əʊ]	[ɛʊ]	*town* <tewn>
	[uː ~ ʉ]	*town* <toon>; *down* <doon>; *pound* <pund>

The MOUTH vowel derives in almost all cases from Middle English /uː/. It was diphthongised by way of the Great Vowel Shift and is typically spelled <ou> or <ow>, as in *out* and *town* (Wells 1982: 152). The mainstream northern vowels in this set are [aʊ] or [əʊ]. Some NEVE speakers have a more localised diphthong [ɛʊ] (Pearce 2009: 179–184; Beal 2004: 124; Devlin et al. 2019). This vowel has been described as a 'shibboleth' of Sunderland English (Beal 2000: 353; see also 2.3) and is sometimes captured orthographically on RTG with <ew>, and possibly <ouw>.

(2) a. I dinnit knaa, cumin te ower **tewn** an' takkin the breed owt uf ower **mouwths**.
 b. Garna cost us a few **pewnd** to turn it **arewnd**.

But the most well-known MOUTH variant in NEVE – a 'marked peculiarity' according to Heslop (1892: 180) – is the preservation of a pre-GVS [uː]-type monophthong. The RTG respellings in (3) represent pronunciations much the same as later OE *dun, hus, muþ, tun, ut, suð* and *pund*, though some 'traditional' speakers have a closer, backer [ʉ], as in [pʉnd] for *pound* (cf. German *Pfund*). The respellings in (3) represent pronunciations found across the linguistic North and are as redolent of Scots as they are of NEVE.

(3) a. The telly was turned reet **doon**.
 b. You could buy a **hoose** for a tenner in those days.
 c. Wash yer **mooth oot**!
 d. Gannin **doon** the **toon** the neet?
 e. Pick that one **oot** of the net.
 f. Didnt he leave cos his lass got a job **doon sooth**?

g. Someone dropped a **pund**.

Although SED reports widespread use of monophthongal [uː] for locations in County Durham and Northumberland (and for some locations in Cumberland, Yorkshire, and North Lincolnshire), this pronunciation has been receding throughout the twentieth century, both geographically and socially, and is now mainly associated with working-class males (Beal 2008: 134). Findings from perceptual dialectology research (Pearce 2012) reveal a linking of [uː] with Newcastle and Tyneside. This could be due to the way in which this pronunciation is prominent in a small set of words associated with Tyneside identity, where the [uː] 'has been lexicalised and reflected in the spelling' (Beal 2004: 124). The most well-known of these is *toon*, which typically does not refer to towns in general, but often occurs in the phrase 'the Toon' as an alternative label for Newcastle and as a nickname for Newcastle United F.C.[1] The saliency of *toon* in North East culture is reflected in the title of a satiric-epic by the Newcastle-based poet, Sean O'Brien, in which a 'water-sprite, a river girl' guides the poet on a phantasmagorical tour of the 'secret Hell of Tyne', prompting him to reflect on aspects of the region's history, mythology, and culture, including what the girl calls 'Geordismo', a distinct variety of North East machismo epitomised by the 'slabs of lard / In dandruffed suits' watching 'dog-headed dancing-girls' perform in a nightclub guarded by a 'triple-headed bouncer'. The poem is called 'On the Toon'. Another poetic example foregrounding the unshifted vowel in MOUTH is the title of Tom Pickard's collected poems and songs: *hoyoot* (2014).

Though in decline, [uː] is by no means entirely 'historical', nor is it exclusively found in MOUTH-words with local cultural significance.

(4) a. Has anyone seen anyone in the **cloods**?
b. Just me or is it gannin **roond**?
c. Has it got torkee and **sproots** in it?
d. No you fekking **cloons** its a no and not a maybe.
e. Alan Brazil has a heed like a borst **cooch**.

As with many vowel respellings on RTG, MOUTH orthographic variants often occur in the context of dialect stylisation. For example, (2a) is a contribution to a thread entitled *mack ya' best Mackem sentence* while the merger of linguistic and social stereotyping in (3d) is from *Things you will only hear a Geordie say*.

---

[1] Other items in this group include *brown* (in relation to a brand of beer called Newcastle Brown Ale which until 2010 was brewed in Gateshead), and possibly *down* and *out* (because people on a night 'oot on the Toon' might 'doon' some 'broons').

7.2.2 GOAT

Table 7.2 *NEVE variants and respellings of the* GOAT *vowel*

'Typical' NEVE vowel(s)	Local vowel variant(s)	Example RTG respelling(s)
[oː]	[eː ~ øː ~ œː]	*coat* <kert>; *hole* <herl>; *covid* <cervid>
	[aː ~ ɑː]	*snow* <snaa>; *cold* <caald>; *own* <arn>; *grow* <gra>
	[aʊ]	*old* <owld; auld>; *cold* <cowld; cauld>; *hold* <howld>
	[ɒ]	*open* <oppen>

The GOAT vowel derives in most cases via the GVS from Middle English /ɔː/, or from /ɔu/. The different origins of words in this set can be seen in spelling contrasts such as *toe/tow, sole/soul, nose/knows*, etc. By 1600 /ɔː/ was raised to /oː/ and /ɔu/ fell in with it soon after (Wells 1982: 210). Although northern dialects preserved diphthongs in some GOAT words, the monophthong [oː] is now mainstream across the north of England.[2]

It is reasonable to assume that unmarked forms do not get respelled as often as marked ones, but there are some RTG respellings which might suggest mainstream [oː]-types, usually in <aw> or <or>, or occasionally <o-a>.

(5)   a. We all speed around in purple **mota bo-ats**, not porple murta burts by the way.
      b. A **Knor** nowt!
      c. Pease pudding – aye or **nor**.
      d. if they manage to fluke a **gawl**, we are more than capable of scoring 2 or 3.
      e. She's had 3 jabs, **cor**vid and now got it again.
      f. **Cawld** out there, get wrapped up folks.

In (5a) the poster seems to be drawing a contrast between a mainstream vowel in *motor* and *boats* (spelled <o> in *mota* and <o-a> in *bo-ats*) and a more localised, fronted vowel, spelled <ur> in *murta burts*, popularly associated with Newcastle (Pearce 2012: 13).

These fronted GOAT vowel variants [eː~øː~øə], and sometimes [œː] (Beal et al. 2012: 31; Rydland 1999: 9–10; Prichard 2014: 98) are captured on RTG.[3]

(6)   a. We all speed around in purple mota bo-ats, not porple **murta burts** by the way.

---

[2] For example, SED records the following diphthongs in *grow* at Northumbrian locations: [ɔʊ], [ʊʊ], [aʊ], [æʊ], [aʊ] (Orton and Halliday 1963: 1014).

[3] A centring diphthong [uə] or [ʊə] also occurs, associated with 'older working-class male speakers' (Beal et al. 2012) – although this variant does not seem to be represented orthographically on RTG.

b. Ive got about 40 **kerts**, around two thirds of which qualify as a winter **kert**.
c. The OP has sang "Sunlans a shit **herl**, a wanna **ger herm**" many a time.
d. 'I widn't gan to the foot o' the stoop to hear him yowl **cerl** down the alley'.
e. Think you'll find it will be wor **cer**vid and injareez that cost us.
f. "Me tattoo. It's a **rerz**. On me arse."
g. Talking of accents I was Just talking to a lass in ashington swimming pool the other day. She said are you **flirting**? I said no I've got one foot on the floor.
h. Byka **grurv**.

The dialectological record reveals a long history for these variants. Prichard suggests – along the lines laid down by Lass (1976) – that in Northumberland, County Durham, and Tyne and Wear it is likely that the [ø:~øə] reflexes of ME 'long o' represent 'a further innovation' of the traditional diphthongs 'found throughout most of the north' (2014: 98).

We must also note that in NEVE some words in this set have an [a:]-type monophthong (Watt and Milroy 1999: 28), but these are lexically restricted to a few GOAT words ending in the cluster [ld] or spelled <ow>, or to open monosyllabic words ending in orthographic <o> (restricted to *go* and *no*).

(7) a. Is it git **cald**?
b. Went to a Cup game, freezin **caald** in January, we got beat I think.
c. Hoping itl not be so **caard**.
d. according to me **ald** Dad Len Shackleton was the best.
e. good to see him rocking the **aald** gadgy clothes.
f. He is a **aad** sack as a footballer.
g. **Haad** on – you drive a transit van?
h. My audi is dreadful in the **snaa**.
i. What in the creation of **craa** shite does that mean?
j. MacGoo gives a **thra** in.
k. Just divvent **blaa** kisses back!
l. As far as I **kna** yes.
m. I've never drank me **arn** piss so I waddant **kna**.
n. Cannit **gar** wrang.
o. **Naa** they're not like.
p. Ours is a right mess as it has ivy all **awa**.

The [a:] in *old, cold*, and *hold* is a preservation of the ME vowel in these words (which itself was lengthened from OE short *a* preceding homorganic clusters like [ld], as shown in the OE forms in *ald, cald,* and *hald*). This lengthened *ā* was rounded to *ō* in later Middle English in the south, but the north has preserved [a]-forms, which for some speakers co-exist alongside the more general forms – a situation recorded for *hold* in South Shields

The soundscape

in Ellis (1889: 673). Typically, the cluster is simplified with the loss of the lateral (7c,f,g). Similarly, GOAT words such as *snow, crow, throw, blow,* and *know* can also be pronounced with an [aː] or [ɑː] vowel in NEVE, echoing the OE forms *snaw, crawe, þrawan, blawan,* and *cnawan.* Such vowels seem mainly confined to older speakers (Watt and Allen 2003: 269; Corrigan et al. 2014: 119), except in the case of *know*, which is widely heard as [naː] across the region (see 3.2.1.2). *Go* and *no* also resemble their OE etymons *gaa* and *na*.[4]

Cold, old, hold, and *told* are also sometimes spelled in such a way as to suggest a diphthong in the region of [aʊ], [əʊ], and even [ɛʊ].

(8) a. Looks canny **cowld** for a hot place like.
 b. **Howld** on a minute.
 c. **Towld** ya.
 d. Just found this git **owld** map from donkey's years ago.
 e. Dunno – it's **cowd** as penguin's chuff here.
 f. Here you go you **owd** nacka. :lol:;)

Nineteenth-century evidence for variation between [aː]-type and [aʊ]-type vowels in this subset can be found in *NW*. For example, 'COWLD, cold; but more frequently *caad*. "It's a *cowld* day." "It's as *caad* as ice"' (Heslop 1892: 189).

We must also note the respelling of *open* as <oppen>.

(9) a. Its **oppen** now man.
 b. SAFC written in ivry inch when cut **oppen**.
 c. Dinnat gan **oppenin** owld wounds.

The <pp> following <o> indicates that an [ɒ]-type vowel is being represented here. Such a pronunciation is recorded as a variant of the word in Wright (1905: 554).

We saw with MOUTH that vowel respellings are often associated with performativity, and this also seems to be the case with GOAT, particularly in relation to the fronted variants represented in (6) which are almost as strongly associated in the region with Newcastle/North Tyneside as [uː] in MOUTH (Pearce 2012: 9–10). For example, in (6e) <cervid> for *covid* appears in an 'impersonation' of the Geordie manager of Newcastle United F.C. justifying a poor performance by the team; in (6f) it is Cheryl Cole who is being lampooned; and the joke in (6g) speaks for itself.

---

[4] Some of the respellings of words in this subset in *NW* overlap with those found on RTG, for example <aad, blaa, caad, craa, knaa, snaa, thraa>.

7.2.3 FACE

Table 7.3 *NEVE variants and respellings of the FACE vowel*

'Typical' NEVE vowel(s)	Local vowel variant(s)	Example RTG respelling(s)
[eː]	[iə ~ ɪə ~ jɛ ~ je] [a] [iː ~ ɪ]	*face* <fyes>; *take* <tyek>; *hame* <hyem> *make* <mack, mak>; *take* <tack, tak> *great* <g(r)eet, g(r)it>; *day* <dee>

This vowel is typically realised in NEVE as the monophthong [eː]. It is unmarked (Watt and Milroy 1999: 40), so we have to assume that standard orthography 'represents' this vowel. Respellings therefore indicate different vowels.

(10) a. The soopa Sunda **feace** off pherto with Fatty and Charver.
 b. The bloke shot himself in the **fyes** with a shotgun.
 c. I heard a local at the match saying "**Tyek** ees **neeeyam**".
 d. Wor rafa needs mer munnie fuck **sayak** man.
 e. Bruce is coming **hyem**.
 f. me dad told me years ago, he was drinking with some danes and he said he was gan **yem** and they couldn't believe it.

(11) a. **Mak** yer minds up. :lol:
 b. Wey man it **taks** months.

(12) a. It blew a **grit** big heavy trampoline, over a 5 foot fence, into my sister's garden.
 b. Just a number mate, mind you a **GREET** BIG NUMBER.
 c. By there's some cack posted on here to read of a **sundee** mornin.
 d. last game of the season in Div 2 in '79 was on a **fridee** neet v Burnley.

The most localised variant is the centring diphthong [ɪə] (approaching [ɛ̣ə] for some speakers). In (10a,b,c,d) it is respelled as <ea, ye>, and <ay>. On RTG, such spellings are often associated with the speech of people from Newcastle and Tyneside. This accords with SED evidence, where diphthongs in FACE are commoner in Nb. than Du. (Orton and Halliday 1963: 1008–1011). The respelling <ye> could also reflect [jɛ] which historically occurred in words in this set (Maguire et al. 2010: 75). *EDG* often records two variants of FACE words in Northumbrian locations – for example, *biək* and *bjek* for *bake*; *giət* and *gjet* for *gate*; *miək* and *mjek* for *make*; *siək* and *sjek* for *sake*. We might also note that the pronunciations [hjɛm] and [jɛm] for *home* (sometimes respelled <hyem>) reflect the fact that in the linguistic North the traditional form of this word is *hame*, preserving the ME unrounded vowel. *Hame* belongs to the

The soundscape 157

FACE set, making the resemblance to Scandinavian forms such as *hjem* coincidental (10e,f).

In (11) the respellings indicate localised pronunciations of *make* and *take* with a pre-GVS [a]-type vowel. SED evidence suggests that traditionally [a] is more frequently found in Durham than it is in Northumberland (Orton and Halliday 1963: 1008–1011). Kerswill (1987: 29) gives the 'Durham vernacular' pronunciation of 'make' and 'take' as [mak] and [tak]. Cooper refers to this vowel as 'short FACE', and notes that it is an enregistered feature of nineteenth-century Yorkshire dialects (2020: 137). The short vowel in *make* and *take* is the origin of the ethnonym *Mackem* (see 2.3).

The front high vowel in *great* is a widespread feature of northern dialects and is recorded in *EDG* for Northumberland and County Durham in nineteenth-century sources, as is a similar vowel in *-day* words (12) (468, 204).

7.2.4 PRICE

Table 7.4 *NEVE variants and respellings of the PRICE vowel*

'Typical' NEVE vowel(s)	Local vowel variant(s)	Example RTG respelling(s)
[aɪ > aɪ]	[ɛi ~ ei ~ aɛ]	*like* <leik>; *shite* <sheite>
	[aː]	*I* <aah>; *my* <mah>
	[iː]	*night* <neet>; *right* <reet>; *died* <deed>

The mainstream northern vowel in the PRICE set – which derives from Middle English /iː/ via the GVS – is a closing diphthong, in the region of [aɪ] (Wells 1982: 149). However, some respellings on RTG suggest a different vowel quality.

(13) a. Mebbies I need to see a psychologist **leik**?
 b. Elmo is **sheite meind**.

Here, <ei> is used to represent an [ɛi]-type diphthong. SED shows a division in Northumbrian locations between [ɛi] and [aɪ], with the marked form occurring in Nb. and the unmarked form in Du. (see phonological maps 103–108 in *LAE*). The proximity of Northumberland to Scotland could be a factor here, since [ɛi]-type vowels in PRICE can also be found in Scottish varieties of English (Wells 1982: 405).[5] It is worth noting that the examples in (13) come from performative contexts in which a poster is 'impersonating' someone from Tyneside, which accords with the distribution given in SED.

---

[5] The presence of [ɛi]-type vowels in PRICE suggests a form of the 'Scottish Vowel Length Rule' (SVLR) is in operation in NEVE (Watt and Ingham 2000).

There is a subset of PRICE consisting of words such as *right, night,* and *light*. The <gh> indicates that they once contained an /h/ phoneme, realised as [ç]. During the Middle Ages, the /h/ was lost, and the preceding vowel was lengthened in compensation, resulting in pronunciations with [i:] which were once general in English but which are now only preserved in certain dialects of northern England and in Scotland.

(14) a. Looks a **reet** mess.
 b. **Reet** so me and a couple of mates ...
 c. **Alreet** bud.
 d. Only had 6 stella so was a**reet** last **neet**.
 e. What you having or had for bait the **neet**?
 f. I dinnat understand why ye felt the need to **leet** a tab up, like.

Beal et al. (2012: 35) suggest words like *night* and *right* take [i:] 'in more conservative varieties' and amongst older male speakers. However, it does occur more widely across the age-range in the fixed phrases 'the neet' (*tonight*) and 'al(l)reet/areet' (*all right* as a greeting), as the examples in (14) demonstrate (see 6.2). We should also note <deed> for *died*. Here, the ME vowel quality is preserved.

(15) a. Thowt he **deed** years ago tbh.
 b. Thought yea must have **deed**.

7.2.5 DRESS

Table 7.5 *NEVE variants and respellings of the DRESS vowel*

'Typical' NEVE vowel(s)	Local vowel variant(s)	Example RTG respelling(s)
[ɛ]	[i:] [ɪ]	*dead* <deed>; *head* <heed> *never* <nivver>; *every* <ivery>; *clever* <clivver>; *chest* <chist>; *ready* <riddy>; *seven* <sivven>

Most speakers of contemporary NEVE have a short [ɛ]-type vowel in this set, which is the mainstream northern – and, indeed, British – vowel (Beal 2004: 121). But some words which belong to the DRESS set in mainstream English can have a different vowel in the region. For example, [i:] is occasionally heard in some monosyllabic words spelled with <ea>, such as *dead* and *head*. On RTG, <ee> is typically used to represent this vowel.

(16) a. Thousands of little **deed** fish along the waterline the neet, when walking from South Bents to Seaburn.
 b. You must store most of your body fat in your **heed**.
 c. I thowt I was gannin' **deef**!

The soundscape

An [iː]-type vowel is also found in contemporary Scots, as in *deid* and *heid* (the <ei> spelling – presumably influenced by Scots orthography – is occasionally found on RTG).

(17) a. Presume Chalky is long **deid**.
     b. Got his **heid** tattooed first n'all.

What are the origins of this? In Middle English there were two long 'e' vowels: /eː/ and /ɛː/ (typically written ē and ẹ̈ by ME scholars). The different historical pronunciation of these vowels has come down to us in a spelling contrast. Some words which had ē are now spelled with the digraph <ee> (as in *teem*), while some words which had ẹ̈ are spelled with the digraph <ea> (as in *team*). In PDE these words are homophones, sharing [iː]. This is the normal development of these ME vowels, via the GVS. However, not all words with ẹ̈ developed in the 'expected' manner in all dialects, because 'in both Middle English and Early Modern English, there was sporadic shortening of long vowels in words of one syllable, especially those ending in a single consonant' (Barber et al. 2009: 204). This shortening was especially prevalent with ẹ̈ and results in the [ɛ] found in words such as *bread, deaf,* and *dead* in most varieties of PDE. But in some dialects (in some ẹ̈ words) this shortening did not happen, and the vowel developed 'normally'; hence the [iː] remains an option in words like *dead* and *head* in some northern varieties of English, particularly in Scotland, but including North East England where it has a long, well-attested history. For example, when the SED fieldworker pointed to his head and asked 'what do you call this?', all but two of the fifteen informants in Northumberland and Durham responded *heed* (Orton and Halliday 1963: 584). Heslop, writing as 'Harry Haldane', pithily points out that 'in reading Chaucer we shall find "head" and "dead" spelled HEED and DEED' (1879: 14).

Similarly, *well* – which typically occurs in the DRESS set in most English varieties – was recorded with an [iː]-type vowel in SED, at various northern locations (Orton and Halliday 1963: 686, 957). This pronunciation is sometimes reflected on RTG.

(18) a. The meal deal is good value **asweel**.
     b. "A'll bray tha **weel**."

EDG records *wīl* across Scotland, the north of England and the north Midlands, suggesting a preservation of the ME vowel quality in this word in regional Englishes (Wright 1905: 672). Evidence of the form's antiquity can be seen in words spoken by Chaucer's Wife of Bath: 'Gat tothed I was / & that bicam me weel'.

The stressed vowel in *never, ever,* and *every* which is typically [ɛ] is sometimes raised to [ɪ] in NEVE. This vowel is also heard in *clever* and *chest*.

EDG shows that such pronunciations were once widely distributed across Scotland, England, and Ireland (379, 425, 540).

(19) a. Heal, thrive & stay for**ivva** egg foo ...
 b. **Nivvor** mind kidda, you can always rely on us for six points.
 c. Only **ivver** seen it the once ower here.
 d. And **ivry** other bugger moves out so there'll be nowt to scavenge.
 e. Put hairs on us **chist** like rusty nails.

7.2.6 LOT/CLOTH

Table 7.6 *NEVE variants and respellings of the LOT/CLOTH vowel*

'Typical' NEVE vowel(s)	Local vowel variant(s)	Example RTG respelling(s)
[ɒ]	[œ]	*job* <jerb>; *dog* <derg>
	[a]	*along* <alang>; *throng* <thrang>
	[ɛ]	*wash* <wesh>
	[ɪ]	*was* <wiz>; *what* <whit>

The mainstream northern vowel in these sets is a low back rounded [ɒ]-type. In NEVE we sometimes encounter [œ(:)], and [a] or [ɛ] in some words which had a (short) /a/ in Old English. An even more lexically restricted [ɪ] can also occasionally be heard.

Some speakers of NEVE have a closer, fronter rounded vowel [œ(:)] in words in these sets, similar to the one in French *jeune* and German *schön*. This is occasionally represented with <er> on RTG.

(20) a. Recommend me a new **jerb**.
 b. Do you have a **derg**?
 c. **Lerg** borna.
 d. prefer **cerd** or hem with chips when in Ashington.
 e. **Terp** blerk.

This fronted variant is first recorded in a collection of dialect speech compiled by Harold Orton between 1928 and 1939 (Rydland 1998). It is also well-attested in SED (see for example the phonological maps for *fox* and *dog* in *LAE*, which locate this vowel in the north of the region). However, it is not mentioned in either Ellis (1889) or *EDG* (Wright 1905). According to Rydland, this does not necessarily mean it is a recent innovation. He suggests that because [œ] 'is not very different from back [o]', it 'could easily have been mistaken for the latter by Wright's and Ellis's sources, most of whom had no phonetic training. In the absence of evidence to the contrary, it may be conjectured that short [œ] developed at an early date, possibly even in early Modern English' (1999: 13).

Another vowel variant in CLOTH, but with better understood origins occurs in some words with orthographic <ong>, such as *long*, *strong*, and *wrong*.

The soundscape 161

(21) a. Anyone wee be**lang**s the town would knarr this.
  b. I'll gan a**lang** with that.
  c. Big **strang** thighs.
  d. Cannit gan **wrang** with a short back & sides & trimmed on the top like.

These respellings represent a pronunciation in which OE short /a/ was preserved before a nasal cluster in the north, rather than rounded to /ɒ/ as it was in the south. Wales comments that such items 'recur so frequently [in writing of northern dialects] as to suggest lexicalisation, and they certainly tend to be (over-) used in stereotypical dialogue' (2010: 70). Evidence for lexicalisation in NEVE can be found in *NW*, where *lang* and *wrang* are given as headwords.

In NEVE *wash* can also preserve an unrounded vowel, but it is an [ɛ]-type spelled with <e> rather than an [a]-type. Heslop also gives it headword status (1893: 770).

(22) a. What's he ganna dee with Bud like? **Wesh** the dog?
  b. Dropping agent orange on the southside to give the residents a **wesh**.

Wright records this pronunciation across Scotland, the north of England, the Midlands, and East Anglia (1905: 667), and it is used by all Northumbrian informants in SED (Orton and Halliday 1963: 565).[6] The respellings <whit> and <wiz(s)> for *what* and *was* are also occasionally found on RTG, representing pronunciations with a close front vowel which have been attested for Scotland (Murray 1873: 219) and which are also recorded in Heslop (1892–1893).

(23) a. **Whit**?
  b. just own up to it, we all nar it **wiz** yay man!!

7.2.7 TRAP/BATH

Table 7.7 *NEVE variants and respellings of the* TRAP/BATH *vowel*

Lexical set	'Typical' NEVE vowel(s)	Local vowel variant(s)	Example RTG respelling(s)
TRAP	[a]	[æ ~ ɛ] [aː]	*Ashington* <Eshington>; *has, had* <hez, hed> *lad* <laad>; *bad* <baad>
BATH	[a]	[ɒː ~ ɑː] [æ ~ ɛ]	*master* <marster>; *plaster* <plarster> *after* <efter>

---

[6] The form represents failure to round historical /a/ in syllables with a /w/-onset. This context 'typically triggers backing and assimilative rounding' (Minkova 2014: 239), resulting in the mainstream pronunciations of words such as *wand* and *watch*. See also the remarks on *water* in 7.2.13.

One of the most well-known accent markers of the north-south divide in England is the quality of the vowel in BATH words. Broadly speaking, in the north and most of the Midlands the typical vowel is an [a]-type and is shared with words in the TRAP set; in the south an innovation which started in the seventeenth century – sometimes referred to as the BATH-TRAP split – lengthened the vowel in BATH to an [ɑːI-type. In common with all varieties of northern English, the typical NEVE vowel in this set remains [a]. There are, however, a few words in which the vowel of the stressed syllable is sometimes longer – typically [ɒː] rather than [ɑː] – and this features in metalinguistic discourse on RTG.

(24) a. We had a very specific "ar" sound in the middle of words like **plarster** and **headmarster** (but only certain words – not glass/grass/bath).
b. Just to be awkward I say '**marster**' and '**plasster**'.
c. I say master and plaster in the same way a Southerner would, but not grass, glass, etc. ... :lol:
d. **Marster** and **Plarster** for me, Durham born and raised.

Wells implies that such pronunciations are due to the influence of 'school and school-inspired standards of correctness' (1982: 354), but this doesn't explain why in the North East a long vowel is largely limited to *master*, *plaster*, and occasionally *disaster*. A more plausible account is supplied by Beal, who argues for 'an internal development ... of the reflexes of ME *ai*' associated with 'burr retraction' (1985: 43) – see 7.3.1.

In NEVE the vowel in TRAP is sometimes lengthened to [aː] if it precedes a voiced consonant/consonant cluster (Wells 1982: 375), particularly in *lad* and *bad*. Here vowel length is determined by phonological environment, as it is in Scottish English. The digraph <aa> is occasionally used on RTG to represent this feature.

(25) a. He seems a canny **laad**.
b. "A **baad** fettle".

Additionally, some speakers have a higher vowel in certain TRAP/BATH words, as reflected in spellings with <e> on RTG.

(26) a. Some of his routines about the **Esh**ington **e**ccent were brilliant.
b. Ah **hev** 2 left.
c. **Hez** 'ee got pineapple balls..???
d. prefer cerd or **hem** with chips when in Ashington.
e. So Ah might well purra Ganzie on and venture up the shops **efter** Chorch in the Morn.

For the south east of England Wright presents widespread evidence of a generally raised TRAP vowel. This phenomenon is rarer in the north,

The soundscape 163

although *EDG* does identify County Antrim (N. Ireland) and parts of eastern Scotland as sites where it is to be found (1905: 22). *EDG* also highlights a raised vowel in Northumberland and County Durham in individual lexical items: *after, ash, axe, fasten, hasp, thank*. In relation to *have* and *has*, Wright notes *ev* and *ez* in Northumberland and County Durham and *hev* and *hez* in Northumberland (1905: 475–476), and all the SED informants from Northumbrian locations have [ɛ] in *have* and *has* (Orton and Halliday 1963: 1046). A raised vowel in *after* is also widely attested in the north, which might be due to early Scandinavian influence (cf. Old Icelandic *eftir*). It is also Scots, as is *esh* (Murray 1873: 109). On RTG posters often associate the raised vowel with the town of Ashington in south east Northumberland, just as the [œ(ː)] in LOT/CLOTH words is linked perceptually to this location.

7.2.8 STRUT

Table 7.8 *NEVE variants and respellings of the STRUT vowel*

'Typical' NEVE vowel(s)	Local vowel variant(s)	Example RTG respelling(s)
[ʊ > ə]	[ɛ]	*curry* <kerry>; *hurry* <herry>; *Durham* <Derram>; *buzz* <bez>
	[a]	*among* <amang>

In northern England, the vowel in this set is [ʊ > ə]. Very occasionally we encounter respellings on RTG which seem to be attempts to capture this mainstream vowel.

(27) a. Just had a **dubble** sossij & egg mcmuffin.
 b. Still think Newcastle are in **trubbel**.

In *double* and *trouble* the standard spelling requires a digraph, but by replacing <ou> with <u> the posters are perhaps making prominent their own pronunciation of the word, which is presumably 'northern' [ʊ]. Alternatively, these might be examples of eye dialect (see 7.1).

In NEVE some words ending orthographically in <urry> (or <orry> as in *worry*), together with the place-name *Durham*, do not always have the expected [ʊ]-vowel in the stressed syllable, but an [ɛ]-type vowel instead, as does *buzz* occasionally (28). The STRUT words *among* and *us* are also respelled on RTG (29).

(28) a. Dinna **werry** Marra.
 b. My dad still gets a prarn **kerry** with extra **kerry** sarse.
 c. **Herry** up will ya.
 d. From **Derram**?
 e. Lost a huge chunk of finger **bezzing** down a hill on mine [a Raleigh 'Chopper' bike].

(29) a. **Amang** other things.
   b. They're watching **iz** dee what?

Forms like *wirry* and *werry* are normal Middle English developments of Old English *wyrgan*. It is possible therefore that *werry* reflects a preservation of the ME pronunciation of this word, which has been extended by analogy to the phonologically similar words *hurry* and *curry* and even *Durham*. However, the dialectological archive seems to be silent on this matter.

The respelling <amang> is easier to account for since it represents the survival of an OE form. Wright records forms in [a] as widespread across the north (1905: 308–9) and SED reports categorical use of *amang* at all Northumbrian locations (Orton and Halliday 1963: 998). It is also Scots.

7.2.9 FOOT

Table 7.9 *NEVE variants and respellings of the* FOOT *vowel*

'Typical' NEVE vowel(s)	Local vowel variant(s)	Example RTG respelling(s)
[ʊ]	[uː]	cook <cewk>; book <bewk>

One of the most well-known indicators of a northern accent in England is the shared [ʊ]-type vowel in words in the STRUT and FOOT lexical sets. But in the North East, as is the case in other parts of northern England, some words ending in orthographic <ook>, which typically have a [ʊ] vowel, have [uː] instead. In the sixteenth and seventeenth centuries words spelled with <oo> that in most dialects now belong to the FOOT set, such as *book*, *cook*, *look*, *took*, *nook*, and *crook* are all recorded with [uː], as are *good*, *stood*, and *foot* (Minkova 2014: 272). Variants with [ʊ] gradually gained ground in the seventeenth century, so that today the vowel has been shortened in most places, but speakers in some locations have preserved the [uː]. *EDG* records both [ʊ] and [uː] in *-ook* words in Northumberland and County Durham (Wright 1905: 145), and similar variation is recorded in SED (see for instance Orton and Halliday 1963: 890).

On RTG there is metalinguistic discourse about the local spatial distribution of these forms, illustrated with respellings.

(30) a. its **cuck buck** not **cewk bewk** :lol:
   b. Oh and pronouncing the oo in words like book and cook so they sound like **boook** and **coook**.
   c. I am 33 years old and pronounce it "**Bewk**" (typical Sunderland pronunciation) informally.

The consensus seems to be that [uː] is more likely to be found in Wearside/County Durham than in Tyneside/Northumberland, where [ʊ~ʊ̈] is believed

The soundscape

to be commoner. The 'Our Dialects' project at the University of Manchester (<https://www.ourdialects.uk/>) found that 85 per cent of the respondents from Tyne and Wear and 83 per cent of respondents from Northumberland claimed to rhyme *book* and *spook* – a much larger proportion than was found in any other part of England. The maps suggest that 'rhymers' are distributed quite evenly across the North East (MacKenzie et al. 2022: 53).

7.2.10 NURSE

Table 7.10 *NEVE variants and respellings of the NURSE vowel*

'Typical' NEVE vowel(s)	Local vowel variant(s)	Example RTG respelling(s)
[ə: > ɜ:]	[ø: ~ ɔ:] [ɑ:] [ə]	*nurses* <norses>; *dirty* <dorty> *German* <Jarman>; *learn* <larn>; *worse* <warse> *first* <fust>; *burst* <bust>

The mainstream North East vowel is an [ə:] or [ɜ:]-type, which most speakers of English in England use in NURSE-words. However, there is considerable social and regional variation in this vowel. Indeed, one of the most well-known shibboleths of North East – particularly 'Geordie' – speech is the so-called 'NURSE-NORTH merger', which has resulted in words like *bird* and *bored* becoming homophones for some speakers, merging on an [ɔ:]-type vowel. The earliest reliable phonetic evidence for NURSE-NORTH homophony is Ellis (1889), but Maguire (2008: 94) also points to respellings in dialect writing and rhymes in dialect poems and songs which indicate it could have been present as early as the mid-1700s. Heslop indicates that the 'merger' is well-established by the late nineteenth century (1892: xxii–xxiii):

> the *ir* and *ur* in the following words become *or*. Bird, sir, first, shirt, fir-tree, &c., are sounded *bord, sor, forst, short, for*-tree; and purse, turn, burn, curse, hurry, &c., are *porse, torn, born, corse, horry*. These rules are applied to all words in which the vowels are sounded as in the examples given.

Interestingly, Heslop does not include here words spelled with <e(a)r>. This is because such words – which developed from Middle English /ɛr/ – had an open [ɑ:]-type reflex. Sometimes, this open reflex becomes the mainstream pronunciation (as in *bark* and *dark*, which descend from the ME /ɛr/-words *berke* and *derc*); sometimes the open reflex is lost to the mainstream but preserved in some traditional dialects. It is still occasionally heard in NEVE in words such as *learn, German*, and *worse*.

On RTG, respellings are used to convey the [ɔ:]-type (31) and, less frequently the [ɑ:]-type (32) vowels sometimes found in NURSE words.

(31) a. what's yer favourite **bord** of prey?
 b. **Forst** I've ever heard of this.
 c. Nivva **hord** orrit.
 d. You'd have to assume Chrissy boy has loosened the **Porse** strings like.
 e. **Torn** reet and gan roond tha roondboot.
 f. Bit of a **bornt** fyace meself Jeff.
 g. Haway **dorty** Leeds!
 h. some strange gannin ons where the **chorch** is concerned;)

(32) a. **Larned** when Ah liv'd in Weshington, that good Pee is high in Nitrogen.
 b. How many **Jarmins** have turned out for the lads?
 c. yer could have **sarved**-up a massive English Chicken Casserole with a Pund of chicken legs.
 d. thas nowt **warse**, but when we win the league it'll be areet.
 e. ffs it's getting **warse**.

A well-known comic guide to North East dialect is called *Larn Yersel' Geordie* (Dobson 1969). The same vowel is reflected in the respelling <warse> for *worse*. This has a long history, as shown in a moving couplet from a song published in Newcastle in 1827 in which a doctor tells a pitman's wife that she has incorrectly administered her husband's enema: 'Stead of making him better, you've sure made him warse, / For you've put in his mouth what should gone up his a—e' (Armstrong 1827, in Hermeston 2009: 74). The rhyme is instructive here.

The development of [ɔː] in NURSE is possibly a consequence of the unusual uvular quality of /r/ in the traditional dialects of North East England (see 7.3.1), which had a retracting and rounding effect on the preceding vowel.

There is also the possibility that <or> reflects another attested NEVE variant for the vowel in NURSE, which is a front rounded [øː]-type – a relatively recent development described by Watt and Milroy as a 'compromise' vowel, associated particularly with young women (1999: 28). But since this vowel is phonetically quite close to mainstream [ɜː], it is perhaps unlikely that this is a target vowel for respellings with <or>.

We also observe some NURSE words ending with <rst>, such as *burst* and *first*, respelled to capture the shortened [əː] sometimes heard in these contexts.

(33) a. a tin of Roses - what gans **fust** in your house?
 b. Always something sad about a **bust** football.

The vowel [ə] is recorded for *first* in SED locations in Du. (Orton and Halliday 1963: 763).

7.2.11 FLEECE

Table 7.11 *NEVE variants and respellings of the FLEECE vowel*

'Typical' NEVE vowel(s)	Local vowel variant(s)	Example RTG respelling(s)
[iː > ɪi]	[ɛi ~ ei]	*cheesy* <cheysey>; *beetroot* <beat rewt>; *ye(e)* <yay>

The mainstream vowel in the north of England in the FLEECE set is a high front [iː] or [i]-type monophthong, and this is the typical NEVE vowel. In open syllables (in words like *three, knee,* and *see*) the diphthong [ɪi] is also heard, and perhaps occasionally represented orthographically on RTG with <eee, eeee>, as in 'Torkey borgas for wa **teeee**'.

Beal et al. (2012: 34) also note the presence of [ei] across the region, but with a tendency for it to occur more frequently in the south. Such diphthongal variants are evident in the nineteenth-century dialectological record: Ellis remarks on what he terms a 'peculiar fracture' in words such as *me, green,* and *meat* across Cumberland, Westmorland, and the south of County Durham (1889: 538). And in SED, diphthongal realisations (e.g. [ɛi] for the vowel in *green* and *cheese*) are also recorded for locations in the south and west of that county (see phonological maps 93 and 94 in *LAE*). It seems this geographical distribution has continued to the present day. In my perceptual dialectology findings, mainstream monophthongal vowels are associated with Newcastle and the north of the region, while diphthongs are associated with County Durham and Sunderland (see Table 2.3). On RTG one FLEECE word sometimes respelled to represent a diphthong is *cheese* (but only in the context of 'cheesy chips' – a culinary delicacy associated with Sunderland). In (34a) 'they' refers to people from Newcastle, some of whom regard both the dish and the diphthong in *cheesy* as indexical of Sunderland identity. Commenting on this gastronomic/linguistic association, one of my informants from Newcastle wrote 'there is the cheesy peas thing where they [speakers from Sunderland] pronounce it cheasy peas (where both rhyme!)' (Pearce 2012: 12). We should also note respellings which represent local pronunciations of the vernacular pronoun *yee*, which in some stressed conditions has this diphthong, and is typically spelled <yay>, or more rarely <yea(h)> (see 3.4.1.3).

(34) a. They reckon we say **cheysey** chips and blew pop. :lol:
 b. I think the mags say chizzy chips and baloo pop. Whereas we all know it should be **cheysey** and blew.

(35) a. **Yay** can dee it in me backyard for 10 grand marra.
 b. Telt **yays**.
 c. Chance to live rent free in Brighton, I will **dae** owt.
 d. **nay** wonder Brucey looked surprised.

The respellings in (35a,b) probably represent the same diphthong recorded in this word in *EDG* for south Durham, which Wright transcribes as *jei* (1905: 691). A similar vowel can sometimes be heard in *dee*, represented in (35c) with <ae> (see 3.2.2) and *nee*, represented in (35d) with <nay> (see 3.5.2).

7.2.12 GOOSE

Table 7.12 *NEVE variants and respellings of the* GOOSE *vowel*

'Typical' NEVE vowel	Local vowel variant(s)	Example RTG respelling(s)
[uː]	[ʉː ~ əʉ]	*skewel* <skewel>; *boots* <beuts>; *beetroot* <beat rewt>

For most NEVE speakers, the vowel associated with this set is an [uː]-type, as it is in most accents of English in England. However, some variation has been noted in the region. Burbano-Elizondo (2008: 292) reports on widespread use of mainstream monophthongal [uː], but also found fronted monophthongs which she describes as [ʉː] or [ʏː] or very occasionally [əː]. On RTG, this is perhaps captured in respellings of GOOSE words using <ew> or, more rarely, <eu>.

(36)   a. **Fewls** rush in.
       b. You from Hartle**pewl**?
       c. Beet roooooot on one side. Beat **rewt** on the other.
       d. How do you pronounce it? **Mewn**?
       e. I probably love a greggs pasty as much as you love a good old portion of cheysey peas with a **spewn**.
       f. They reckon we say cheysey chips and **blew** pop. :lol:
       g. Fine pair of **beuts**.

It is also possible that <ew> is being used to represent a diphthong. Burbano-Elizondo records some rare diphthongal realisations of the GOOSE vowel, in the region of [əu] or [əʉ], 40 per cent of which occurred in the word *school*. Some RTG respellings of *school* (and words rhyming with *school*) which use <ew(w)e> are possibly more likely than <ew> and <eu> to be attempts to capture this diphthong.

(37)   a. Burra use to gan to **skewel** (Hudson Rard Juniors) wirra lass called Theresa Green.
       b. Heaven forbid anyone who might say skool instead of **scewwel**. :lol:
       c. Well done to you for garn to **scewel**.
       d. **Fewel** hasn't worked out how to stop the Green Bay passing game.
       e. Sunlun f***ing **rewel**.
       f. It's **cewel** man.

The soundscape 169

EDG records diphthongal variants of the vowel in *school* for locations in Northumberland and County Durham (Wright 1905: 585–586).

As we saw in Chapter 2, different vowel qualities in GOOSE words – especially *school* – are believed to distinguish people from Sunderland and Newcastle (see Table 2.3).

7.2.13 THOUGHT, NORTH, FORCE

Table 7.13 *NEVE variants and respellings of the* THOUGHT/NORTH/FORCE *vowel*

Lexical set	'Typical' NEVE vowel(s)	Local vowel variant(s)	Example RTG respelling(s)
THOUGHT	[ɔː]	[aː ~ ɑː] [a ~ ɑ] [aʊ]	*talk* <taalk>; *fall* <faal> *water* <watta>; *scald* <scad> *daughter* <dowter>; *thought* <thowt>; *Houghton* <Howton>
NORTH/FORCE	[ɔː]	[aʊ] [aː] [ɒ]	*four* <fower> *sauce* <sarce> *horse* <hoss>; *sauce* <soss>

Because NEVE is non-rhotic, words in THOUGHT (e.g. *caught, fraught, gnaw, walk*) and words in NORTH/FORCE (e.g. *fork, horse, lord, floor, worn*) typically share the same [ɔː]-type vowel, which is mainstream across the north of England. However, there is some variation in NEVE within these sets which is sometimes captured on RTG.

THOUGHT has two historical subsets: DRAW (made up of words such as *claw, draw, law, thaw*) and FALL (*all, ball, call, fall, salt, talk, walk, bald, scald*, etc.). The vowel in DRAW words is derived from northern Middle English /au/; the vowel in FALL words is derived from /a/+/l/(C) (Rydland 1999: 9). In NEVE, FALL words sometimes preserve this historical form, which can still be heard in the speech of working-class males (Maguire 2008: 215–216). In spelling it is typically represented by the <aa> digraph.

(38) a. She can **taalk** under watta.
 b. I'd rather **waalk**.
 c. Preferably, a CB!!! (Not RB, Onuoha) who can heed the **baall**.
 d. So-called because they winnit **faall** off.
 e. Divennt **caal** me a Southern Jessie.
 f. "Stop stottin' the **baall** off me **waall**".
 g. Agree, he'd be bowkin **aal** ower.
 h. Not in the market for a haircut (**baald**) but wouldn't mind a shave and that nose thing.
 i. Bruce is from Corbridge but was brought up in **Waalsend**.

Occasionally, <ar> is used (usually – but not always – in words of 'non-native' stock).

(39) a. Two seats, 4 **smarl** bags £91.
 b. Cruise is owa **tarl**, man.
 c. My dad still gets a **prarn** kerry with extra kerry **sarse**.
 d. Go on say **prarn** sarnie with a **strar**biree myilk shyake.
 e. Basically sausages should only be enhanced by English mustard or Chop **sarce**.
 f. Ah went to the shops to buy some **sarse**. The man says "HP?" Ah says nor I'll pay for it.

Some DRAW words have fallen in with FALL words in the north, hence respellings like the following.

(40) a. he'd asked one of the lads what the score was, he said "it was a **draa**".
 b. Me fatha would've eloquently put it as "That bloke from Friends has turned up in a **claa** hammer coat!"
 c. Say nowt an **sar** wood.

Occasionally, we encounter spellings suggesting a shorter vowel [a~ɑ].

(41) a. She can taalk under **watta**.
 b. You can socialise on pints of **watta**.
 c. A cup of **scad** and several slices of white bread.
 d. it was hotter than the earths f***ing core, f***ing **scadded** my gob!

Across northern England ['watə, 'wata] are well-known pronunciations of *water* which preserve the ME unrounded vowel quality.[7] The short vowel in *water* and *sca(l)d* is also found in Scotland and the north of Ireland.

In THOUGHT words ending in orthographic <ght>, sometimes the quality of the ME diphthong /au/ has been preserved, typically as [aʊ] (though the fricative has of course been lost). This is represented on RTG with the spelling <ow>.

(42) a. Well I **thowt** it was funny.
 b. me **dowter** tried to fill up the oil in her car through the dipstick barrel.
 c. I've **bowt** some wax to hoy owa the sharp edge.
 d. Anar **nowt** and what anar ye **towt** us.
 e. Wish ad **browt** me brolly.
 f. Snarmaggedon in **Howton** [Houghton] like.

The number *four*, which belongs to the modern NORTH/FORCE set can also share this vowel in NEVE.

---

[7] As Tony Harrison remarks in 'Them & [uz]', for northern poets like himself or William Wordsworth '*matter/water* are full rhymes'.

The soundscape

(43) a. I was there when we got beat **fower** nowt on telly!!
 b. If you mean gilets, I've got **fower**.
 c. Last player to get **fowa** in a game?
 d. Neen, nee bairns nee marriage and I'm **fowty** this year.

The pronunciation represented here is presumably ['faʊə] or ['faʊɐ]. In the stressed syllable of *four*, [aʊ] or [ɒʊ] was recorded at Northumbrian locations in SED (Orton and Halliday 1963: 750), and [aʊ] was also noted by Wright (1905: 452). On RTG we also encounter respellings of *more*.

(44) a. **Mer** posh than that, Wardley.
 b. Nee one keeps Budgies nee **mair**.

The vowel implied here is [ɛː] or possibly [ɛə]. *EDG* records the diphthong in south Northumberland and County Durham and the monophthong in south east Northumberland (Wright 1905: 531). Spellings like those in (44) echo forms going back to the Middle English period in the north (see 3.5.2).

Horse is also respelled to indicate an [ɒ]-type vowel.

(45) a. didnt someone ride a **hoss** into B and M at Houghton, or is that an urban myth?
 b. good luck on the **hosses**.

<Hoss> (cf. Old High German *hros* and Old Icelandic *hross*) captures a vowel pronunciation widely recorded in dialects of English (see Wright 1905: 490). In SED, [hɒs] and [ɒs] are the prevalent forms in Du. (Orton and Halliday 1963: 88–92).

7.2.14 PALM, START

Table 7.14 *NEVE variants and respellings of the PALM/START vowel*

Lexical set	'Typical' NEVE vowel(s)	Local vowel variant(s)	Example RTG respelling(s)
PALM	[aː > ɑː]	[ɒː ~ ɔː] [a]	*half* <hawf>; *father* <fatha>
START	[aː > ɑː]	[ɒː ~ ɔː]	*car* <cor>; *start* <stort>

The non-rhoticity of NEVE means that words in PALM and START share the same [ɑː]-type vowel. Words belonging to START historically had postvocalic /r/ and this is retained in their spelling (as in *start, car, barn,* etc.). On RTG, some START words are respelled to convey a rounder vowel in the region of [ɒː], which is sometimes used in NEVE in words in this set (Beal et al. 2012: 36).

(46) a. "Well Ando, d ya not think he should **stort** Andy Carrall now?"
 b. Jesus was born in a **born**.
 c. Why don't we find it funny when they ask for a **Mors Bor**.

As with [ɔː] in NURSE, 'burr retraction' (7.3.1) is possibly implicated in the development of [ɔː] in START. Some words in PALM, despite the absence of etymological /r/, also have [ɔː], represented on RTG as <or> or <aw>.

(47) a. Me **maw** makes great pies.
 b. Radiuur Newcassel, **Hawf** teyme heyleyts!!

EDG records [ɔː]-type vowels in *half* for Northumbrian locations (Wright 1905: 471–472) and in *EDD hawf* is given as a form of *half* in Northumberland, Cumberland, and Yorkshire.

In relation to the PALM word *father*, spellings such as <fatha> almost certainly indicate an [a]-type vowel in the stressed syllable which has a long history in NEVE (see Wright 1905: 431). In SED, ['faðə] is the prevalent form in Du. (Orton and Halliday 1963: 869).

(48) a. Me **Fatha** used to sleep starkers.
 b. Me **fathas** there.

The short /a/ in *father* echoes the earliest form of the word recorded in Northumbrian Old English: *fador* (in the Lindisfarne Gospels).

7.2.15 CURE

Table 7.15 *NEVE variants and respellings of the CURE vowel*

'Typical' NEVE vowel(s)	Local vowel variant(s)	Example RTG respelling(s)
[uə > ʊə]	[uɐ]	*pure* <pyuwah>

The mainstream North East vowel in this set is the centring diphthong [uə], in contrast to monophthongal [ɔː]-types prevailing in the south, where the lexical sets CURE and FORCE have merged. Sometimes the second element is more open, resulting in [uɐ]. In NEVE, words in this set which are normally monosyllabic become disyllabic for some speakers, resulting in pronunciations like ['pju.ɐ] for *pure* and ['pu.ɐ] for *poor* (rhyming with *fewer/sewer*). On RTG, words such as *pure, poor,* and *sure* are sometimes respelled with <ah> or <a> to convey the quality of the vowel in the second element of the diphthong (or in a disyllabic pronunciation the vowel in the final syllable). The roundedness of the first vowel can also be conveyed with <w>, while <y> is sometimes used to represent the yod in *pure* (see 3.7.1.4 for *pure* as an intensifier).

The soundscape 173

(49) a. "Hya meee Granda **pyuah** where's [wears] them man".
 b. **Pyuwah** shithousery.
 c. It's **pyuwa** Matty not pure.
 d. **Puah** bantz that like.
 e. **Puwah** nyucassal.
 f. "Yannow……wuh didn't give wurselves a chance. That's fah **shoowa**".

SED records disyllabic pronunciations of *sure* in County Durham (Orton and Halliday 1963: 1067).

7.2.16 NEAR

Table 7.16 *NEVE variants and respellings of the* NEAR *vowel*

'Typical' NEVE vowel(s)	Local vowel variant(s)	Example RTG respelling(s)
[iə]	[ə:] [ia]	*years* <yerz> *beer* <beeah, beeya>

In NEVE, the most typical vowel in NEAR words is the centring diphthong [iə], but for some speakers – as we saw with CURE – these words become disyllabic, sometimes with [j] (rather than [w]) as a hiatus breaker. In (50a,b) it seems that <-> is used to indicate a syllable boundary, and in (d) and (e) we see <y> for [j].

(50) a. Finish ya **bee-ah**, grab wa bairns, wa gannin' on wa holly-bobs!
 b. **CHEE-AZ** TOE KNEE AV HAD A REET LAFF MAN! A REET LAFF!
 c. Was trying to remember the tattoo blerk. **Cheeaz**.
 d. Hoy the hamma owa **heeya** hinny.
 e. **Beeya**, Shirley?

We also see some variation in the NEAR word *year(s)*, as pointed out in this comment which suggests [jə:z] is found on Wearside and [jɛ:z] on Tyneside.

(51) I'll be honest, to me the South Shields accent sounds Geordie for the most part but has some Mackem inflections such as the pronunciation of *'years'* which is phonetically more like **YERZ** (same as Sunderland) and unlike **YAIRZ** (Newcastle).

There is some dialectological evidence to support this claim. In SED, half of the eighteen elicitations of *year(s)* resulted in [jə:(z)] in Du., whereas none of the twenty-seven elicitations in Nb. produced this vowel (Orton and Halliday 1963: 778–779, 793).

7.2.17 SQUARE and CHOICE

In NEVE there is little of dialectological interest in relation to the vowels in these lexical sets, which tend to be [ɛ:] and [ɔɪ] respectively. One exception is illustrated in (52).

(52) a. Haway, have a **choss** day everyone.
 b. Standy-up slides? Where you ran and slid on your feet? **Choss** them.
 c. Blink 182 were **chos** man! :cool: ...

Choice is a venerable slang adjective meaning 'excellent' – these respellings represent a local pronunciation with an [ɒ] vowel.

7.2.18 Unstressed vowels

Unstressed vowels can have a distinctive quality in NEVE (Moisl and Maguire 2008: 61), as illustrated in these RTG respellings of words ending in *-er*.

(53) a. "wu deserve **betta**. wu desoaaarve a trophy".
 b. **Troosaz** not talking to ya shoes?
 c. "Can a yooose tha **computa** to gan on the SMB and wind the mackems up like".
 d. And the bloke who hoyed beer at club legend **peetah** Reed.
 e. They might not buy him any new **playaz** if he upsets them.
 f. Alreet? Whee, ya **fuckaz**.

The examples in (53) reflect the fact that in NEVE the quality of the unstressed vowel in lettER words is [ɑ~ɛ] (Wells 1982: 376) or [ɐ] (Beal et al. 2012: 36), rather than the [ə] found in most other non-rhotic accents of British English. The origins of this vowel quality can be ascribed to the influence of the highly distinctive [ʁ] which historically followed the vowel in lettER words (Wells 1982: 376). As we saw in relation to the NURSE-NORTH merger (7.2.10), uvular /r/ can have a powerful backing and rounding effect on a preceding vowel, hence the traditional forms [ɔʁ, ɔ̞] in lettER words recorded in Ellis and SED (Maguire 2008: 124), and occasionally found on RTG (e.g. *nivvor, ivvor*). The present-day forms [ɑ~ɛ~ɐ] come about when the rounding and backing influence of [ʁ] is lost due to the absence of post-vocalic /r/.

When is the vowel quality captured in the respellings in (53) first recorded in the dialectological literature? Not in the SED. For Northumbrian locations, *-er* words (e.g. *adder, flowers, mourners*) generally end in [ɔʁ] in Nb. and [ə~əʁ] in Du. (Orton and Halliday 1963). Given that in Ellis and Wright there is also no evidence of the [ɑ~ɛ~ɐ] vowel quality which is so salient in contemporary NEVE, we might assume it is a relatively recent innovation.

The soundscape

However, in the earliest known audio recordings of voices from the North East (which were made in 1916–1917 in German prisoner of war camps and are available through the British Library – see 2.2.3) a male speaker from South Shields born in 1892 pronounces *hunger* as [ˈhʊŋɐ], although '[ə] is the most common form across the four recordings' (Watt and Foulkes 2017: 156). Here is early evidence of the effect of burr retraction on the preceding vowel.

We also see respellings of di-syllabic words ending in *-ow*. And occasionally *piano*.

(54) a. So if we don't **folla** ya rules, we can't take part?
 b. Ye can **borra** mine, if ye like, Cluffy, son.
 c. You've got nee **marras** that's why.
 d. Chin up, **fella**.
 e. The wheel come off me **barra** as well of course.
 f. People who live in Hebburn want to live in **Jarra** [Jarrow] but aren't lucky enough.
 g. Morning, me owld cock **sparra**.
 h. Help! Me fuckin **pianna**'s on fire!

The vowel represented by <a> here is typically [ə] (occasionally [ɑ~ɐ] in NEVE) and was recorded by Wright as widespread in dialect speech across the country (1905: 211).

We might also note in this context that on RTG the placename *Penshaw* is sometimes spelled <Pensha> or <Pensher>, with <a> and <er> standing for [ə].

7.2.19 HappY

The unstressed vowel in happY is generally [i] in NEVE, particularly in the north of the region, where it might be longer in duration than further south (Beal et al. 2012: 36–37). On RTG this is reflected in the respelling of *Geordie*, especially when the intent is to be abusive towards Tynesiders and/or their speech (see also 7.1).

(55) a. I don't know anyone from Whitburn who talks even remotely that **jawdee**.
 b. "There'll be 52,000 screaming **jawdeez**..."

7.2.20 Epenthetic vowels

Vowel epenthesis is a phonological process involving the insertion of a vowel into a consonant cluster. Epenthesis occurs in Irish varieties of English, but it is unlikely that this feature was 'imported' into NEVE via Irish migration, as is sometimes claimed, since it has also been a feature – albeit a rare one – of English and Scots dialects throughout their histories. Maguire (2018: 495) notes that North East England (specifically Northumberland and the north of County Durham) 'was traditionally a hotspot for epenthesis'. Pronunciations such as [wəɹəmz] for *worms* and [beːʁən] for *bairn* (Orton and Halliday 1963: 429, 870) are rarely heard today, due to the loss of postvocalic /r/, but an epenthetic vowel can be found in the /lm/ cluster in the word *film*, which is sometimes respelled on RTG. *Blue* is also occasionally respelled to indicate epenthesis.

(56)   a. Best **fillum** ive seen in a while.
      b. Which **fillim**?
      c. I think the mags say chizzy chips and **baloo** pop.

EDG records epenthesis in the word *film* from Aberdeen in the north to Devon in the south (Wright 1905: 438).

7.3 Consonants

While the inventory of consonant phonemes accords with other varieties of English in England, NEVE shows some interesting realisational variation in relation to /r/, voiceless stops, /h/, and /l/ (Beal et al. 2012: 37–42). However, as was mentioned in 7.1, some of this variation can be challenging to capture in respelling (though it does sometimes become the subject of metalinguistic commentary).

7.3.1 /r/

In North East England today, /r/ is an alveolar approximant [ɹ], as it is in most parts of the country. However, metalinguistic discussions on RTG indicate some level of awareness of a sound which was once regarded as '*the* characteristic' of Northumberland speech (and was also present in other parts of the region): the so-called 'Northumberland/Northumbrian burr' (Ellis 1889: 641–644). The burr is a uvular pronunciation of /r/, transcribed as [ʁ] or occasionally [R] (for reference, [ʁ] is the default realisation of /r/ in French). This feature, which has been the subject of commentary since the early eighteenth century, is highly recessive.[8] Despite its rarity, it is occasionally referred to on RTG, typically in threads devoted to linguistic topics.

---

[8] In an oft-cited passage from volume 3 of his *Tour Thro' the Whole Island of Great Britain*, Daniel Defoe describes the natives of Northumberland as having 'difficulty in pronouncing the Letter R, which they cannot deliver from their Tongues without a hollow Jarring in the Throat' (1727: 196). But his first published reference to the phenomenon appears in *Mere Nature Delineated*, a pamphlet on the subject of 'Peter the Wild Boy', a so-called 'feral child' discovered in a German forest. In his account, he mentions a young woman

The soundscape 177

(57) a. The Northumbrian Burr has almost died out now. Although some young lads use it if they do an impression of old folk. My granny's rolled Rs were so broad I used to think she had a speech impediment when I was a kid.
b. the 'Northumbrian burr': that throat-clearing sound still heard north of the Tyne.
c. we would always stop and ask directions from the oldest guy we could find just to hear the Northumbrian dialect, even if we knew exactly where we were going. It was so different from the "Geordie" accent because they rolled their "R's" and was far more guttural.

These comments place the burr mainly in the past, or in the mouths of the elderly, accurately reflecting the situation as described in the dialectological record – see for example Påhlsson (1972), and Maguire, who reports that while [ʁ] can still be heard in the speech of older men in remote Northumberland locations like Lindisfarne, 'it will not be long before this unique feature of the dialects of north-east England disappears' (2017: 101). The sound is hardly ever captured in respelling on RTG, presumably because of its rarity, but also because 'English orthography has no way of representing uvular fricatives' (Honeybone 2020: 225). Nevertheless, one poster, in what they describe as a 'poor attempt' does use <g> for the /r/ in the initial clusters /kr/ and /pr/ to convey the velar/uvular quality of the burr (Craster is a village on the Northumberland coast).

(58) **Pgonounced Cgaster**, of course.

These spellings have a striking appearance, given that /pg/ and /kg/ are impermissible onsets in English.
One other variant of /r/ is mentioned on RTG.

(59) a. There used to be a groundsman at Whitburn Cricket Club who came from Thompson road area. He called the big roller the **voarla**. I've known plenty of Sunderland folk who have this speech quirk.
b. My brothers partner speaks like this. She has a thick mackem accent. Ewa **tevvy** [Terry] purra bet on the orses **buvvees** [but his] mate **fvom** werk **davven** [Darren] arny bets on the dogs. Is a typical sentence she might say.
c. It's not a V sound. I know what the OP means in terms of the way some people pronounce their Rs but it doesn't sound like a V. I can't describe what it sounds like mind.
d. It's like a really soft W, only half pronounced.

brought up by her deaf sisters whose speech was delayed; when she eventually learned to speak 'she spoke always like a Foreigner; and particularly it was remarkable, that she found great Difficulty in pronouncing some of the Letters of the Alphabet, as the *R* especially, which she always pronounced as the *Northumbrians* do, and which is therefore called, the *Northumberland R*, speaking in the Throat, and harsh, like *Ghr*' (1726: 76).

While it is not possible to be certain about what is intended by <v> here, it seems likely that it represents a labiodental approximant [ʋ] (a 'soft W, only half pronounced' sums it up elegantly). The use of the word 'quirk' is interesting. In English, this sound is often regarded as a speech defect, infantilism, or affectation (Foulkes and Docherty 2000: 31). The discussion from which the posts in (59) are taken was split between people who regarded the pronunciation as 'wrong', and those who claimed it was a part of the Sunderland accent. There is, indeed, some dialectological evidence to suggest it has been a variant of /r/ in the region (albeit a rare one) for some time. For example, Ellis (1889) claims that North and South Shields 'are celebrated for not pronouncing the letter (r)', going on to describe the quality of /r/ there as a 'stiff lip trill' – which he writes as (W) and describes elsewhere as a 'defective lip trill' (1869: 9). Ellis claims that although this sound is 'naturally confounded with (w) by ordinary ears ... the speaker always feels the difference between (w, W), for the sides of the upper lip are inflated for (w), but not at all for (W)' (1889: 664–665). In modern phonetic terms it seems that Ellis is describing a bilabial fricative [β] or the labiodental approximant [ʋ].⁹

/r/ is also significant in NEVE because of the effect the uvular variant has had on nearby sounds. For example, it has been associated with the so-called NURSE-NORTH merger (see 7.2.10) in which the vowel in NURSE words was retracted to [ɔː] prior to loss of rhoticity in the dialect (Beal 2004: 126). This process of 'burr-modification' (Påhlsson 1972: 20) is also implicated in vowel variation in START (7.2.14), CURE (7.2.15), NEAR (7.2.16), and lettER (7.2.18), as well as in localised pronunciations of *plaster* and *master* (7.2.7).

7.3.2 /p t k/

A widely cited feature of NEVE is the glottalisation or glottal reinforcement of the voiceless stops /p t k/, described by Wells (1982: 374) as 'glottal masking of the oral plosive bursts' and Gimson as 'oral closure reinforced by a glottal closure' (1989: 159). These double articulations – typically transcribed as [ʔ͡p], [ʔ͡t], [ʔ͡k] – mainly occur intervocalically. They were not recorded in SED, though they are 'frequently reported in the literature as a characteristic feature of Newcastle and Tyneside English' (Beal et al. 2012: 38). It is, however, difficult to know how they could be represented using the orthographic resources available in the context of online writing, so unsurprisingly they do not seem to feature on RTG as respellings.

---

[9] The picture is complicated by the presence, amongst younger speakers recorded in urban contexts throughout England (including Newcastle), of a [ʋ] for /r/ which has been ascribed to regional dialect levelling (see Foulkes and Docherty 2000). However, since the comments on RTG do not refer to young people it is more likely that posters have in mind the older sound described by Ellis.

7.3.3 /h/

In contrast to double articulations of /p t k/, variation in relation to /h/ is represented on RTG.

(60) a. **oy** the **amma** owa **eeya inny** [hoy the hammer over here hinny]
b. I'm from **Artlepool** [Hartlepool] speak English man :lol:
c. "I'm garn back to the **'ouse**. I've got a reet **angowa** off the beer".
d. She used to read the "**Hecho**", eat "**heggs**" and any other word that began with a vowel was always pronounced with an "h" at the start.
e. Remember a guy who loved talking about 1973, especially beating **Harsenal** at **Illsborough**.

The deletion of /h/ at the start of stressed syllables – described by Wells as 'the single most powerful pronunciation shibboleth' in the country (1982: 254) – is widespread in England. However, so-called 'h-dropping' – as represented in (60a,b,c) – is particularly salient in North East England because Newcastle, unusually for a large city, is associated with the retention of the glottal fricative, while its deletion is seen as a marker of Sunderland speech (Hughes et al. 2005: 66; Beal 2000: 352).

How long has this intra-regional contrast been a feature of the dialectological landscape? We can be sure it goes back to at least the middle of the nineteenth century, based on Heslop's remarks in a paper he gave at a meeting of the Newcastle Society of Antiquaries.

> The South Shields man is jealous of his aspirate and never omits it, whilst his neighbour at Sunderland is reckless of the matter, and talks of Hartlepool as "Aht-le-powl." (Heslop 1885: 93)

SED (as summarised by Burbano-Elizondo 2008) shows that County Durham was an area where /h/ was variably dropped (although it was retained in Northumberland), and analysis of data from the Millennium Memory Bank component of the British Library's accent and dialect recordings associates *h*-dropping with south west County Durham and a narrow coastal strip extending as far north as Sunderland (Pearce 2009: 183). Interestingly, Burbano-Elizondo's research shows that despite its high perceptual salience (see Table 2.3), *h*-dropping appears to be less common in Sunderland than might be expected, although it is more common than on Tyneside (2008: 215–216).

Examples (60d,e) illustrate a further aspect of variability in /h/. Some speakers who perceive *h*-dropping to be stigmatised engage in hypercorrection, inserting /h/ where it is not normally found.

7.3.4 Alveolarisation of velar nasals

A common feature of varieties of English around the world is the shift of /ŋ/ > [n̩] (popularly known as 'g-dropping') in words like *running* and *walking*. In spoken NEVE this shift is almost categorical and is therefore quite often represented on RTG.

(61) a. Fuck knows what they were **deein'** like.
 b. I'm **shittin'** mesel.

7.3.5 [t] → [tʲ] → [tʃ]

On RTG we occasionally encounter spellings such as the following: <chew> for *tew*, <chebble, cheble> for *table*, and <chetty, chatty> for *tatie/tatty*.

(62) a. I can't be **chewed** following people on social media.
 b. Someone's hoyed a **chebble** in the sleck.
 c. Roast **Chetties**. Lush.

Here, it appears *tew, table,* and *taties* have been respelled to indicate an initial [tʃ] rather than [t].[10] The spelling of *tew* reflects a general development beginning in EME in which /j/, when it followed alveolar obstruents like [s] and [t], was absorbed into the consonant, with outcomes such as [sj-] > [ʃ], as in *sugar*; [dj-] > [dʒ], as in *dune*, and [tj-] > [tʃ], as in *tune* (Minkova 2014: 143; see also Beal et al. 2020). Some posters on RTG seem to prefer <t> rather than <ch> (suggesting a pronunciation closer to [tj] than [tʃ]), but they are in the minority.

(63) Can't be **tewed** with another warning.

The process behind *cheb(b)le* and *chetty/chatty* is phonologically different, associated with the palatalisation of the on-glide in the traditional diphthong in words in the FACE set (see 7.2.3). *Cheble* is a rare variant of *table* on RTG, occurring mainly in expressions comparing penises with table legs (see 5.2). It is not recorded in this form in *EDD* or SED, though *tyeble* with 'intermediate' [tj] orthographically represented as <ty> appears in *The Pitman's Pay* (1826–1830). *Chetty* and *chatty* as variants of *tatie* and *tattie* ('potato') are also unrecorded in nineteenth-century sources, though spellings in <ty> occur in printed material going back to before the Second World War

---

[10] *Tew* is a traditional dialect word (see Chapter 5) defined in *EDD* as 'To annoy, vex; to tease, importune, pester; to urge, persuade.' The phrase 'can't be tewed' is the equivalent of 'can't be bothered', while 'a chew on' is an annoying or bothersome situation or task (cf. 'clart on' – see 6.5).

The soundscape 181

('Dorfy', whose dialect column appeared regularly in South Shields newspapers, uses <tyetty> in 1936, for example).

7.4 Connected speech processes

As we saw in Chapter 1, there are four main categories of connected speech processes (natural phonetic changes to word forms which occur in spontaneous speech): deletion, insertion, modification, and reduction. Most of these are common to all varieties of spoken English (see 1.1.1.). However, some are associated with particular dialects. In NEVE we encounter the modification known as T-to-R (7.4.1), and the more localised insertion of intervocalic /v/ in specific contexts (7.4.2).

7.4.1 T-to-R

On RTG, respelling is used to indicate a geographically widespread and frequent feature of northern and midland varieties of English in which [ɹ] replaces [t] in foot-internal intervocalic position, usually across word boundaries in high frequency words with historic short vowels, resulting in outputs such as *ge*[ɹ] *off*, *ge*[ɹ] *in*, *shu*[ɹ] *up* (Wells 1982: 370). There is a small core of words that have been found to undergo this process in all dialects that have been studied, although as Honeybone et al. point out, while it is clear all dialects with T-to-R share these words, 'different dialects may have slightly different inventories of words which undergo the process' (2017: 97). Buchstaller et al. suggest that 'a full list of the lexical items which have been claimed to permit T-to-R takes up relatively little space', going on to record 'every word that we are aware of' (2013: 89). Most of the items identified can be found on RTG.

Buchstaller et al. note several cross-lexical and word-internal conditions in which T-to-R occurs (the * indicates T-to-R being triggered after *h*-deletion).

(64) Final /t/ in conjunctions, particles, and determiners
    a. There's a reason I'm **norra** [*not a*] engineer.
    b. It's good, but still **norraz** [*not as*] good as the one up towards Nursery Road way.
    c. **Wharra** [*what a*] loada shite.
    d. Ah could'n mack out **wharree*** [*what he*] was saying.
    e. Bit naffed **tharra** [*that I*] dinnut gerra look-in, mind.
    f. An Ah cannut berlieve **tharree*** [*that he*] achully At/Et/Ate this efter all that time.
    g. Nor, **burree*** [*but he*] nivva lets the side down when ye need a pile of hoss shit fer yer rurzes.
    h. **Burrits** [*but it's*] got nowt to dee with binned Salmon.

i. Sh'looked up **arruz** [*at us*].
j. he said 'nah marra, a hoss. It's in the bar if you wanna have a look **orrit'** [*at it*].
k. Norman Wisdom a hero over there, **tharrul** [*that'll*] do for me.

(65) Final /t/ in complex determiners
   a. Bruce Lee wad bray the **lorra** [*lot of*] them.
   b. Everyone likes a **birra** [*bit of*] Jornee don't they?
   c. Borrom level marra, **birrovva** private "do".

(66) Final /t/ in monosyllabic verbs[11]
   a. he's not really working out, might have to **lerrim*** [*let him*] gan.
   b. The girl said 'carrier bag?', and I said 'nah, **lerra*** [*let her*] walk'.
   c. **Gorra** [*got a*] reet headache me like.
   d. **Gerroff** [*get off*] the pitch man Hancock!!
   e. **GerrrrrrrrrrrRRRRIN** [*get in*] yafukaz [*you fuckers*]!
   f. **Gerrim*** [*get him*] telt.
   g. **Gerrup** [*get up*] Moyesy lad!
   h. The PE teacher telt me ma ter **gerruz** [*get us*] on a Guinness & steak diet.
   i. **Shurrup** [*shut up*] man you horse fiddler.
   j. **Hirrim*** [*hit him*] in the eye, **hirrim** in the eye, **hirrim** in the eye with a Roker pie whey aye.
   k. Ye can't **purra** [*put a*] price on it, marra.
   l. A **berrits** [*bet it's*] fuckin rivetin.
   m. **serrit** [*set it*] aleet when he puts it on the weshin line.
   n. Hey .. **currit** [*cut it*] out.

(67) Word-internal, morpheme-final /t/
   a. "me dah is **gerrin** a bit edgy cos he's not seen ya fer reassurance like".
   b. Am **gerrin** upset cos you didn't realise this you inconsiderate individual you.
   c. **Worrevah**!

(68) Morpheme-internal /t/
   a. **Berra** not look anymore then.
   b. what's tha **marra** with you man.
   c. Tak yer boots this **sarradee** then.
   d. Should be a canny **lirrul** atmosphere.
   e. **Borrom** level marra, birrovva private "do".
   f. **Tarra** lad!
   g. When the Broon **borrul** met Cider woman in the park man!!

[11] RTG evidence suggests deverbal nouns can also take part in this process: e.g. 'What a **Serra** [*set of*] bastards'.

The soundscape   183

The earliest dialectological reference to the phenomenon is in Wright who gives '**ger əm** ... **ler it bī, ser it, wor iz it**' as outcomes of a process he describes as 'change of final t to r in monosyllables with short stem-vowel ... when the next word begins with a vowel' (1905: 230). Wright describes this modification occurring 'sporadically in most parts of England', but associates it particularly with 'Yorkshire, Lancashire and the north Midlands'. Buchstaller et al. record a similar 'core' distribution, with the addition of the west and east Midlands, some varieties of Irish English, Merseyside, and Tyneside (2013: 91–92).[12]

Occasionally, what looks like TH-to-R can be found, but only with *with*.

(69) a. Wot Can Ya Dee **Wirra** [*with a*] Fone That's Been Drowned?
      b. sometimes he used to gan off it **wirruz** [*with us*] in chaplins.
      c. Knarr that **wirrout** [*without*] even checking.

In fact, this is not TH-to-R. It is an instance of epenthetic /r/ being inserted as a hiatus breaker between [wɪ] (a typical reduced northern form of *with* – as represented in orthographic representations on RTG such as 'Me **wimmee** Davy Crocket Hat on') and the initial vowel in the following syllable (/j/ is also sometimes found in this context). Epenthetic /r/ can also occur as a hiatus breaker between phonologically reduced *of* and the initial vowel in the following syllable, as in the respelling <orrit> for 'of it' (see also 7.4.2).

7.4.2 Hiatus breaker [v]

More localised than T-to-R is a process involving the insertion of a cross-lexical intervocalic [v] at the end of traditional pronunciations of the prepositions *to* [ti~ti~tɪ] and *with* [wi~wɨ~tɪ], and the primary auxiliary verb *do* with an unrounded front vowel.

(70) a. Beat yer **tiv** it.
      b. Or 1977 if you prefer to gan **tiv** Abigail's party.
      c. "Wu gannun for a borrrrrga **wiv** a serssssseggge rerrrrrlll man Ant n Dec SheeeeeRA".
      d. I **divvent** care if the cool kids say they're shite.

Where does the [v] come from? It appears to be the remnant of a more extensive system where speakers could vary forms 'at discretion to suit the euphony of the sentence in which they occur' (Heslop 1892: xx).

---

[12] The origins of this feature probably lie with an earlier process in which /t/ was replaced intervocalically with the alveolar tap [ɾ] (found, for example, in American English in words like [bɛɾəɹ] *better*). The [ɾ] was then phonologically reinterpreted as /r/, resulting in the use of the prevailing /r/ variant – typically [ɹ] – in place of [ɾ], though as we have seen this was mainly restricted to word boundaries (Wells 1982: 370).

The following examples of variant forms of *to, with, in, by,* and *from* are from *NW*.

(71) a. He's shrunk **tiv** a spelk.
      b. A foreign sailor **wiv** a gully **iv** a sheth **biv** his side.
      c. Did ye get it **fre** Tom, or **frev** Anty?

Heslop – like Ellis – claims that forms in -*v* occur before vowels, which suggests they arose as a hiatus breaker. In some languages, including English, it is phonologically undesirable for two separate vowels to occur adjacently (both within words and across word boundaries). When such a 'hiatus' occurs, a number of strategies can be deployed to resolve it, including the insertion of an epenthetic consonant. In the case of *tiv*, it seems the [v] represents a fortition of the epenthetic [w], which is the normal hiatus resolution mechanism in contexts such as 'to a' [tuːwə] and 'to his' [tuːwɪz] (Rowe 2007). In order to explain *wiv*,[13] we need to take into account the fact that, as Wright (1905: 240) observes

> *with* has gen. become **wi** ... in all dialects. **wi** was formerly used in the dialects before a following consonant and **wiþ**, **wið** before a following vowel. But most dialects now have **wi** in both positions. A few dialects have **wid** when the next word begins with a vowel ... and also a few have **wiv** s. Nhb. n.Dur. nw. snw. e.m. & nm. Yks.

In addition, *tiv* has become lexicalised. Evidence for this lies with the fact that it can also appear before consonants.

(72) a. It's not a club foot, man, he's just **intiv** glam rock.
      b. Mair **tiv** that byuk than meets the eye.

This lexicalisation goes back to at least the mid-nineteenth century, as these *EDD* examples show.

(73) a. **Tiv** sike time is the day daws, an' the cloods is a' flown, ROBSON *Sng. Sol.* (1859)
      b. Then away on the dowie road **tiv** Shields, HALDANE *Geordy* (1878)

EDD also points to a historically wider distribution across the north of England, with numerous examples given from all three Ridings of Yorkshire.

---

[13] Another explanation for the respelling <wiv> is that it represents *th*-fronting, though this is infrequent in contemporary NEVE (Watt and Foulkes 2017: 153). When it does appear on RTG it typically does so in dialect stylisations of southern accents: 'Knees up **muvver** braaawn. Jog on maayyyyte.'

The origins and development of *div* are similar to *tiv*, though the fact that *div* is commoner in negative clauses might suggest that the [v] element first arose as a hiatus breaker between the verb and the negative enclitic, as in *divent*, and was then introduced in positive contexts (see 3.2.2 and 4.3.1).

7.5 Prosodic features

When we move through a territory where the dialect is new and unfamiliar to us, we do not separate out the consonants from the vowels, submitting them to scrutiny before noting other aspects of the sound experience: 'a dialect is normally perceived as a whole, rather than by listening for individual features' (Kerswill and Williams 2002: 184). The *dialekt-gestalt* includes suprasegmental as well as segmental aspects of language. Indeed, the prominence of prosody – pitch, tempo, intonation, duration, volume, and voice quality – in the auditory experience of dialect gestalts has been revealed in perceptual dialectology. In research on perceptions of North East speech (e.g. Pearce 2012), the salience of prosody is reflected in the remarks of survey respondents from across the region who were asked to describe any differences they were aware of between Sunderland and Newcastle accents. Many of the adjectives used suggest prosodic features: for example, pitch (*deeper, high, higher, piercing, squealy*); tempo (*fast, faster, clipped*); intonation (*melodic, flat, flatter, sing-song*). Paralinguistic features such as voice quality are also evoked (*harsh, harsher, rough, rougher, hard, harder, rounded, smooth, softer*).

An early reference to the distinctiveness of North East prosody appears in a set of letters written by an 'English commercial traveller' journeying from London to Scotland in the summer of 1815. In County Durham the author encounters people whose speech combines 'indistinct singing and drawling' (reminiscent of 'the Scots') with 'a high tone of voice, a sort of falsetto, which, with the other peculiarities, has, to me, a ludicrous effect' (Anon. 1817: 54–55). In a less condescending fashion, the author of an essay published in *The Phonetic Journal* in 1852 recalls how an acquaintance from the south of England, after 'a single week's residence in Newcastle-on-Tyne' adopted the 'Northumbrian intonation; the peculiarity of which is, the use of the "rising inflexion" of the voice at the close of almost every sentence' (Anon. 1852: 105). Towards the end of the century, we find this passage on the dialect of Tyneside from the biography of the locally renowned teacher and musician Thomas Haswell, describing 'a curious and quite characteristic singing intonation', which

> from a strange inflection and a certain indescribable inversion of cadence at once arrests the ear of every stranger. "How I admire your *recitative*" said a gentleman once to a Shields lady in a London drawing-room, and the epithet is not altogether inapt, though the

"recitative," owing to its utter lack of tonal relationship, could never be scored for musical accompaniment. (G. H. Haswell 1895: 268)

The perception of the 'musicality' of the North East accent was bought to the attention of an informant in the Tyneside Linguistic Survey:

I was in down London on the BRS [British Rail Services] and I just used to talk the way I'm talking now and this fellow says listen him you know Cockney like the way them talk listen him he's singing he's singing (TLSG19) [male 41–50 recorded in 1960s]

'Singing and drawling', 'rising inflexion', 'inversion of cadence', 'recitative', 'he's singing he's singing'. What is being described here? Research on prosodic features of English dialects is somewhat limited, although where it has been undertaken North East English has attracted attention, probably because amongst English cities Newcastle – like Liverpool and Birmingham – has a particularly characteristic intonation type (Wells 1982: 55–56). The fullest accounts of North East intonation are in publications based on the Intonational Variation in English (IViE) corpus (see Grabe et al. 2008 for a summary). Amongst the findings for Tyneside is the presence of a rise-plateau 'tune' in declarative sentences, described impressionistically by Wells (1982: 376) as 'a low-to-high rise, with high level tail, in certain contexts where RP would have a high fall'. This contributes to the perception of Newcastle – and North East speech generally – as musical. Prosody is a topic of metalinguistic discussion on RTG.

(74) a. The Geordie accent pisses me off, it sounds like they are singing and when they get to the end of the sentence they go higher pitched like they are asking a question.
b. Its not just the dialect, it's the intonation.
c. People from pennywell and south hylton speak ridiculously fast.
d. Has anyone noticed that there seems to be a huge amount of people from Sunderland that have a really high pitched voice?
e. its quite remarkable how the accent 'softens' from the harsher geordie thru the slightly softer wearside and durham tones thru to starting to soften right off darlo hartlepool and down to boro.
f. I find the Colliery accent much less harsh and more gentle.

Perceptual dialectology research has revealed a tendency for the speech of Newcastle to be associated with 'musical' intonation, quicker tempo, and harsh voice quality, while Sunderland speech has a narrower intonational range and is 'softer' in terms of voice quality (Pearce 2012: 17–18).

Finally in relation to prosody, some respellings might be attempts to convey a marked pattern of lexical stress in NEVE: a 'tendency to level stress or heavier second element stress in compounds, so that the city of

Newcastle (upon Tyne) is pronounced by many inhabitants [njʊ'kasl] (as opposed to ['nju:kasl])' (Upton 2015: 266).

(75) a. a "must see game" for anyone except Sunderland & **Newcassel** fans.
 b. they knew how important the cup was to **Newcassil**.

The <ass> here perhaps draws attention to both the vowel quality in the nucleus of the second syllable, and its stressed nature. This respelling has regularly appeared in print since the late eighteenth century. For example, Brockett's definition of *canny* exemplifies the standard and the 'local' spelling: 'a genuine Newcastle word, applied to any thing superior, or of the best kind; hence, "Canny Newcassel," *par excellence*, has become proverbial' (1829: 61).

7.6 Conclusion

This chapter has shown how posters on RTG use orthographic means to convey information about the sounds of spoken NEVE. While some respellings are eye dialect, serving to impart an informal flavour, and some portray connected speech processes found in the casual conversation of most English speakers everywhere, many respellings capture details of accent. This is most clearly shown in the treatment of vowels, with evidence of respelling observable in relation to almost every vowel in the dialect's phoneme inventory. Although respellings are often used to represent vowel variants heard widely across the region, some forms demonstrate posters' perceptions of intra-regional variation, especially differences between mainstream accents and the marked accents of Tyneside (e.g. <toon, tyek>) and Wearside (e.g. <tewn, tak>). The respelling of vowels often appears in stylisations of North East accents on RTG, but the only consonantal feature evoked orthographically in this context is /h/, the absence of which at the start of stressed syllables is sometimes used to index a Sunderland accent. Localised connected speech processes also make an appearance, with T-to-R particularly well represented. RTG is also a repository of metalinguistic commentary on speech sounds, containing detailed and perceptive observations about the soundscape of NEVE, some of which would have been difficult – if not impossible – to access using more conventional means.

In this and in previous chapters I have shown how RTG is an environment where dialect is not simply surviving but flourishing. Participants exploit this linguistic resource in a variety of ways: sometimes non-standard morphosyntax, lexis, and respelling seem to be reflecting posters' everyday, subconscious usage offline, where these features are an instinctive and intrinsic part of their linguistic repertoire (Dent 2013: 114); sometimes NEVE is used more consciously as part of a rhetorical performance, or its features become objects of metalinguistic scrutiny. But why should this be the case? Why do we see so much dialect on the site, and why is it of such interest to some participants? Is there something special about North East England itself which encourages the maintenance of these vernacular forms? The region is distant from London and the South East, and, broadly speaking, dialect features (particularly of the more 'traditional' kind) are becoming confined to geographically peripheral areas (Trudgill 2000: 126). Furthermore, since the 1970s the policies of successive governments have condemned the North East to social, economic, and cultural marginalisation, resulting in limited in-migration from other parts of the UK. Peripherality and marginalisation are conditions that encourage a degree of insularity, meaning that the forces which lead to dialect levelling, compared with other parts of England, are not as strong there for socio-psychological as well as demographic reasons. An additional brake on the large-scale attrition of dialect in the North East might be its unique cultural status. While other urban varieties of English in England, such as those associated with Merseyside and the West Midlands (enregistered as *Scouse* and *Brummie* respectively) are well known to British people, urban North East English (enregistered as *Geordie* – see 2.3), though equally recognisable, typically receives somewhat more favourable assessments in language attitudes research, consistently outranking many other varieties on affective dimensions like social attractiveness and solidarity (Montgomery 2018). Such positive exogenous regard helps to preserve distinctive dialect forms.

We can also point to the concept of sociolinguistic change – defined by Coupland as 'a broad set of language-implicating changes' within a society (2014: 69) – as a possible reason for the proliferation of NEVE features on RTG. Of relevance here is the realignment of power relations in the UK, which has been in progress since at least the middle of the twentieth century, involving a loosening of rigid hierarchies of social class, increased social mobility, and a redrawing of the boundaries between 'high' and 'low' cultural forms. The linguistic reflex of this realignment is described by the critical discourse analyst Norman Fairclough as the 'democratization' of discourse: 'the removal of inequalities and asymmetries in the discursive and linguistic rights, obligations and prestige of groups of people' (1992: 201). The democratisation of discourse involves what Coupland calls 'vernacularization': a weakening of the hegemony of standard languages and a 'valorization of vernacularity' (Coupland 2014: 85–86). On RTG, evidence of the shifting status of SE can be seen in the willingness of posters to use non-standard forms in writing (a mode traditionally seen as the domain of the standard). And while metalinguistic comments about accent and dialect can sometimes be negative and derogatory (usually in the context of intraregional rivalries) we also encounter comments which 'valorise' dialect in various ways, from positive assessments of how accents sound (76a,b), to expressions of personal pride (76c,d,e) and interest in the dialect's historical pedigree (76f), to forms of vernacular prescriptivism (Pearce 2015b) which assert what is 'permissible' linguistically for North East folk (76g,h,i).

(76) a. Some North East accents sound lovely.
  b. I love the South Durham and Sunderland accents.
  c. I've a quite strong Geordie accent and am proud of my roots.
  d. I am very proud of my pitmatic dialect.
  e. My accent is one of the things I can be really proud of.
  f. I think it's a fantastic dialect, as we speak the nearest form of English to that brought here by the Anglo Saxons.
  g. There's nowt worse than someone from the NE trying to change their accent.
  h. If you're from the north east there's no other word but charver, which has been used around these parts for decades.
  i. *Anyone from the north east who says 'Mum' should be shot.*

Vernacularisation does not proceed at the same pace across all social domains, though the participatory web is an arena where we are especially likely to see it in action. In these sites of virtual encounter, interactants are limited mainly to the written verbal mode. Lacking the range of semiotic resources available to people engaged in 'real-world' conversations – such as facial expression, posture, gait, dress, and hairstyle – posters rely heavily on the words and structures they use (and the metalinguistic knowledge they display) to *construct* a place in the social landscape, creating 'social meaning through deploying and recontextualizing linguistic resources' (Coupland 2014: 177). Because *Ready to Go* is a highly local project, in which the symbolic value of local knowledge and humour is used in the construction of a virtual community of practice, use of and interest in dialect are potent and concentrated ways to demonstrate affiliations and loyalties, pungently evoking 'a constellation of ideologically related meanings' (Eckert 2008: 464) connected with North East people, places, landscapes, working lives, sports, pastimes, and histories.

References

Aalen, Fred (2006) 'North-eastern landscapes', in Fred Aalen and Colm O'Brien (eds), *England's Landscape: The North East*, London: Collins, pp. 11–16.

Agha, Asif (2003) 'The social life of cultural value', *Language and Communication* 23: 231–273.

Aitken, A. J. (1981) 'Angus McIntosh and Scottish Studies', in Michael Benskin and Michael Samuels (eds), *So Meny People Longages and Tonges: Philological Essays in Scots and Mediaeval English presented to Angus McIntosh*, Edinburgh: Edinburgh University Press, pp. xix–xxvi.

Aitken, A. J. and Caroline Macafee (2002) *The Older Scots Vowels: A History of the Stressed Vowels of Older Scots from the Beginnings to the Eighteenth Century*, Guildford: Biddles Limited (for the Scottish Text Society).

Alameen, Ghinwa and John Levis (2015) 'Connected speech', in Marnie Reed and John Levis (eds), *The Handbook of English Pronunciation*, Oxford: Blackwell, pp. 159–174.

Allen, Will, Joan Beal, Karen Corrigan, Warren Maguire, and Hermann Moisl (2007) 'A linguistic "time capsule": The Newcastle Electronic Corpus of Tyneside English', in Joan Beal, Karen Corrigan, and Hermann Moisl (eds), *Creating and Digitizing Language Corpora. Volume 2: Diachronic Databases*, New York/Basingstoke: Palgrave Macmillan, pp. 16–48.

Amand, Maelle (2019) 'A sociophonetic analysis of Tyneside English in the DECTE corpus', unpublished PhD thesis, University of Paris.

Anderwald, Lieselotte (2002) *Negation in Non-standard British English*, London: Routledge.

Anderwald, Lieselotte (2009) *The Morphology of English Dialects: Verb Formation in Non-standard English*, Cambridge: Cambridge University Press.

Androutsopoulos, Jannis (2000) 'Non-standard spellings in media texts: The case of German fanzines', *Journal of Sociolinguistics* 4: 514–533.

Androutsopoulos, Jannis (2010) 'Localizing the global on the participatory web', in Nicolas Coupland (ed.), *The Handbook of Language and Globalization*, Oxford: Wiley-Blackwell, pp. 203–231.

Androutsopoulos, Jannis (2013) 'Participatory culture and metalinguistic discourse: Performing and negotiating German dialects on YouTube', in Deborah Tannen and Anna Marie Trester (eds), *Discourse 2.0: Language and New Media*, Washington, DC: Georgetown University Press, pp. 47–72.

References

Anon. (1817) *Letters from Scotland by an English Commercial Traveller Written During a Journey to Scotland in the Summer of 1815*, London: Longman.

Anon. (1852) 'The moral influence of Romanic spelling', *The Phonetic Journal* 14(11): 105–106.

Astley, Neil (ed.) (2017) *Land of Three Rivers: The Poetry of North-East England*, Hexham: Bloodaxe Books.

Bakhtin, Mikhail M. (1981) *The Dialogic Imagination: Four Essays*, edited by Michael Holquist, translated by Caryl Emerson and Michael Holquist, Austin: University of Texas Press.

Barber, Charles, Joan Beal, and Philip Shaw (2009) *The English Language: A Historical Introduction*, 2nd edition, Cambridge: Cambridge University Press.

Barton, David and Carmen Lee (2013) *Language Online: Investigating Digital Texts and Practices*, London: Routledge.

Beal, Joan (1985) 'Lengthening of *a* in Tyneside English', *Current Issues in Linguistic Theory* 41: 31–44.

Beal, Joan (1993) 'The grammar of Tyneside and Northumbrian English', in James Milroy and Lesley Milroy (eds), *Real English: The Grammar of English Dialects in the British Isles*, Harlow: Longman, pp. 187–213.

Beal, Joan (2000) 'From Geordie Ridley to *Viz*: Popular literature in Tyneside English', *Language and Literature* 9(4): 343–359.

Beal, Joan (2004) 'English dialects in the north of England: Phonology', in Edgar Schneider, Kate Burridge, Bernd Kortmann, Rajend Mesthrie, and Clive Upton (eds), *A Handbook of Varieties of English. Vol. 1: Phonology*, Berlin: Mouton de Gruyter, pp. 114–141.

Beal, Joan (2006) *Language and Region*, London: Routledge.

Beal, Joan (2008) 'English dialects in the north of England: Morphology and syntax', in Bernd Kortmann and Clive Upton (eds), *Varieties of English I: The British Isles*, Berlin: Mouton de Gruyter, pp. 373–403.

Beal, Joan (2009) 'Enregisterment, commodification and historical context: "Geordie" versus "Sheffieldish"', *American Speech* 84(2): 138–156.

Beal, Joan (2010) *An Introduction to Regional Englishes*, Edinburgh: Edinburgh University Press.

Beal, Joan (2017) 'Nineteenth-century dialect literature and the enregisterment of urban vernaculars', in Jane Hodson (ed.), *Dialect and Literature in the Long Nineteenth Century*, Abingdon and New York: Routledge, pp. 15–32.

Beal, Joan (2018) 'Dialect as heritage', in Angela Creese and Adrian Blackledge (eds), *The Routledge Handbook of Language and Superdiversity*, Abingdon and New York: Routledge, pp. 165–181.

Beal, Joan and Paul Cooper (2015) 'The enregisterment of northern English', in Raymond Hickey (ed.), *Researching Northern English*, Amsterdam and Philadelphia, PA: John Benjamins, pp. 27–50.

Beal, Joan and Karen Corrigan (2005) '"No, nay, never": Negation in Tyneside English', in Yoko Iyeiri (ed.), *Aspects of English Negation*, Amsterdam: John Benjamins, pp. 139–156.

Beal, Joan and Karen Corrigan (2009) 'The impact of nineteenth century Irish-English migrations on contemporary Northern Englishes: Tyneside and Sheffield compared', in Esa Penttilä and Heli Paulasto (eds), *Language Contacts Meet English Dialects*, Newcastle-upon-Tyne: Cambridge Scholars, pp. 231–258.

Beal, Joan, Lourdes Burbano-Elizondo, and Carmen Llamas (2012) *Urban North-Eastern English: Tyneside to Teesside*, Edinburgh: Edinburgh University Press.

Beal, Joan, Ranjan Sen, Nuria Yáñez-Bouza, and Christine Wallis (2020) 'En[dj] uring [tʃ]unes or ma[tj]ure [dʒ]ukes? Yod-coalescence and yod-dropping in the *Eighteenth-Century English Phonology Database*', *English Language and Linguistics* 24(3): 493–526.

Beeching, Kate (2016) *Pragmatic Markers in British English*, Cambridge: Cambridge University Press.

Benson, Erica and Megan Risdal (2018) 'Variation in language regard: Sociolinguistic receptivity and acceptability of linguistic features', in Betsy Evans, Erica Benson, and James Stanford (eds), *Language Regard: Methods, Variation and Change*, Cambridge: Cambridge University Press, pp. 80–95.

Besnier, Niko (1990) 'Language and affect', *Annual Review of Anthropology* 19: 419–451.

Biber, Douglas, Susan Conrad, and Geoffrey Leech (2002) *The Longman Student Grammar of Spoken and Written English*, London: Longman.

Biber, Douglas, Stig Johansson, Geoffrey Leech, Susan Conrad, and Edward Finegan (1999) *The Longman Grammar of Spoken and Written English*, Harlow: Longman.

Bolinger, Dwight (1972) *Degree Words*, The Hague: Mouton.

Brinton, Laurel (2012) '"The ghosts of old morphology": Lexicalization or (de)grammaticalization?', in Kristin Davidse, Tine Breban, Lieselotte Brems, and Tanja Mortelmans (eds), *Grammaticalization and Language Change*, Amsterdam: John Benjamins, pp. 135–166.

Britain, David (2010) 'Grammatical variation in the contemporary spoken English of England', in Andy Kirkpatrick (ed.), *The Routledge Handbook of World Englishes*, London: Routledge, pp. 37–58.

Brockett, John Trotter (1825) *A Glossary of North Country Words in Use*, Newcastle-upon-Tyne: T. and J. Hodgson.

Brockett, John Trotter (1829) *A Glossary of North Country Words in Use*, 2nd edition, Newcastle-upon-Tyne: Emerson Charnley.

Buchstaller, Isabelle, Karen Corrigan, Anders Holmberg, Patrick Honeybone, and Warren Maguire (2013) '"T-to-R" and the "Northern Subject Rule"', *Journal of English Linguistics* 17: 85–128.

Buchstaller, Isabelle and Karen Corrigan (2015) 'Morphosyntactic features of Northern English', in Raymond Hickey (ed.), *Researching Northern English*, Amsterdam: John Benjamins, pp. 71–98.

Bueltmann, Tanja, Andrew Hinson, and Graeme Morton (2013) *The Scottish Diaspora*, Edinburgh: Edinburgh University Press.

Bunting, Basil (2000) *Complete Poems*, Hexham: Bloodaxe Books.

Burbano-Elizondo, Lourdes (2003) 'First approaches to the unexplored dialect of Sunderland', *Miscelánea: A Journal of English and American Studies* 27: 51–68.

Burbano-Elizondo, Lourdes (2008) 'Language variation and identity in Sunderland', unpublished PhD thesis, University of Sheffield.

Burke, Isabelle and Kate Burridge (2023) 'From *a bit of processed cheese* to *a bit of a car accident* and *a little bit of "oh really"* – The journey of Australian English *a bit (of)*', *Journal of Pragmatics* 209: 15–30.

Carter, Ronald and Michael McCarthy (2006) *Cambridge Grammar of English: A Comprehensive Guide*, Cambridge: Cambridge University Press.

Chamson, Emile (2012) 'Etymology in the *English Dialect Dictionary*', in Manfred Markus, Yoko Iyeiri, Reinhard Heuberger, and Emil Chamson (eds), *Middle and Modern English Corpus Linguistics: A Multi-dimensional Approach*, Amsterdam: John Benjamins, pp. 225–240.

Cheshire, Jenny, Viv Edwards, and Pamela Whittle (1993) 'Non-standard English and dialect levelling', in James Milroy and Lesley Milroy (eds), *Real English: The Grammar of English Dialects in the British Isles*, Harlow: Longman, pp. 53–96.
Childs, Claire (2016) 'Canny good, or quite canny?' *English World-Wide* 37(3): 238–266.
Colls, Robert and Bill Lancaster (2005a) '1992 Preface', in Robert Colls and Bill Lancaster (eds), *Geordies: Roots of Regionalism*, 2nd edition, Newcastle: Northumbria University Press, pp. xi–xviii.
Colls, Robert and Bill Lancaster (2005b) 'Preface to the second edition', in Robert Colls and Bill Lancaster (eds), *Geordies: Roots of Regionalism*, 2nd edition, Newcastle: Northumbria University Press, pp. vii–x.
Colls, Robert and Bill Lancaster (2005c) 'Guide to further reading', in Robert Colls and Bill Lancaster (eds), *Geordies: Roots of Regionalism*, 2nd edition, Newcastle: Northumbria University Press, pp. 184–194.
Common, Jack (1951) *Kiddar's Luck*, London: Turnstile Press.
Cooper, Paul (2019) 'The enregisterment of "Barnsley" dialect: Vowel fronting and being "broad" in Yorkshire dialects', *Language and Communication* 64: 68–80.
Cooper, Paul (2020) 'Russian dolls and dialect literature: The enregisterment of nineteenth-century "Yorkshire" Dialects', in Patrick Honeybone and Warren Maguire (eds), *Dialect Writing and the North of England*, Edinburgh: Edinburgh University Press, pp. 126–146.
Corrigan, Karen, Adam Mearns, and Hermann Moisl (2014) 'Feature-based versus aggregate analyses of the DECTE corpus: Phonological and morphological variability in Tyneside English', in B. Szmrecsanyi and B. Wälchli (eds), *Aggregating Dialectology, Typology, and Register Analysis: Linguistic Variation in Text and Speech*, Berlin: De Gruyter, pp. 113–149.
Corrigan, Karen, Isabelle Buchstaller, Adam Mearns, and Hermann Moisl (2012) *The Diachronic Electronic Corpus of Tyneside English*, Newcastle University <https://research.ncl.ac.uk/decte>.
Coupland, Nikolas (2001) 'Dialect stylization in radio talk', *Language in Society* 30(3): 345–375.
Coupland, Nikolas (2007) *Style: Language Variation and Identity*, Cambridge: Cambridge University Press.
Coupland, Nikolas (2014) 'Sociolinguistic change, vernacularization and broadcast British media', in Jannis Androutsopoulos (ed.), *Mediatization and Sociolinguistic Change*, Freiburg: Linguae and Litterae, Publications of the School of Language and Literature, Freiburg Institute for Advanced Studies, pp. 67–98.
Crowley, Tony (2003) *Standard English and the Politics of Language*, 2nd edition, Basingstoke: Palgrave Macmillan.
Culpeper, Jonathan and Merja Kytö (2010) *Early Modern English Dialogues: Spoken Interaction as Writing*, Cambridge: Cambridge University Press.
Davies, Mark (2018) 'Establishing corpora from existing data sources', in Christine Mallinson, Becky Childs, and Gerard Van Herk (eds), *Data Collection in Sociolinguistics: Methods and Applications*, 2nd edition, London: Routledge, pp. 211–213.
Defoe, Daniel (1726) *Mere Nature Delineated*, London: T. Watson.
Defoe, Daniel (1727) *A Tour Thro' the Whole Island of Great Britain* (volume 3), London: Strahan, Mears, and Stagg.
Dent, Susie (2013) 'Mapping the word: Local vocabulary and its themes', in Clive Upton and Bethan C. Davies (eds), *Analysing 21st Century British English: Conceptual and Methodological Aspects of the 'Voices' Project*, London: Routledge, pp. 110–123.

Devlin, Thomas, Peter French, and Carmen Llamas (2019) 'Vowel change across time, space, and conversational topic: The use of localized features in former mining communities', *Language Variation and Change* 31: 303–328.

Di Martino, Emilia (2020) *Celebrity Accents and Public Identity Construction: Analyzing Geordie Stylizations*, London: Routledge.

Dobson, Scott (1969) *Larn Yersel' Geordie*, Newcastle: Frank Graham.

Durham, Mercedes (2011) 'Right dislocation in Northern England: Frequency and use–perception meets reality', *English World-Wide* 32(3): 257–279.

Durkin, Philip (2009) *The Oxford Guide to Etymology*, Oxford: Oxford University Press.

Durkin, Philip (2015) '*Mackems, Geordies* and *ram-raiders*: Documenting regional variation in historical dictionaries', *English Language and Linguistics* 19(2): 313–326.

Eckert, Penelope (2008) 'Variation and the indexical field', *Journal of Sociolinguistics* 12(4): 453–476.

Eckert, Penelope (2013) 'Ethics in linguistic research', in Robert Podesva and Devyani Sharma (eds), *Research Methods in Linguistics*, Cambridge: Cambridge University Press, pp. 11–26.

Ellis, Alexander John (1869) *On Early English Pronunciation* (Early English Text Society, Extra Series 2). Repr. 1968. London: Greenwood Press.

Ellis, Alexander John (1889) *On Early English Pronunciation, Part V, The Existing Phonology of English Dialects Compared with that of West Saxon*, London: Trübner and Co.

Fairclough, Norman (1992) *Discourse and Social Change*, Cambridge: Polity Press.

Fennell, Barbara and Ronald Butters (1996) 'Historical and contemporary distribution of double modals in English', in Edgar Schneider (ed.), *Focus on the USA. Varieties of English around the World*, Amsterdam: John Benjamins, pp. 265–288.

Foulkes, Paul and Gerard Docherty (2000), 'Another chapter in the story of /r/: "Labiodental" variants in British English', *Journal of Sociolinguistics* 4: 30–59.

Freud, Sigmund (1930) *Das Unbehagen in der Kultur*, Wien: Internationaler Psychoanalytischer Verlag.

Gimson, Alfred (1989) *An Introduction to the Pronunciation of English*, 4th edition, revised by Susan Ramsaran, London: Edward Arnold.

Görlach, Manfred (1999) *English in Nineteenth-Century England*, Cambridge: Cambridge University Press.

Grabe, Esther, Greg Kochanski, and John Coleman (2008) 'The intonation of native accent varieties in the British Isles', in Katarzyna Dziubalska-Kołaczyk and Joanna Przedlacka (eds), *English Pronunciation Models: A Changing Scene*, Bern: Peter Lang, pp. 311–337.

Great Britain Tourism Survey (2023) VisitBritain/VisitEngland <https://www.visitbritain.org/>.

Green, Joanne and J. D. A. Widdowson (2003) *Traditional English Language Genres: Continuity and Change, 1950–2000. Vol. 1*, Sheffield: The National Centre for English Cultural Tradition.

Green, Jonathon (2016) *Slang: A Very Short Introduction*, Oxford: Oxford University Press.

Gregory, Derek (2000) 'Regions and regional geography', in R. J. Johnston, Derek Gregory, Geraldine Pratt, and Michael Watts (eds), *The Dictionary of Human Geography*, Oxford: Blackwell, pp. 687–690.

References

Grieve, Jack (2009) 'A corpus-based regional dialect survey of grammatical variation in written Standard American English', unpublished PhD thesis, Northern Arizona University.
Grieve, Jack (2015) 'Dialect variation', in Douglas Biber and Randi Reppen (eds), *The Cambridge Handbook of English Corpus Linguistics*, Cambridge: Cambridge University Press, pp. 362–380.
Grieve, Jack, Andrea Nini, Diansheng Guo, and Alice Kasakoff (2015) 'Using social media to map double modals in modern American English', paper given at NWAV44, University of Toronto, 25 October 2015.
Griffiths, Bill (2005) *A Dictionary of North East Dialect*, 2nd edition, Newcastle: Northumbria University Press.
Griffiths, Bill (2006) *Stotty 'n' Spice Cake: The Story of North East Cooking*, Newcastle: Northumbria University Press.
Grose, Francis (1787) *A Provincial Glossary*, London: S. Hooper.
Hagan, Holly (2014) *Not Quite a Geordie*, London: John Blake Books.
Haldane, Harry (1879) *Geordy's Last* and *Newcastle Folk Speech*, 2nd edition, Newcastle-upon-Tyne: The Daily Journal Office.
Hall, David (2012) *Working Lives: The Forgotten Voices of Britain's Post-War Working Class*, London: Transworld Publishers.
Hancil, Sylvie (2018) 'Transcategoriality and right periphery', *Cognitive Linguistic Studies* 5(1): 61–76.
Harrison, Tony (2016) *Collected Poems*, London: Penguin.
Haswell, George H. (1895) *The Maister: A Century of Tyneside Life*, London: Walter Scott Ltd.
Hermeston, Rodney (2009) 'Linguistic identity in nineteenth-century Tyneside dialect songs', unpublished PhD thesis, University of Leeds.
Hernández, Nuria (2011) 'Personal pronouns', in Nuria Hernández, Daniela Kolbe, and Monika Schultz (eds), *A Comparative Grammar of British English Dialects*, Berlin, pp. 53–191.
Heslop, Richard Oliver (1885) 'The Permian people of north Durham', *Archæologia Æliana* vol.10, Society of Antiquaries of Newcastle-upon-Tyne, pp. 93–102.
Heslop, Richard Oliver (1892–1893) *Northumberland Words*, London: English Dialect Society.
Hickey, Raymond (2007) *Irish English: History and Present-day Forms*, Cambridge: Cambridge University Press.
Hickey, Raymond (2014) *A Dictionary of Varieties of English*, Oxford: Wiley-Blackwell.
Hickey, Raymond (2015) 'The north of England and northern English', in Raymond Hickey (ed.), *Researching Northern English*, Amsterdam: John Benjamins, pp. 1–24.
Hickey, Raymond (2016) 'Society, language and Irish emigration', in Raymond Hickey (ed.), *Sociolinguistics in Ireland*, London: Palgrave Macmillan, pp. 224–268.
Higgins, Michael and Angela Smith (2017) *Belligerent Broadcasting: Synthetic Argument in Broadcast Talk*, Abingdon: Routledge.
Hogg, Richard (2006) 'English in Britain', in Richard Hogg and David Denison (eds), *A History of the English Language*, Cambridge: Cambridge University Press, pp. 352–383.
Holmes, Janet and Nick Wilson (2017) *An Introduction to Sociolinguistics*, 5th edition, London: Routledge.
Honeybone, Patrick (2020) 'Which phonological features get represented in dialect

writing? Answers and questions from three types of Liverpool English texts', in Patrick Honeybone and Warren Maguire (eds), *Dialect Writing and the North of England*, Edinburgh: Edinburgh University Press, pp. 211–242.

Honeybone, Patrick and Warren Maguire (2020) 'Introduction: What is dialect writing? Where is the North of England?', in Patrick Honeybone and Warren Maguire (eds), *Dialect Writing and the North of England*, Edinburgh: Edinburgh University Press, pp. 1–28.

Honeybone, Patrick and Kevin Watson (2013) 'Salience and the sociolinguistics of Scouse spelling: Exploring the phonology of the Contemporary Humorous Localised Dialect Literature of Liverpool', *English World-Wide. A Journal of Varieties of English* 34(3): 305–340.

Honeybone, Patrick, Kevin Watson, and Sarah van Eyndhoven (2017) 'Lenition and T-to-R are differently salient: The representation of competing realisations of /t/ in Liverpool English dialect literature', in Joan Beal and Sylvie Hancil (eds), *Perspectives on Northern Englishes*, Berlin: De Gruyter, pp. 83–109.

Honkanen, Mirka (2020) *World Englishes on the Web: The Nigerian Diaspora in the USA*, Amsterdam: John Benjamins.

Howard, Robert (2008) 'The vernacular web of participatory media', *Critical Studies in Media Communication* 25(5): 490–513.

Hughes, Arthur, Peter Trudgill, and Dominic Watt (2005) *English Accents and Dialects*, 4th edition, London: Hodder Arnold.

Ihalainen, Ossi (1994) 'The dialects of England since 1776', in Robert Burchfield (ed.), *The Cambridge History of the English Language Volume 5: English in Britain and Overseas*, Cambridge: Cambridge University Press, pp. 197–276.

Jackson, Dan (2019) *The Northumbrians: North-East England and its People: A New History*, London: Hurst.

Jackson, Howard (2002) *Lexicography: An Introduction*, London: Routledge.

Jamieson, John (1808) *An Etymological Dictionary of the Scottish Language. Vol. 1*, Edinburgh: Edinburgh University Press.

Johnston, Paul (1997) 'Older Scots orthography and its regional variation', in C. Jones (ed.), *The Edinburgh History of the Scots Language*, Edinburgh: Edinburgh University Press, pp. 47–111.

Johnstone, Barbara (2010) 'Indexing the local', in Nikolas Coupland (ed.), *The Handbook of Language and Globalization*, Oxford: Blackwell, pp. 386–405.

Johnstone, Barbara (2013) *Speaking Pittsburghese: The Story of a Dialect*, Oxford: Oxford University Press.

Jones-Sargent, Val (1983) *Tyne Bytes: A Computerised Sociolinguistic Study of Tyneside*, Frankfurt am Main: Peter Lang.

Kellett, Arnold (2004) 'Wright, Joseph (1855–1930), philologist and dialectologist', in *Oxford Dictionary of National Biography*, Oxford: Oxford University Press.

Kerswill, Paul (1987) 'Levels of linguistic variation in Durham', *Journal of Linguistics* 23(1): 25–49.

Kerswill, Paul and Ann Williams (2002) 'Dialect recognition and speech community focusing in New and Old Towns in England', in Daniel Long (ed.), *Handbook of Perceptual Dialectology, Volume 2*, Philadelphia, PA: John Benjamins, pp. 173–204.

Kilgarriff, Adam, Vít Baisa, Jan Bušta, Miloš Jakubíček, Vojtěch Kovář, Jan Michelfeit, Pavel Rychlý, and Vít Suchomel (2014) 'The Sketch Engine: Ten years on', *Lexicography* 1: 7–36.

References

Kjellmer, Göran (2001) '"IT'S A INTERESTING BOOK": On the use of the indefinite article *a* before a vowel in English', *Neuphilologische Mitteilungen* 102(3): 307–315.

Koch, Peter and Wulf Österreicher (1985) 'Sprache der Nähe – Sprache der Distanz. Mündlichkeit und Schriftlichkeit im Spannungsfeld von Sprachtheorie und Sprachgeschichte', in *Romanistisches Jahrbuch 36*, Berlin and New York: Walter de Gruyter, pp. 15–43.

Kortmann, Bernd (2008) 'Synopsis: Morphological and syntactic variation in the British Isles', in Bernd Kortmann and Clive Upton (eds), *Varieties of English 1: The British Isles*, Berlin: Mouton de Gruyter, pp. 478–479.

Kortmann, Bernd (2020) 'Global variation in the Anglophone world', in Bas Aarts, Jill Bowie, and Gergana Popova (eds), *The Oxford Handbook of English Grammar*, Oxford: Oxford University Press, pp. 630–653.

Kortmann, Bernd and Christian Langstrof (2017) 'Regional varieties of British English', in Alexander Bergs and Laurel Brinton (eds), *The History of English: Volume 5 Varieties of English*, Berlin: De Gruyter Mouton, pp. 121–150.

Kristiansen, Tore (2018) 'Sociodialectology', in Charles Boberg, John Nerbonne, and Dominic Watt (eds), *The Handbook of Dialectology*, Oxford: Wiley-Blackwell, pp. 106–122.

Kurath, Hans (1952) *Middle English Dictionary Vol. 1*, Ann Arbor: University of Michigan Press.

Lancaster, Bill (2005) 'Newcastle – capital of what?' in Robert Colls and Bill Lancaster (eds), *Geordies: Roots of Regionalism*, 2nd edition, Newcastle: Northumbria University Press, pp. 53–70.

Lass, Roger (1997) *Historical Linguistics and Language Change*, Cambridge: Cambridge University Press.

Lass, Roger (2006) 'Phonology and morphology', in Richard Hogg and David Denison (eds), *A History of the English Language*, Cambridge: Cambridge University Press, pp. 43–108.

Lawless, Richard (1995) *From Ta'izz to Tyneside: An Arab Community in the Northeast of England during the Early Twentieth Century*, Exeter: University of Exeter Press.

Lazer, D., A. Pentland, L. Adamic, S. Aral, A.-L. Barabási, D. Brewer, and M. Alstyne (2009) 'Computational social science', *Science* 323: 721–723.

Leech, Geoffrey (2014) *The Pragmatics of Politeness*, Oxford: Oxford University Press.

Llamas, Carmen (2001) 'Language variation and innovation in Teesside English', unpublished PhD thesis, University of Leeds.

Llamas, Carmen (2010) 'Convergence and divergence across a national border', in Carmen Llamas and Dominic Watt (eds), *Language and Identities*, Edinburgh: Edinburgh University Press, pp. 227–236.

Macafee, Caroline (1991) '"Acumsinery": Is it too late to collect traditional dialect?', *Folk Life* 30(1): 71–77.

Macafee, Caroline (ed.) (1996) *A Concise Ulster Dictionary*, Oxford: Oxford University Press.

McColl Millar, Robert (2007) *Northern and Insular Scots*, Edinburgh: Edinburgh University Press.

MacKenzie, Laurel, George Bailey, and Danielle Turton (2022) 'Towards an updated dialect atlas of British English', *Journal of Linguistic Geography* 10(1): 46–66.

Macleod, Iseabail, with Pauline Cairns, Caroline Macafee, and Ruth Martin (eds) (1990) *The Scots Thesaurus*, Aberdeen: Aberdeen University Press.

MacMahon, M. K. C. (2006) 'Ellis, Alexander John (né Sharpe) (1814–1890)', in Keith Brown (ed.), *Encyclopedia of Language and Linguistics Volume 4*, 2nd edition, Amsterdam: Elsevier, p. 114.

Maguire, Warren (2008) 'What is a merger, and can it be reversed? The origin, status and reversal of the "nurse-north merger" in Tyneside English', unpublished PhD thesis, Newcastle University.

Maguire, Warren (2012) 'Mapping the existing phonology of English dialects', *Dialectologia et Geolinguistica* 20(1): 84–107.

Maguire, Warren (2015) 'The north above the North: Scotland and Northern English', in Raymond Hickey (ed.), *Researching Northern English*, Amsterdam: John Benjamins, pp. 437–458.

Maguire, Warren (2017) 'Variation and change in the realisation of /r/ in an isolated Northumbrian dialect', in Emma Moore and Chris Montgomery (eds), *Language and a Sense of Place*, Cambridge: Cambridge University Press, pp. 87–104.

Maguire, Warren (2018) 'The origins of epenthesis in liquid+sonorant clusters in Mid-Ulster English', *Transactions of the Philological Society* 116(3): 484–508.

Maguire, Warren, April MacMahon, Paul Heggarty, and Dan Dediu (2010) 'The past, present, and future of English dialects: Quantifying convergence, divergence, and dynamic equilibrium', *Language Variation and Change* 22: 69–104.

Mair, Christian (2006) *Twentieth Century English: History, Variation and Standardization*, Cambridge: Cambridge University Press.

Mair, Christian (2020) 'World Englishes in cyberspace', in Daniel Schreier, Marianne Hundt, and Edgar W. Schneider (eds), *The Cambridge Handbook of World Englishes*, Cambridge: Cambridge University Press, pp. 360–383.

Mair, Christian and Stefan Pfänder (2013) 'Vernacular and multilingual writing in mediated spaces: Web forums for post-colonial communities of practice', in Peter Auer, Martin Hilpert, Anja Stukenbrock, and Benedikt Szmrecsanyi (eds), *Space in Language and Linguistics: Geographical, Interactional, and Cognitive Perspectives*, Berlin: De Gruyter, pp. 529–556.

Markus, Manfred (2014) 'Spoken features of interjections in English dialect (based on Joseph Wright's *English Dialect Dictionary*)', in Irma Taavitsainen, Merja Kytö, Claudia Claridge, and Jeremy Smith (eds), *Developments in English: Expanding Electronic Evidence*, Cambridge: Cambridge University Press, pp. 116–134.

Markus, Manfred (2020) 'What did Joseph Wright mean by *meaning*: The complexity of lexical semantics in the *English Dialect Dictionary Online*', *International Journal of English Studies* 20(1): 1–25.

Markus, Manfred (2021) *English Dialect Dictionary Online: A New Departure in English Dialectology*, Cambridge: Cambridge University Press.

Martin, William (1993) *Marra Familia*, Hexham: Bloodaxe Books.

Matras, Yaron (2010) *Romani in Britain: The Afterlife of a Language*, Edinburgh: Edinburgh University Press.

Mearns, Adam (2015) 'Tyneside', in Raymond Hickey (ed.), *Researching Northern English*, Amsterdam: John Benjamins, pp. 161–182.

Mearns, Adam, Karen Corrigan, and Isabelle Buchstaller (2016) 'The Diachronic Electronic Corpus of Tyneside English and The Talk of the Toon: Issues in preservation and public engagement', in Adam Mearns and Karen Corrigan (eds), *Creating and Digitizing Language Corpora*, London: Palgrave Macmillan, pp. 177–210.

Meinig, Donald (ed.) (1979) *The Interpretation of Ordinary Landscapes*, Oxford: Oxford University Press.

References

Milani, Tomasso and Sally Johnson (2010) 'Critical intersections: Language ideologies and media discourse', in Sally Johnson and Tomasso Milani (eds), *Language Ideologies and Media Discourse*, London: Continuum, pp. 3–14.

Miller, Jim (1993) 'The grammar of Scottish English', in James Milroy and Lesley Milroy (eds), *Real English: The Grammar of English Dialects in the British Isles*, Harlow: Longman, pp. 99–138.

Miller, Jim (2004) 'Scottish English: Morphology and syntax', in Edgar Schneider, Kate Burridge, Bernd Kortmann, Rajend Mesthrie, and Clive Upton (eds), *A Handbook of Varieties of English Volume 2*, Berlin: Mouton de Gruyter, pp. 47–72.

Miller, Jim and Regina Weinert (1995) 'The function of LIKE in dialogue', *Journal of Pragmatics* 23: 365–393.

Milne, Graeme J. (2007) 'Business regionalism: Defining and owning the industrial North East, 1850–1914', in Adrian Green and A. J. Pollard (eds), *Regional Identities in North-East England, 1300–2000*, Woodbridge: The Boydell Press, pp. 113–132.

Milroy, James and Lesley Milroy (eds) (1993) *Real English: The Grammar of English Dialects in the British Isles*, Harlow: Longman.

Minkova, Donka (2014) *A Historical Phonology of English*, Edinburgh: Edinburgh University Press.

Moisl, Hermann and Warren Maguire (2008) 'Identifying the main determinants of phonetic variation in the *Newcastle Electronic Corpus of Tyneside English*', *Journal of Quantitative Linguistics* 15(1): 46–69.

Montgomery, Chris (2018) 'The perceptual dialectology of England', in Natalie Braber and Sandra Jansen (eds), *Sociolinguistics in England*, London: Palgrave Macmillan, pp. 127–164.

Montgomery, Michael (2017) *From Ulster to America: The Scotch-Irish Heritage of American English*, Ullans Press.

Moore, Emma and Julia Snell (2011) '"Oh, they're top, them": Right dislocated tags and interactional stance', in Frans Gregersen, Jeffrey Parrott, and Pia Quist (eds), *Language Variation: European perspectives III*, Amsterdam: John Benjamins, pp. 97–110.

Morley, John and Alan Partington (2009) 'A few frequently asked questions about semantic – or evaluative – prosody', *International Journal of Corpus Linguistics* 14(2): 139–158.

Mortensen, Janus, Nikolas Coupland, and Jacob Thøgersen (eds) (2017) *Style, Mediation, and Change*, Oxford: Oxford University Press.

Murray, James (1873) *The Dialect of the Southern Counties of Scotland*, Hertford: Stephen Austin and Sons.

Mustanoja, Tauno F. (1960) *A Middle English Syntax*, Helsinki: Société Néophilologique.

Myers, Alan (1995) *Myers' Literary Guide: The North East*, Manchester: Carcanet Press.

Nevalainen, Terttu and Helena Raumolin-Brunberg (2017) *Historical Sociolinguistics: Language Change in Tudor and Stuart English*, 2nd edition, Abingdon: Routledge.

Newby, Astrid (2020) 'Multicultural Northeastern English (MNE): 'Could the North East be host to a new centre for the emergence of a multiethnolect?', unpublished undergraduate dissertation, Sunderland University <https://priestman.wordpress.com/volume-7-august-2020/>.

Norrick, Neal (2006) 'Humor in language', in Keith Brown (ed.), *Encyclopedia of Language and Linguistics Volume 5*, 2nd edition, Amsterdam: Elsevier, pp. 425–426.

O'Brien, Sean (2012) *Collected Poems*, London: Picador.

Orton, Harold (1962) *Survey of English Dialects: Introduction*, Leeds: E. J. Arnold and Son.
Orton, Harold and Wilfrid Halliday (1962–1963) *Survey of English Dialects (B) the Basic Material Vol. 1, The Six Northern Counties and the Isle of Man Parts I–III*, Leeds: E. J. Arnold and Son.
Orton, Harold and Philip Tilling (1971) *Survey of English Dialects (B) the Basic Material Vol. 3, The East Midland Counties and East Anglia Part III*, Leeds: E. J. Arnold and Son.
Orton, Harold, Stewart Sanderson, and John Widdowson (1978) *The Linguistic Atlas of England*, London: Croom Helm.
Påhlsson, Christer (1972) *The Northumbrian Burr*, Lund: C. W. K. Gleerup.
Palgrave, Francis (1896) *A List of Words and Phrases in Every-day Use by the Natives of Hetton-Le-Hole in the County of Durham*, London: Published for the English Dialect Society by Henry Frowde.
Paterson, Laura (2014) *British Pronoun Use, Prescription, and Processing*, London: Palgrave Macmillan.
Pattison, Vicky (2014) *Nothing but the Truth: My Story*, London: Sphere.
Pearce, Michael (2009) 'A perceptual dialect map of North East England', *Journal of English Linguistics* 37(2): 162–192.
Pearce, Michael (2011) '"It isn't geet good, like, but it's canny": A new(ish) dialect feature in North East England', *English Today* 27(3): 1–7.
Pearce, Michael (2012) 'Folk accounts of dialect differences in Tyne and Wear', *Dialectologica et Geolinguistica* 20: 5–25.
Pearce, Michael (2013) '"That word so fraught with meaning": The history, cultural significance and current use of *canny* in North East England', *English Studies* 94(5): 562–581.
Pearce, Michael (2014) '"Not quite a Geordie": The folk-ethnonyms of north-east England', *Nomina* 37: 1–34.
Pearce, Michael (2015a) 'The ethnonym *Geordie* in North East England', *Names: A Journal of Onomastics* 63(2): 75–85.
Pearce, Michael (2015b) '*Mam* or *mum*? Sociolinguistic awareness and language-ideological debates online', *Sociolinguistic Studies* 9(1): 115–135.
Pearce, Michael (2017) 'The linguistic landscape of North-East England', in Joan Beal and Sylvie Hancil (eds), *Perspectives on Northern Englishes*, Berlin: De Gruyter, pp. 61–82.
Pearce, Michael (2020) 'The survival of traditional dialect lexis on the participatory web', *English Studies* 101(4): 487–509.
Pearson, Harry (1994) *The Far Corner: A Mazy Dribble through North-East Football*, London: Abacus.
Pearson, Harry (2010) *Slipless in Settle: A Slow Turn Around Northern Cricket*, London: Little, Brown.
Pease, Howard (1899) *Tales of Northumbria*, London: Methuen.
Penhallurick, Robert (2009) 'Dialect dictionaries', in Anthony Cowie (ed.), *The Oxford History of English Lexicography Vol. 2*, Oxford: Oxford University Press, pp. 290–313.
Penhallurick, Robert (2018) *Studying Dialect*, London: Palgrave Macmillan.
Periyan, Natasha (2018) '"Altering the structure of society": An institutional focus on Virginia Woolf and working-class education in the 1930s', *Textual Practice* 32(8): 1301–1323.

References

Pichler, Heike (2016) 'Introduction: Discourse-pragmatic variation and change', in Heike Pichler (ed.), *Discourse-pragmatic Variation and Change in English: New Methods and Insights*, Cambridge: Cambridge University Press, pp. 1–18.

Pickard, Tom (2014) *hoyoot: Collected Poems and Songs*, Manchester: Carcanet.

Pietsch, Lukas (2012) 'Verbal concord', in Raymond Hickey (ed.), *Areal Features of the Anglophone World*, Berlin: Mouton de Gruyter, pp. 355–378.

Preston, Dennis (1985) 'The Li'l Abner syndrome: Written representations of speech', *American Speech* 60(4): 328–336.

Preston, Dennis (1993) 'Folk dialectology', in Dennis Preston (ed.), *American Dialect Research*, Amsterdam: John Benjamins, pp. 333–377.

Prichard, Hilary (2014) 'Northern dialect evidence for the chronology of the Great Vowel Shift', *Journal of Linguistic Geography* 2: 87–102.

Quirk, Randolph, Sidney Greenbaum, Geoffrey Leech, and Jan Svartvik (1985) *A Comprehensive Grammar of the English Language*, London: Longman.

Research and Development Unit for English Studies (2022) *WebCorp Linguist's Search Engine* (version 2), Birmingham City University <https://www.webcorp.org.uk/lse>.

Robinson, Jonnie (2021) *A Thesaurus of English Dialect and Slang: England, Wales and the Channel Islands*, Cambridge: Cambridge University Press.

Robinson, Jonnie, Jon Herring, and Holly Gilbert (2013) 'Voices of the UK: The British Library description of the *BBC Voices Recordings* collection', in Clive Upton and Bethan C. Davies (eds), *Analysing 21st Century British English: Conceptual and Methodological Aspects of the 'Voices' Project*, London: Routledge, pp. 136–161.

Rowe, Charley (2007) '"He divn't gan tiv a college ti di that, man!": A study of *do* (and *to*) in Tyneside English', *Language Sciences* 29: 360–371.

Ruano-García, Javier (2014) 'ON JOHN T. BROCKETT'S GLOSSARY OF NORTH COUNTRY WORDS: NOTES ON THE RECEPTION OF WHITE KENNETT'S PAROCHIAL ANTIQUITIES (1695), AND MS LANSDOWNE 1033', *Notes and Queries* 61(4): 536–542.

Ruano-García, Javier, Pilar Sanchez-García, and Miguel García-Bermejo Giner (2015) 'Northern English: Historical lexis and spelling', in Raymond Hickey (ed.), *Researching Northern English*, Amsterdam: John Benjamins, pp. 131–157.

Rupp, Laura and David Britain (2019) *Linguistic Perspectives on a Variable English Morpheme: Let's Talk About –s*, London: Palgrave Macmillan.

Rupp, Laura and Hanne Page-Verhoeff (2005) 'Pragmatic and historical aspects of definite article reduction in northern English dialects', *English World-Wide* 26: 325–346.

Rydland, Kurt (1995) 'The Orton Corpus and Northumbrian phonology: The material from Bamburgh and Bellingham (Northumberland)', *English Studies* 76: 547–586.

Rydland, Kurt (1998) *The Orton Corpus. A Dictionary of Northumbrian Pronunciation 1928–1939*, Studia Anglistica Norvegica 10, Oslo: Novus Press.

Rydland, Kurt (1999) 'Front rounded vowels in Northumberland English: The evidence of the Orton corpus', in Clive Upton and Katie Wales (eds), 'Dialectal variation in English: Proceedings of the Harold Orton Centenary Conference 1998', *Leeds Studies in English* 30: 1–15.

Rymes, Betsy (2020) *How We Talk About Language: Exploring Citizen Sociolinguistics*, Cambridge: Cambridge University Press.

Samuels, Michael (1985), 'The Great Scandinavian Belt', in Roger Eaton, Olga Fischer, Willem Koopman, and Federike van der Leek (eds), *Papers from the Fourth International Conference on English Historical Linguistics*, Amsterdam: John Benjamins, pp. 269–281.

Sandow, Rhys and Justyna Robinson (2018) '"Doing Cornishness" in the English periphery: Embodying ideology through Anglo-Cornish dialect lexis', in Natalie Braber and Sandra Jansen (eds), *Sociolinguistics in England*, London: Palgrave Macmillan, pp. 333–362.

Schilling, Natalie (2013) *Sociolinguistic Fieldwork*, Cambridge: Cambridge University Press.

Schneider, Edgar (2004) 'The English dialect heritage of the southern United States', in Raymond Hickey (ed.), *Legacies of Colonial English: Studies in Transported Dialects*, Cambridge: Cambridge University Press, pp. 262–309.

Schneider, Edgar (2013) 'Investigating historical variation and change in written documents: New perspectives', in J. K. Chambers and Natalie Schilling (eds), *The Handbook of Language Variation and Change*, 2nd edition, Oxford: Wiley-Blackwell, pp. 57–82.

Scott, Maggie (2020) 'The Scottish dictionary tradition', in Sarah Ogilve (ed.), *The Cambridge Companion to English Dictionaries*, Cambridge: Cambridge University Press, pp. 315–323.

Scottish Language Dictionaries (2017) *Concise Scots Dictionary*, 2nd edition, Edinburgh: Edinburgh University Press.

Seppänen, Aimo (1997) 'The genitives of the relative pronouns in present-day English', in Jenny Cheshire and Dieter Stein (eds), *Taming the Vernacular: From Dialect to Written Standard Language*, Harlow: Longman, pp. 152–169.

Siemund, Peter (2020) 'Regional varieties of English: Non-standard grammatical features', in Bas Aarts, Jill Bowie, and Gergana Popova (eds), *The Oxford Handbook of English Grammar*, Oxford: Oxford University Press, pp. 604–629.

Sisson, C. H. (1998) *Collected Poems*, Manchester: Carcanet.

Smith, Jennifer, David Adger, Brian Aitken, Caroline Heycock, E. Jamieson, and Gary Thoms (2019) *The Scots Syntax Atlas*, University of Glasgow <https://scotssyntaxatlas.ac.uk>.

Snell, Julia (2017) 'Enregisterment, indexicality and the social meaning of "howay": Dialect and identity in north-east England', in Emma Moore and Chris Montgomery (eds), *Language and a Sense of Place*, Cambridge: Cambridge University Press, pp. 301–324.

Stuart-Smith, Jane (1999) 'Voice quality in Glaswegian', *Proceedings of the International Congress of Phonetic Sciences* 14: 2553–2556.

Swinney, Paul (2019) *The Mackem Dictionary*, 3rd edition, Sunderland: ALS Publications.

Szmrecsanyi, Benedikt (2013) *Grammatical Variation in British English Dialects: A Study in Corpus-Based Dialectometry*, Cambridge: Cambridge University Press.

Szmrecsanyi, Benedikt and Lieselotte Anderwald (2018) 'Corpus-based approaches to dialect study', in Charles Boberg, John Nerbonne, and Dominic Watt (eds), *The Handbook of Dialectology*, Oxford: Blackwell, pp. 300–313.

Tagliamonte, Sali (2012) *Variationist Sociolinguistics: Change, Observation, Interpretation*, Oxford: Wiley-Blackwell.

Tagliamonte, Sali (2013) *Roots of English: Exploring the History of Dialects*, Cambridge: Cambridge University Press.

Tagliamonte, Sali (2016) *Making Waves: The Story of Variationist Sociolinguistics*, Oxford: Wiley-Blackwell.

Tomaney, John (2010) 'Contemporary Britain and its regions', in Michael Higgins, Clarissa Smith, and John Storey (eds), *The Cambridge Companion to Modern British Culture*, Cambridge: Cambridge University Press, pp. 79–95.

Traugott, Elizabeth (2010) '(Inter)subjectivity and (inter)subjectification: A reassessment', in Kristin Davidse, Lieven Vandelanotte, and Hubert Cuyckens (eds), *Subjectification, Intersubjectivication and Grammaticalization*, Berlin and New York: De Gruyter Mouton, pp. 29–71.

Trousdale, Graham (2013) 'English dialects in the north of England', in Bernd Kortmann and Kerstin Lunkenheimer (eds), *The Mouton World Atlas of Variation in English*, Berlin and Boston, MA: De Gruyter Mouton, pp.70–77.

Trudgill, Peter (2000) *The Dialects of England*, 2nd edition, Oxford: Blackwell.

Trudgill, Peter (2016) *Dialect Matters: Respecting Vernacular Language*, Cambridge: Cambridge University Press.

Trudgill, Peter and J. K. Chambers (1991) *Dialects of English: Studies in Grammatical Variation*, London: Longman.

Upton, Clive (2000) 'Maintaining the Standard', in Robert Penhallurick (ed.), *Debating Dialect: Essays on the Philosophy of Language*, Cardiff: University of Wales Press, pp. 66–83.

Upton, Clive (2015) 'British English', in Marnie Reed and John Levis (eds), *The Handbook of English Pronunciation*, Oxford: Wiley-Blackwell, pp. 251–268.

Upton, Clive and Bethan C. Davies (eds) (2013), *Analysing 21st Century British English: Conceptual and Methodological Aspects of the 'Voices' Project*, London: Routledge.

Upton, Clive and J. D. A. Widdowson (1999) *Lexical Erosion in English Regional Dialects*, Sheffield: The National Centre for English Cultural Tradition.

Upton, Clive, David Parry, and J. D. A. Widdowson (1994) *Survey of English Dialects: The Dictionary and Grammar*, London: Routledge.

Wakelin, Martin (1972) *English Dialects*, London: The Athlone Press.

Wales, Katie (1996) *Personal Pronouns in Present-day English*, Cambridge: Cambridge University Press.

Wales, Katie (2006) *Northern English: A Social and Cultural History*, Cambridge: Cambridge University Press.

Wales, Katie (2010) 'Northern English in writing', in Raymond Hickey (ed.), *Varieties of English in Writing. The Written Word as Linguistic Evidence*, Amsterdam and Philadelphia, PA: John Benjamins, pp. 61–80.

Wales, Katie and Clive Upton (1998) 'Celebrating variation: Harold Orton and dialectology, 1898–1998', *English Today* 14(4): 27–33.

Walkden, George (2013) 'The status of *hwæt* in Old English', *English Language and Linguistics* 17(3): 465–488.

Watt, Dominic (1998) 'Variation and change in the vowel system of Tyneside English', unpublished PhD thesis, Newcastle University.

Watt, Dominic (2002) '"I don't speak with a Geordie accent, I speak, like, the Northern accent": Contact induced levelling in the Tyneside vowel system', *Journal of Sociolinguistics* 6(1): 44–63.

Watt, Dominic and William Allen (2003) 'Tyneside English', *Journal of the International Phonetic Association* 33: 267–271.

Watt, Dominic and Paul Foulkes (2017) 'Tyneside English', in Raymond Hickey (ed.), *Listening to the Past: Audio Records of Accents of English*, Cambridge: Cambridge University Press, pp. 142–170.

Watt, Dominic and Catherine Ingham (2000) 'Durational evidence of the Scottish Vowel Length Rule in Berwick English', *Leeds Working Papers in Linguistics* 8: 205–228.

Watt, Dominic and Lesley Milroy (1999) 'Patterns of variation and change in three Newcastle vowels: Is this dialect levelling?', in Paul Foulkes and Gerard Docherty (eds), *Urban Voices: Accent Studies in the British Isles*, London: Arnold, pp. 25–46.
Wells, John (1982) *Accents of English*, Cambridge: Cambridge University Press.
Williams, Raymond (1977) *Marxism and Literature*, New York: Oxford University Press.
Williams, Raymond (1979) *Politics and Letters: Interviews with the New Left Review*, London: New Left Books.
Wolfram, Walt and Natalie Schilling (2016) *American English. Dialects and Variation*, 3rd edition, Oxford: Wiley Blackwell.
Wright, Elizabeth (1913) *Rustic Speech and Folk-lore*, Oxford: Oxford University Press.
Wright, Joseph (1896–1905) *The English Dialect Dictionary*, Oxford: Henry Frowde.
Wright, Joseph (1905) *The English Dialect Grammar*, Oxford: Henry Frowde.

Index

adjectives (morphology), 84
adverbial clauses, 107–8
adverbial -s morpheme, 89–90
adverbs (morphology), 84–91
  degree adverbs, 85–9
agreement, 67, 94–7
agriculture, 27, 116, 118, 123–4
all right, 137
allegro spellings, 15, 148–9
alveolarisation, 180
and all, 8, 85, 90
Anglian(s), 29–30, 33, 46n, 56
Anglo-Norman, 112
Angloromani, 111–12, 127–8; see also Romani
angloversals, 16, 25, 55, 71, 101, 102
Ant and Dec, 50
articulatory setting, 149
Ashington, 52, 161, 163
Auf Wiedersehen, Pet, 47, 50, 136
aye, why aye, 10, 16, 23, 130, 141–2

bairn, 16, 23, 61, 111, 115, 119, 122, 124, 176, 143–4
bait, 111, 119, 124
Beal, Joan, 50–2, 162
Beowulf, 61, 137
Bernicia, 26, 29, 32
Blenkinsop, Tom, 48
Bonaparte, Prince Louis-Lucien, 34n
bonny, 61n, 112, 115, 124, 133–4, 135–6
Brecht, Bertolt, 2
British Library, 37–8, 175, 179

British National Corpus, 102, 138
Brockett, John T., 24n, 39, 41, 59, 89, 110, 132, 134, 141, 187
Brontë, Emily, 135
Brummie, 188
Bunting, Basil, 24
Burns, Robert, 85, 98, 135
burr retraction/modification, 87, 162, 172, 175, 178

Camus, Albert, 2
canny, 16, 23, 85–6, 93, 115–17, 119, 134, 187
charver, 127–8
Chaucer, Geoffrey, 84, 96, 107, 159
chav, 126–7
cheesy chips, 21, 167
CHOICE vowel, 174
Cleveland, 48, 96
Cleveland, John, 136
coal-mining and miners, 27, 41, 42–3, 44n, 116, 123n, 135, 136, 139
Cole, Cheryl, 50, 74, 155
commodification, 24, 50, 52, 53, 143–4
Common, Jack, 136
complement clauses, 12, 106, 107–8, 109
Concise Ulster Dictionary, A (CUD), 39, 113–17, 118
connected speech processes, 8, 15, 147, 181–5
Conrad, Joseph, 144n
consonantal features, 176–81; see also alveolarisation, glottalisation, *h*-dropping

corpus linguistics, 22–4; *see also* sample corpus
County Durham, 3n, 19n, 26–7, 30, 32, 34–5, 37, 38, 41, 44n, 46, 52, 58, 63n, 66, 70, 73, 74, 81, 87n, 98, 101, 110, 111, 134, 152, 154, 156, 157, 163, 164–5, 166, 167, 168–9, 171, 172, 173, 174, 176, 179, 185
crack, 32, 117, 122
Cumberland, 26n, 30, 32, 34, 89, 91, 101, 110, 111n, 134, 151, 152, 167, 172
Cumbria, 26n, 29, 76
CURE vowel, 172, 173, 178
Cursor Mundi, 59, 61, 83, 84

Danelaw, 32
Darlington, 3n, 27, 52
dead, 88, 158–9
definite articles, 81–2
Defoe, Daniel, 176n
Deira, 26, 29, 32
determiners
 demonstrative determiners, 68, 78–9, 81
 possessive determiners, 51, 68, 73–6, 81
 quantifying determiners, 81, 83–4
Diachronic Electronic Corpus of Tyneside English (DECTE), 17, 23–4, 38, 82; *see also* Tyneside Linguistic Survey (TLS)
dialect gestalt, 185
dialect writing, 20–2, 49, 149–50, 165
dialectscape, 25, 52–3
dialect stylisation, 19, 20–2, 25, 109, 119, 130, 147, 152, 184n, 187
diatopic variation, 26
Dictionaries of the Scots Language (DSL), 30n, 39, 40, 41n, 62, 70, 88, 112, 113–17, 128, 142
Dictionary of North East Dialect, A (DNED), 39, 50, 111, 128
Dictionary of the Older Scottish Tongue, A, 30n, 39
Dieth, Eugen, 36
discourse-pragmatic features
 attention signals, 10, 130, 133, 136–7
 discourse markers/particles, 7, 9, 10, 62, 72, 86, 130, 137–41, 142, 144, 146

 expressions, 9, 126n, 129, 130, 136, 142–4, 180
 greetings, 6, 10, 13, 130, 136–7, 142, 146, 158
 interjections, 7, 9, 10, 12, 130, 131–3
 quotatives, 86, 130, 137–8, 139, 146
 response forms, 6, 9, 10, 79, 130, 141–2
 vocatives, 7, 10, 67, 130, 133–7, 144
dislocation, 130, 144–6
Dobson, Scott, 50, 166
Dorfy, 46n, 181
double modals, 97, 98–9, 109
DRESS vowel, 158–60
Dunbar, William, 135
Dutch, 24n, 68, 110, 111–12

Early Modern English (EME), 65, 76, 99, 159, 160
Eliot, T. S., 144n
Ellis, A. J., 33, 34–5, 36, 90, 139, 165, 167, 178
English Dialect Dictionary (EDD), 35–6, 38, 39, 111–12
English Dialect Society (EDS), 35–6
enregisterment, 25, 49–52, 53, 62, 69, 72, 76, 135, 149, 157, 188
epenthetic consonants, 183, 184
epenthetic vowels, 32, 175–6
ethnonyms, 33n, 39–52, 64, 157
expressive spelling, 18, 148–9
eye dialect, 15, 148–9, 150, 163, 187

FACE vowel, 45, 63, 156–7, 180
Fender, Sam, 50, 142n
Ferry, Bryan, 50n
FLEECE vowel, 50, 65, 167–8
football, 1, 23, 42, 46–7
FOOT vowel, 164–5
French, 68, 112, 160, 176
Freud, Sigmund, 44n

Gateshead, 3n, 27, 33n, 42, 139, 143, 152n
geet/git, 86–7, 138–9
Geordie, 21, 39–44, 48–52, 68, 74, 129, 136n, 148, 152, 155, 165, 175, 188
Geordie Shore, 42–3
German, 2, 67–8, 92, 111, 151, 160, 171
Germanic, 29, 67–8

Index

Gibbon, Edward, 57
glottalisation, 178
GOAT vowel, 62, 148, 153–5
GOOSE vowel, 51, 65, 168–9
Great Vowel Shift (GVS), 63, 151, 153, 157, 159
Griffiths, Bill, 39, 50, 111

Hagan, Holly, 43–4
HappY, 148, 175
Harrison, Tony, 170n
Hartlepool, 3n, 27, 44n, 179
Haswell, Thomas, 185–6
haway/howay, 132
h-dropping, 50, 179
Hebburn, 31
hellish, 88–9, 128n
Heslop, Richard O., 36
hiatus breaker [v], 183–5
hinny, 115, 130, 136
howk, 116, 124–5
hoy, 16, 111, 116, 119, 129
hypercorrection, 179
hyperdialectalism, 121, 149

indefinite articles, 82–3
indexicality, 49, 120, 139
industry, 3, 27, 30, 31, 41–2, 45, 48, 117
informality, 1, 4, 7, 15–16, 17, 102, 109, 119, 125–6, 130, 148, 187
interactivity, 6–11, 130, 144, 146
intonation, 14, 85, 131, 185–6
Ireland, 29–32, 52, 89, 134, 135, 140, 141, 143, 160, 163, 170
Irish language, 31

Jackson, Dan, 3
Johnson, Brian, 50n

Knopfler, Mark, 50n, 142

lad(s), 23, 61, 115, 117, 133, 136, 162
lass(es), 23, 61, 74, 111, 115, 133–36
Lawson, Jack, 32
Learmouth, Jimmy, 136
lexical erosion, 123–4; *see also* traditional dialect lexis
lexicalisation, 161, 184
lexical/semantic fields, 113–17

animals, 113
building(s), architecture, 117
character, emotions, social behaviour, 117
environment, 114
food and drink, 116
lifecycle, family, 115
physical states, 115–16
plants, 114
trades and occupations, 116
water, sea, ships, 114–15
like (as discourse marker and quotative), 137–8; *see also* terminal elements
Likely Lads, The, 50
Lindisfarne, 27, 177
Lindisfarne Gospels, 59, 61, 172
Linguistic Survey of Scotland (LSS), 30
LOT/CLOTH vowel, 160–1, 163
Low Countries, 32

McIntosh, Angus, 30
Mackem, 39, 43–6, 48–52, 64, 129, 142n, 152, 157, 173
Mackem Dictionary, The, 52
mam, 136
man (terminal), 134
Markus, Manfred, 36
marrow/marra, 115, 133–5, 175
Martin, William, 134n
master and *plaster*, 162
measure phrases, 68, 94
Merseyside, 31, 183, 188
metalinguistic commentary, 22, 50–1, 109, 118, 122–3, 136, 147, 162, 164, 176, 186, 187–9
Middle English (ME), 49, 61, 64, 66, 68, 69, 71, 83, 92, 99, 101, 102, 142, 151, 153, 154, 156, 157, 158, 159, 162, 164, 165, 169–71
Middlesbrough, 27, 29, 43–4, 47–8, 52, 99, 146
Midlands, 69, 76, 159, 161, 162, 183, 188
Millennium Memory Bank, 37n, 179
modal verbs, 12, 32, 94, 97–9, 100–1, 109
Monkey Hanger, 44n
MOUTH vowel, 21, 49, 51, 151–2, 149, 155
Murray, James, 29–30, 34n, 96

na, 142
-na(t), 100–1
naturalistic language, 4, 6, 17–19, 20–1, 22–3, 25
NEAR vowel, 173
nee, 16, 23, 79, 83–4, 168
negation
  enclitic negation of *DO*, 99–100
  enclitic negation of modal verbs, 100–1
  multiple negation, 16, 99, 101–2
  never, 102
Newcastle Brown Ale, 152n
Newcastle Society of Antiquaries, 179
Newcastle United F.C., 21, 42, 46, 74, 121, 132, 152, 155
Newcastle-upon-Tyne, 3, 21, 27, 29, 31, 39, 40, 41–4, 51–2, 74, 75, 90, 132, 136, 141, 149–50, 152, 153, 155, 156, 166, 167, 169, 178, 179, 185–7
Norse, 109, 111, 125; *see also* Vikings
northern fronting, 65, 91
Northern Ireland, 29, 30–32, 134, 141, 170
northern subject rule, 95
Northumberland, 3n, 26–30, 32, 34–5, 37, 38, 41, 52, 58, 64, 66, 69, 70, 74, 75, 79n, 81, 82, 89, 98, 101, 105, 110, 111, 123, 134, 135, 144, 152, 154, 157, 159, 163, 164–5, 169, 171, 172, 176–7, 179
Northumbria(n), 3, 26–7, 29, 30–2, 37, 41, 59–61, 62–3, 66, 68, 69, 74, 75, 76, 77, 78, 80, 81–3, 89–90, 95, 96, 109, 111, 124, 127, 141–2, 153n, 156, 157, 161, 163, 164, 171, 172, 174, 176–7, 185
Northumbrian/Northumberland burr, 176–8; *see also* burr retraction/modification
nouns (morphology), 66–8
nowt, 16, 23, 61n, 79, 134, 143
NURSE vowel, 148–9, 165–6, 172
NURSE-NORTH merger, 32, 49–50, 165, 174, 178

O'Brien, Sean, 152
of-deletion, 68
Old English (OE), 33, 56, 59, 61, 62, 63, 66–8, 69, 71, 76, 83, 101, 111–12, 128n, 134, 137, 142, 151, 154–5, 160–1, 164, 172
-ook words, 51, 164–5
Orton, Harold, 36–7, 160
Our Dialects project, 165
over, 89, 92
owt, 23, 61n, 79–80
Oxford English Dictionary (*OED*), 29, 38–9

pagger(ed), 111–12, 115–16
palatalisation, 180–1
Palgrave, Francis, 36
PALM, START vowel, 171–2
panackelty, 19
parmo, 52
Pattison, Vicky, 43–4
Pearson, Harry, 46–7
Penshaw, 175
perceptual dialectology, 51–2, 74, 152, 167, 185–6
performativity, 2, 19–22, 49–50, 74, 82, 109, 119–21, 129, 147, 155, 157, 187
pet, 16, 47, 50, 115, 130, 133, 115, 130, 133–4, 136
Pickard, Tom, 152
Pit Yacker, 44n
pitch, 185–6
Pitmatic, 44n
ploat, 110–12, 116, 118–19, 122, 124, 129
plodge, 24, 114, 116
poke, 111–12, 117
politeness, 10, 11–14
prepositions, 91–2, 103–5
PRICE vowel, 21, 157–8
pronouns
  demonstrative pronouns, 68, 78–9, 93
  indefinite pronouns, 12, 68, 79–80, 83, 93
  interrogative pronouns, 68, 80–1
  personal pronouns, 68, 69–73
  possessive pronouns, 73–6
  pronouns in *th-*, 69, 72, 73, 75, 77
  reflexive pronouns, 68, 76–8, 93, 109
  relative pronouns, 80–1, 106
proper (as intensifier), 87–8
prosodic features, 14, 86, 185–7
pure (as intensifier), 87–8

Index

railways, 27
Ramsey, Chris, 50
Ramsey, Rosie, 50
Ready to Go (RTG), 1–24
regiolectal spelling, 15–16, 148–50
relative clauses, 80, 106–7
Republica, 1n
respelling, 15–16, 21, 52, 70, 75–6, 98, 131, 132, 137, 148–50, 151–87
River Tees, 27–9
River Tyne, 27–9, 31, 43, 81, 152
River Wear, 27–9, 31, 45
Romani, 32, 122, 127–8; *see also* Angloromani

sample corpus, 9n, 18, 23, 40n, 61n, 79, 90, 119, 134, 136n, 141
Sand Dancer, 33n, 44n
saveloy dip, 2, 4
Scandinavia(n), 32, 109, 111, 134, 156–7, 163
school, 51, 168–9
Scotland, 27, 29–33, 34, 41n, 57, 59, 64–5, 66, 70–1, 73–4, 79n, 80, 88, 89, 98, 104n, 105, 109, 110, 111n, 127, 134, 135–6, 138, 140, 141, 143–4, 157–8, 159–60, 161, 163, 170, 185
Scots, 29–31, 32, 33, 34n, 39, 40, 41, 57, 59, 64, 68, 76, 79–80, 83, 87, 90, 97–9, 101, 103, 107, 110, 113, 128n, 151, 159, 163, 164, 176, 185
Scots Syntax Atlas (SSA), 57
Scottish English, 31, 76, 103, 108, 162
Scottish National Dictionary, The, 30n, 39
Scottish vowel length rule, 157n
Scouse, 188
Shakespeare, W., 91, 135
shared context, 6, 11–14
Shearer, A., 50
shibboleth, 51, 56–7, 80n, 85, 107, 151, 165, 179
shipbuilding, 3, 27, 31–2, 41, 45, 114–15
Simpsons, The, 99n
Sisson, C. H., 27n
slang, 39, 122, 126, 124–9, 174
Smoggie, 40, 43–4, 46–9, 51–2, 68
sociodialectology, 2, 17, 25, 34, 38, 53, 148

sociolinguistic change, 188–9
South Shields, 29, 31, 33n, 43, 44n, 45, 91, 154–5, 175, 178, 179, 181
speech representation, 7–8, 19–21
spelk, 112, 119
SQUARE vowel, 174
Stadium of Light, 1n, 132
stereotyping, 42n, 99n, 141, 152
Sting, 50
stress, 49, 64, 69, 70–1, 73, 91, 92, 148, 159, 162, 163, 167, 171, 172, 174–5, 179, 186–7; *see also* unstressed vowels
structure of feeling, 3–4, 17
STRUT vowel, 163–4
Sturgeon, Nicola, 46
style *see* dialect stylisation
style-shifting, 18
styling, 19, 147
stylistic variation, 19, 54
Sunderland, 2–3, 21, 27–30, 34, 38, 43–6, 50–2, 72, 80n, 99, 132, 147, 151, 167, 169, 178, 179, 185–7
Sunderland A. F. C., 1, 12n, 42, 46–7, 80n, 121, 132
swearing, 17–18, 24

taboo, 10, 15, 18, 126
Teesside, 27, 29, 42, 46–8, 52, 132–3
telt, 16, 55–7
tempo, 14, 185–6
terminal elements
  but, 139–40
  like, 138
  mind, 139–40
  thou knows, 139
tew(ed), 117, 180–1
th-fronting, 184n
Thirlwall, Jade, 33n, 50
thou knows, 62, 72, 95; *see also* terminal elements
THOUGHT, NORTH, FORCE vowel, 169–71
Thunberg, Greta, 2
tiv, 91, 93, 183–5; *see also* prepositions
Tomaney, John, 3
toon, 152, 187
traditional dialect lexis, 111–25; *see also* lexical/semantic fields

TRAP/BATH vowel, 161–3
T-to-R, 8, 32, 149, 181–3, 187
Tyne and Wear, 26–8, 51–2, 123, 154, 165
Tyneside, 3n, 17, 21, 27, 29, 30–1, 33n, 38, 39–40, 41–3, 45–6, 49–50, 52, 57, 74, 87, 136n, 149–50, 152, 155, 156, 157, 164, 173, 175, 178, 179, 183, 185, 185–7
Tyneside Linguistic Survey (TLS), 38, 123–4, 186; *see also* Diachronic Electronic Corpus of Tyneside English (DECTE)

Ulster, 30, 99n
Ulster Scots, 31–2, 108, 113
unstressed vowels, 49, 70–1
Upton, Clive, 2n, 37–8, 123

Vera, 50
verb forms, 58–65
　gan/go, 59–62, 116
　know, 62–3
　make/take, 63–4
verb paradigms, 54, 55–8

vernacular(ity), 1–20, 148
　vernacular prescriptivism, 188
　vernacularisation, 188–9; *see also* sociolinguistic change
Vikings, 32, 112; *see also* Norse
Viz, 50n, 150
voice quality, 149, 185–6
Voices project, 37–8, 110, 111, 118–19, 127, 140

wad, 98, 109
Wearside, 27, 29, 42, 45, 46, 164, 173, 187
Westmorland, 26n, 85, 89, 107, 110, 134, 167
Williams, Raymond, 3n
Wilson, Thomas, 139
Woolf, Virginia, 35n
wor(s), 51, 73, 74, 76, 77, 81, 109
Wright, Elizabeth, 36n
Wright, Joseph, 35–6, 37n

Yorkshire, 27, 29, 32, 35n, 72, 76, 80, 81, 89, 96, 110, 111n, 112, 134, 135, 138, 144, 151, 152, 157, 172, 183, 184
yous(e), 16, 31–2, 69, 71–2, 75, 109

EU representative:
Easy Access System Europe
Mustamäe tee 50, 10621 Tallinn, Estonia
Gpsr.requests@easproject.com

www.ingramcontent.com/pod-product-compliance
Lightning Source LLC
Chambersburg PA
CBHW071715160426
43195CB00012B/1682